Presented to

....

From

....

Date

....

STRENGTH
for the
CHALLENGE

—— **365** ——
DEVOTIONS FOR MEN

STRENGTH
for the
CHALLENGE

—365—
DEVOTIONS FOR MEN

BARBOUR
PUBLISHING

Our mission is to inspire the world with the life-changing message of the Bible.

Member of the
Evangelical Christian
Publishers Association

GUYS, YOU KNOW LIFE CAN BE TOUGH.

BUT NEVER FORGET HOW STRONG GOD IS.

This encouraging daily devotional builds off the inspired message of 2 Corinthians 12:10 (NIV):

*For Christ's sake, I delight in
weaknesses, in insults, in hardships,
in persecutions, in difficulties.
For when I am weak, then I am strong.*

Why would the apostle Paul find strength in his own weakness? Because reaching the end of his own abilities allowed God to demonstrate what *He* could do through Paul. That's the ultimate message of the 365 readings that follow.

Featuring more than two hundred contemporary entries and scores of "classics" from figures such as D. L. Moody, Andrew Murray, Charles Spurgeon, and John Wesley, *Strength for the Challenge* promises insight and inspiration for men of all ages.

Whatever your current circumstances, you'll be encouraged to seek your daily strength from God through Jesus Christ. Sure, life can be tough. But with the all-powerful Creator and Sustainer on your side, how can you lose?

MORE GRACE

*Lest I should be exalted above measure through the
abundance of the revelations, there was given to me a thorn
in the flesh, the messenger of Satan to buffet me, lest I should be
exalted above measure. For this thing I besought the Lord thrice,
that it might depart from me. And he said unto me, My grace
is sufficient for thee: for my strength is made perfect in
weakness. Most gladly therefore will I rather glory in my
infirmities, that the power of Christ may rest upon me.*
2 CORINTHIANS 12:7–9 KJV

As Moses takes up more room in the Old Testament than any other character, so it is with Paul in the New Testament, except, perhaps, the Lord Himself. Yet Paul did not know how to pray for himself. He besought the Lord to take away "the thorn in the flesh." His request was not granted; but the Lord bestowed upon him a greater blessing. He gave him more grace.

It may be we have some trial—some thorn in the flesh. If it is not God's will to take it away, let us ask Him to give us more grace in order to bear it. We find that Paul gloried in his reverses and his infirmities, because all the more the power of God rested upon him.

It may be there are some of us who feel as if everything is against us. May God give us grace to take Paul's platform and say: "All things work together for good to them that love God" (Romans 8:28 KJV). So when we pray to God we must be submissive and say, "Thy will be done."

GODLY THOUGHTS

"This book of the Law must not leave your mouth. Think about it day and night, so you may be careful to do all that is written in it. Then all will go well with you."
JOSHUA 1:8 NLV

Imagine how Joshua felt after the death of Moses. Tasked with leading God's people across the Jordan River and into the Promised Land, Joshua was sure to face battles—both from the inhabitants of the land and from the Israelites themselves. Joshua took the reins knowing that God had promised to be faithful to him, just as He had with Moses. Even so, God gave Joshua two key instructions.

First, he was to have strength of heart (1:6)—that is, courage—and to be careful to obey all the Law which Moses had taught him (1:7). In fact, the book of the Law was to permeate Joshua's thoughts night and day (1:8). That was how he could be certain to do everything written in it.

The challenges we face today are different than Joshua's: Some of us lead people at the office, some of whom aren't easy to manage. Some of us teach a Sunday school class or small group, serving people from difficult family or spiritual backgrounds. Many of us lead families, which is never easy. But God's advice remains the same regardless of our circumstance. We can do well when the scriptures are on our minds continually.

Thankfully, that's something we can control.

JOSEPH'S CHOICE

Joseph, to whom she was engaged, was a righteous man and did not want to disgrace her publicly, so he decided to break the engagement quietly. As he considered this, an angel of the Lord appeared to him in a dream. "Joseph, son of David," the angel said, "do not be afraid to take Mary as your wife. For the child within her was conceived by the Holy Spirit."
MATTHEW 1:19–20 NLT

Joseph, a working-class man, didn't expect drama when he invited Mary to be his wife. Then Mary got pregnant and Joseph found himself in a frightening situation.

If Mary was unfaithful in their engagement, might she be unfaithful during their marriage? Would the community assume Joseph had had premarital sexual relations? What if the baby looked nothing like Joseph? Mary's infidelity might become obvious, and people would shun the couple. Joseph's livelihood in carpentry might be jeopardized.

So he decided to break things off. If Joseph did that publicly, Mary's infidelity would be punishable by death. If he divorced her quietly, she would be shamed, but live. Joseph held Mary's life—and the life of her unborn child—in his hands.

Then an angel appeared. Joseph was to marry Mary as planned. He was to trust God over the evidence of Mary's seeming infidelity.

And Joseph did trust God. He took Mary as his wife and adopted Jesus as his son. Jesus' life was saved so He could save the entire world from sin.

Perhaps the angel's request—God's request—seemed unfair to Joseph. There will be times when God's expectations of us will be tough too. Will we choose to trust anyway? Joseph did. So can we.

THE LORD HIMSELF IS MY SALVATION

*"Surely God is my salvation; I will trust and not be afraid.
The Lord, the Lord himself, is my strength and my
defense; he has become my salvation."*

Isaiah 12:2 niv

Isaiah 12 is essentially tied with Jeremiah 45 as the shortest chapter in all the books of the prophets. But "small" doesn't imply "weak." The theme of Isaiah 12—praising the Lord for being Israel's salvation—foreshadows the great prophecies of the Messiah in Isaiah 40 and following.

Today's verse spells out some practical implications of praising the Lord, and each is more relevant today than ever.

First, trust in the Lord. Know that He is bigger and stronger than any current national or international upheaval, personal uncertainty, or other dire circumstance.

Second, don't be afraid. In Isaiah's day, the Babylonians, Persians, or Medes were the issue; in our day, it may be foreign nations, climate change, disease, you name it. Isaiah says we can choose not to fear.

Third, grab hold of God's strength. This reminds us of Paul's affirmation, "I can do all [these] things because Christ gives me the strength" (Philippians 4:13 nlv). That is, the apostle could do each thing he had just commanded the believers of Philippi to do.

Fourth, appreciate God's protection. Know that death cannot touch us until the Lord's appointed time—until then, He defends us every second.

These truths will give us the strength to face the worst life throws at us.

—— ALL THE LIGHT YOU NEED ——

*And thou shalt make a candlestick of pure gold: of beaten work
shall the candlestick be made: his shaft, and his branches,
his bowls, his knops, and his flowers, shall be of the same.
And six branches shall come out of the sides of it; three
branches of the candlestick out of the one side, and three
branches of the candlestick out of the other side.*
EXODUS 25:31–32 KJV

The tabernacle had no windows; all its light was candlelight, which
notes the comparative darkness of that dispensation, while the Sun
of righteousness was not as yet risen, nor had the Daystar from on
high visited His church.

Yet God left not Himself without witness, nor them without
instruction; the commandment was a lamp, and the law a light,
and the prophets were branches from that lamp, which gave light
in their several ages.

The church is still dark, as the tabernacle was, in comparison
with what it will be in heaven: but the Word of God is the candlestick, a light burning in a dark place.

FAITH IN MOTION

After saying this, he was taken up into a cloud while they were watching, and they could no longer see him. As they strained to see him rising into heaven, two white-robed men suddenly stood among them. "Men of Galilee," they said, "why are you standing here staring into heaven? Jesus has been taken from you into heaven, but someday he will return from heaven in the same way you saw him go!"

ACTS 1:9–11 NLT

After Jesus' work on earth was over, He ascended into heaven. The disciples watched Him leave, staring up into the sky even after He was completely out of sight. Were they hoping for another glimpse? The disciples stood and looked for so long that God sent two angels to tell them to move. Their apprenticeship was over. It was time to do the work their Lord had called them to do.

When God asks *us* to work, we may be tempted to stand still and continue to look for absolutely clarity. How often do we hope that God will give us more instruction or make our pathway absolutely certain. But the apostle Paul has written, "We live by faith, not by sight" (2 Corinthians 5:7 NIV). In other words, as followers of Christ we move through life one faithful step at a time.

To keep us from staring up into the clouds—to get us moving in our work—Jesus uses words like *ask, seek,* and *knock* (Matthew 7:7). These active words build motion into our faith. And we live *by* faith, trusting and following our Lord even when we might wish for more sight.

—— THE REWARD WILL COME ——

And let us not be weary in well doing:
for in due season we shall reap, if we faint not.
GALATIANS 6:9 KJV

Don't let anybody fool you: the Christian life is tough. If it weren't, why would the apostle Paul write what he did in Galatians 6:9?

There is a weariness in well doing. There are those moments when we feel like fainting—or giving up, as newer translations of the Bible say. In the context, Paul was describing the difficulties of restoring a fellow Christian who's fallen into sin. We are to carry each other's burden to fulfill the law of Christ (verse 2). But we must beware of the danger of falling into sin ourselves, perhaps by thinking we are better than our sinning brother (verses 1, 4).

This is the well-known passage that describes sowing and reaping, spiritually speaking: "Be not deceived; God is not mocked: for whatsoever a man soweth, that shall he also reap" (verse 7 KJV). It's all work! Sowing, reaping, restoring fellow believers who stumble. . .

The good news is in verse 9, where Paul—speaking for God—promises a harvest. There will be a payoff for the hard work we put into our Christian lives. But we can't faint. We don't dare give up. Stay on task, do your work faithfully, allow God to provide the strength. . .and then wait for the reward. It will come.

THE LONG VICTORY

*Joshua waged war against all these kings for a
long time. . . . For it was the LORD himself who
hardened their hearts to wage war against Israel.*
JOSHUA 11:18–20 NIV

Various sources suggest it took Joshua and his men five to seven years to conquer the kings of northern Canaan. That was a long time, but it makes sense, given that the Israelites started in the south. By the time they reached the north, the enemy kings—having heard of the Israelites' advance—had probably dug in and formed alliances.

Notice that the Lord himself hardened the kings' hearts, causing them to wage war against Israel. But these nations in the north were destined to fall. In Deuteronomy 31:8, Moses made a comforting promise to Joshua: "The LORD himself goes before you and will be with you; he will never leave you nor forsake you. Do not be afraid; do not be discouraged" (NIV). Still, it took Joshua and his army *years* to conquer their enemies. Not even a promised victory was instantaneous. That's often the case for us too.

Have you been fighting a spiritual battle for years, only to become discouraged by your lack of victory? As soldiers in the fight, our job is to obey our Commander and leave the result to Him—no matter how long it takes.

Today, take heart. God goes before you and He will be with you.

OFTEN AND LONG ALONE WITH GOD

*Speak unto all the congregation of the children
of Israel, and say unto them, Ye shall be holy:
for I the LORD your God am holy.*
LEVITICUS 19:2 KJV

If you wish to strengthen yourself in the practice of this holy Presence, take up the holy Word. Take, for instance, the book of Leviticus and notice how God seven times gives the command: "Ye shall be holy, for I am holy.". . . Nothing but the knowledge of God, as the Holy One, will make us holy.

And how are we to obtain that knowledge of God, save in the Inner Chamber? It is a thing utterly impossible unless we take time and allow the holiness of God to shine on us. How can any man on earth obtain intimate knowledge of another man of remarkable wisdom if he does not associate with him and place himself under his influence? And how can God Himself sanctify us if we do not take time to be brought under the power of the glory of His holiness?

Nowhere can we get to know the holiness of God and come under its influence and power save in the Inner Chamber. It has been well said: "No man can expect to make progress in holiness who is not often and long alone with God."

WILL WE SAY YES?

This is what the Sovereign Lord, the Holy One of Israel, says:
"In repentance and rest is your salvation, in quietness and
trust is your strength, but you would have none of it."
ISAIAH 30:15 NIV

In Isaiah 30 and 31, the Lord drives home a point to His people Israel: it's futile and absurd to rely on Egypt for salvation from the upcoming Babylonian conquest. What in the world could Pharaoh and his armies do to save the Israelites? Human power is nothing compared to the infinite and eternal greatness of the Lord God.

Two descriptions of God echo throughout this section of Isaiah. The first is "the Sovereign Lord" or "Lord Almighty"; the second is "the Holy One of Israel." How good that we can know God in His sovereignty (greatness), providence (goodness and guidance), holiness (glory), love (graciousness), and mystery ("God alone knows").

Do these descriptions of the Lord God move our souls and echo from our lips? If yes, we will have the strength to face any and every challenge that comes our way. If no, what futile and absurd plan are we pursuing?

Scripture, history, and contemporary experience all call us to rely on the Lord alone. How do we do that? Today's verse prescribes repentance (confession of sin), rest (in God Himself), quietness (while waiting for His salvation), and trust (focusing on the Lord and no one else). How heartbreaking to see the prophet's words, "but you would have none of it." May that never be true of us!

SHADOWS AND LIGHT

*Yea, though I walk through the valley of the shadow of death,
I will fear no evil; for You are with me; Your rod and Your staff,
they comfort me. You prepare a table before me in the presence
of my enemies; You anoint my head with oil; my cup runs over.
Surely goodness and mercy shall follow me all the days of
my life; and I will dwell in the house of the LORD forever.*
PSALM 23:4–6 NKJV

Fear is like a shadow. It's a small thing. But when we give it permission to stand in front of the light of Christ, it will block that light and spread a terrifying blackness over our lives. This shadow-deceiver can cause a legitimate panic that rages like wildfire, jumping from one light-starved heart to another. When we focus on the growing darkness the shadow creates, we can find ourselves paralyzed by an enemy that looks unassailable—but does not even exist.

When our peace fades into the shadows, the solution lies in removing the darkness that stands in front of God's Word. The only way that Satan's lies can block the light is if we allow them to—if we seek the lies, rather than God's kingdom—first.

When you are God's child, you can claim His presence and protection in any and every situation. . .up to and including the valley of the shadow of death.

A TOKEN FOR GOOD

And the blood shall be to you for a token upon the houses where ye are: and when I see the blood, I will pass over you, and the plague shall not be upon you to destroy you, when I smite the land of Egypt.
EXODUS 12:13 KJV

There are some, as we have said, who desire a token of their safety from man, a poor thing when they get it and not worth asking for; and there are others who desire it from God in the form of a sign or a wonder, or else they will not believe. "Show me a token for good" is a prayer which is often used in a very mistaken sense.

They desire some special transaction of providence or remarkable or singular feeling; but God says to all those who desire a token for good, "The blood shall be to you for a token." What more can we desire?

All the squadrons of the angelic host could not better assure us if each one brought a message from heaven. The best of all evidences of divine love is the cross. The strongest of all assurances of safety, the surest of all pledges of favor, the best token of grace that a man can possibly behold is the sprinkled blood, by which he is cleansed from sin. "The blood shall be to you for a token."

GOD IS MORE WILLING TO BLESS

And I, brethren, when I came to you, came not with excellency of speech or of wisdom, declaring unto you the testimony of God. For I determined not to know any thing among you, save Jesus Christ, and him crucified.
1 CORINTHIANS 2:1–2 KJV

It was not enticing words; it was not eloquence that Paul had. Why, he said his speech was contemptible! He did not profess to be an orator; but he preached Christ, the power of God and the wisdom of God, Christ and Him crucified.

And this is what the whole world wants—Christ and Him crucified. And the world will perish for want of Christ. Let every man and woman that loves the Lord Jesus begin to publish the tidings of salvation. Talk to your neighbors and your friends. Run and speak to that young man! Talk to him of heaven and of the love of Christ! Tell him that you want to see him saved; and bear in mind this, that God is far more willing to bless us than we are to have Him.

Let us then keep close to Christ.

ACCEPTANCE

Then the Lord said to Cain, "Why are you angry? Why is your face downcast? If you do what is right, will you not be accepted? But if you do not do what is right, sin is crouching at your door; it desires to have you, but you must rule over it."

GENESIS 4:6–7 NIV

Very early in the Bible, we encounter the disappointing story of Cain and Abel. The two oldest sons of Adam and Eve are presenting offerings to the Lord, but Cain, the firstborn, brings a sacrifice that does not follow God's standard. When Abel presents an acceptable offering, Cain responds in sinful anger.

Cain wanted God's acceptance even though his offering did not warrant it. The obvious solution is that Cain should have used his God-given abilities to acquire and make an appropriate offering. His decision to murder his younger brother, who gave the acceptable offering, is one of the greatest failures in human history.

Jealousy is just one of many challenges that we as men face. It easily leads to anger which easily leads to sin. How much better is it to simply do the right thing in the first place, to approach all of life with simple obedience to the Word of God. As the prophet Samuel said to the erring King Saul, "Does the LORD delight in burnt offerings and sacrifices as much as in obeying the LORD? To obey is better than sacrifice" (1 Samuel 15:22 NIV).

When God's direction is clear, let us be obedient.

DON'T BE SLACK

And Joshua said unto the children of Israel,
How long are ye slack to go to possess the land,
which the Lord God of your fathers hath given you?
JOSHUA 18:3 KJV

After subduing the Promised Land, Israel assembled at Shiloh and set up the tabernacle. Seven tribes of Israel had yet to receive their inherited land, causing Joshua to question their "slackness." The word in Hebrew can mean to abate, cease, fail, faint, forsake, idle, let alone, or be feeble, among other meanings. None are particularly desirable!

Why might those tribes have hesitated to step into the land God had provided for them? Perhaps they preferred their current state, living in a large community. Or maybe the idea of settling down lacked appeal after their years of nomadic existence. We don't know for sure. But their "slackness" was something displeasing to God.

Today, we should also beware of that problem. As Christians, we are called to a different type of conquering—not of land, but of our sin. According to Hebrews 12:1, we should "lay aside every weight, and the sin which doth so easily beset us, and. . .run with patience the race that is set before us" (KJV). And we cannot be slack in doing that.

Thankfully, we don't have to conquer on our own. As the apostle Paul wrote, "If the Spirit of him that raised up Jesus from the dead dwell in you, he that raised up Christ from the dead shall also quicken your mortal bodies by his Spirit that dwelleth in you" (Romans 8:11 KJV).

THE SAME SPIRIT

*As soon as Jesus was baptized, he went up out of the
water. At that moment heaven was opened, and he saw
the Spirit of God descending like a dove and alighting
on him. And a voice from heaven said, "This is my Son,
whom I love; with him I am well pleased."*
MATTHEW 3:16–17 NIV

Jesus' baptism, mentioned in all four Gospels, precedes His formal ministry. It is one of the few situations in scripture depicting the Trinity together. As Jesus came out of the water, the Holy Spirit descended from heaven and the Father audibly declared His love.

The spoken declaration calls to mind Isaiah 42:1, which says, "Here is my servant, whom I uphold, my chosen one in whom I delight; I will put my Spirit on him, and he will bring justice to the nations" (NIV).

Observers on the shore watched as Jesus stepped into His role as justice-bringer, endorsed by God the Father and empowered by the Holy Spirit. People may have assumed Jesus' baptism would be followed by a dramatic march to Rome, where He would overthrow the emperor and take His rightful place as ruler. Instead, Jesus went into the wilderness to be tempted by the devil.

Though His ministry defied human expectations, Jesus did bring justice to the nations: He satisfied His Father's justice by being a worthy sacrifice for human sin. Jesus' strength was shown in the form of weakness.

Now, if we are willing to show weakness and admit we need a savior, the same Holy Spirit that descended on Jesus will empower us. There is no greater strength for our challenges.

CLASSICS: CHARLES SPURGEON

IN ALL THINGS OBEY THE LORD

And an angel of the LORD came up from Gilgal to Bochim, and said, I made you to go up out of Egypt, and have brought you unto the land which I sware unto your fathers; and I said, I will never break my covenant with you. And ye shall make no league with the inhabitants of this land; ye shall throw down their altars: but ye have not obeyed my voice: why have ye done this?
JUDGES 2:1–2 KJV

If you turn aside from God's words by a hair's breadth you know not where it will end. The rail diverges but a little where the switches are turned, but before long the branch line is miles away from the main track. Backslide a little and you are on the way to utter apostasy. The mother of mischief is small as a midge's egg: hatch it, and you shall see an evil bird larger than an ostrich.

The least wrong has in it an all but infinity of evil. You cannot say to sin, "Hitherto shalt thou go, and no farther, and here shall thy proud waves be stayed" (see Job 38:11 KJV). Like the sea when the dyke is broken, it stretches forth its hand to grasp all the surrounding country.

The beginning of sin is like the beginning of strife, and that is said to be as the letting out of water: no man knows what a flood may come when once the banks are burst. So Israel went aside farther and farther from God because they regarded not their way and did not in all things obey the Lord.

LOOK BEYOND
THE STARS TO GOD

Who hath measured the waters in the hollow
of his hand, and meted out heaven with the span?
ISAIAH 40:12 KJV

God's greatness can be compared to the vastness of space. Today, our basic unit of measurement is a foot. In ancient times, it was a span, the width of a hand from the end of the thumb to the tip of the little finger—a distance of about nine inches.

If we were to mark off the distance from here to the moon by spans, it would take more than fifty years to do it. . .assuming someone could mark a span every second of every minute of every hour of every day of every week of every month for every one of those years. Yet in no time the Lord God marked off every span across the universe, nearly 100 billion light years (as far as we can tell right now). Beyond that, He knows each of the countless billions of stars by name (Isaiah 40:26).

The point isn't just that the Lord is a lot smarter than us. He is infinitely and completely beyond us. God didn't go to school to learn how to make a universe. He didn't have to read a book to know how to keep the entire cosmos running. He never had to learn, because He is the all-knowing, all-powerful sovereign of all.

No one will ever explain to God a better way to run human lives, no matter how hard they try. So relax and let Him lead. If He can manage the universe, He can handle your circumstances.

—— GOD HAS THE POWER ——

While the man held on to Peter and John, all the people were astonished and came running to them in the place called Solomon's Colonnade. When Peter saw this, he said to them: "Fellow Israelites, why does this surprise you? Why do you stare at us as if by our own power or godliness we had made this man walk?"
ACTS 3:11–12 NIV

Peter and John were two of Jesus' closest disciples. They were taught by the greatest teacher in the world, God in flesh. They were given the Holy Spirit to equip them to carry out God's plans. It could have been easy for Peter and John to become arrogant. Instead, they gave glory to God, knowing full well the power behind their miracles was the heavenly Father.

Unfortunately, we don't always see miracles in our daily experience.

When we experience a life-altering event like a job loss or a troubling diagnosis, it's easy to succumb to a sense of hopelessness. We may think we'll never get out of our pit of hardship. We feel powerless to do anything but sulk.

But just as God was with Peter and John, He is with us too. We don't have to pull ourselves out of our circumstances. As believers in Jesus, we can call on His name and power to do the heavy lifting. The One who had power to let the blind see, the lame walk, and the dead rise to life two thousand years ago still has that power today. And He will give us strength to weather whatever storms our life can muster.

RUN TO CHRIST

The Lord said to Joshua, "Say to the people of Israel, 'Choose the cities where you may go and be safe when you are in trouble, as I said to you through Moses. So the man who kills any person without meaning to or planning to may run to one of these cities.' "
JOSHUA 20:1–3 NLV

At God's instruction, Israel chose six sanctuary cities that were spread out across Canaan. If an Israelite took someone's life by accident, he or she could flee to one of these cities for protection from an avenger. (You can learn more about the sanctuary cities in Numbers 35:9–15.)

These special cities protected anyone who had killed another person unintentionally. But the killer could be avenged legally if he chose to go outside the city. The sanctuary was always available, but never to be disregarded.

Today, Christians know how often they sin—both unintentionally and with full knowledge. Some days are better than others, and some more challenging. We all fight against the "old man" and the wickedness of our own hearts every day. As the prophet Jeremiah said, "The heart is fooled more than anything else, and is very sinful. Who can know how bad it is?" (17:9 NLV).

That's the bad news. The good news is this: even when we've failed for the hundredth (or thousandth) time, we can always run to Jesus to confess our sins. He is our sanctuary city.

INSTRUMENTS OF USEFULNESS

And it came to pass on a certain day, as he was teaching, that there were Pharisees and doctors of the law sitting by, which were come out of every town of Galilee, and Judaea, and Jerusalem: and the power of the Lord was present to heal them.
LUKE 5:17 KJV

Luke, the writer of this Gospel, was a physician, and therefore had a quick eye for cases of disease and instances of cure; you can trace throughout the whole of his Gospel the hand of one who was skilled in surgery and medicine.

From which I gather that whatever may be our calling, or in whatever art or science we may have attained proficiency, we should take care to use our knowledge for Christ; and that if we be called being physicians we may understand the work of the Lord Jesus all the better by what we see in our own work, and we may also do much for our Lord in real substantial usefulness among our patients.

Let no man despise his calling; whatever instrument of usefulness God hath put into thine hand, consider that the Great Captain knew what weapon it were best for thee to wield. See what it is that thou canst do where thou art, and use such things as thou hast in glorifying thy Lord and Master.

Day 22

— RUN AND NOT GROW WEARY —

Do you not know? Have you not heard? The LORD is the everlasting God, the Creator of the ends of the earth. He will not grow tired or weary, and his understanding no one can fathom. He gives strength to the weary and increases the power of the weak. Even youths grow tired and weary, and young men stumble and fall; but those who hope in the LORD will renew their strength. They will soar on wings like eagles; they will run and not grow weary, they will walk and not be faint.

ISAIAH 40:28–31 NIV

Elsewhere in this chapter of Isaiah, the Lord God's infinite and eternal greatness is compared to the vastness of the oceans. Scientists tell us the earth has more than 300 million cubic miles of water on it. That's enough to cover the entire planet with water upwards of two miles deep. Yet the Lord can hold it all "in the hollow of his hand" (verse 12).

What's more, God's greatness can be compared to the vastness of the earth itself. Our planet's volume is about 260 *billion* cubic miles of land mass. We can't imagine how tedious it would be to weigh the dirt in a small knoll. Yet God knows exactly how much each massive hill and mountain weighs.

We begin to form a right view of God's greatness, goodness, and glory only after we first remove our small, finite, and very misshapen ideas. Does God ever grow tired or weary? Of course not—that's a human trait. Does God understand our situation? Yes, He does—He understands everything! Let's put our hope in *Him* again today.

THE CREATOR IS YOUR GUIDE

And they will tell it to the inhabitants of this land: for they have heard that thou Lord art among this people, that thou Lord art seen face to face, and that thy cloud standeth over them, and that thou goest before them, by day time in a pillar of a cloud, and in a pillar of fire by night.

NUMBERS 14:14 KJV

All that the children of Israel had to do in the wilderness was to follow the cloud. If the cloud rested, they rested; if the cloud moved forward, then they moved as it did. I can imagine the first thing Moses, or any of the people, did, when the grey dawn of morning broke, was to look up and see if the cloud was still over the camp. By night it was a pillar of fire, lighting up the camp and filling them with a sense of God's protecting care; by day it was a cloud shielding them from the fierce heat of the sun's rays and sheltering them from the sight of their enemies.

Israel's Shepherd could lead His people through the pathless desert. Why? Because He made it. He knew every grain of sand in it. They could not have had a better leader through the wilderness than its Creator.

—— STRENGTH IN SURRENDER ——

Finally, my brethren, be strong in the Lord,
and in the power of his might.
EPHESIANS 6:10 KJV

Men, generally speaking, like to be in control. From earliest childhood, we like to say, "I can do it myself!" All through life, we want to impress others with our own strength—physical, emotional, intellectual, even spiritual. But God's ways are often very different than ours (see Isaiah 55:8). He calls us to surrender.

God does assign certain tasks to us, giving us areas of responsibility. We are expected to do our best, develop our gifts, and accomplish as much as we can for His glory. But we are never in total control. Our strength comes from God, from the power of *His* might. Many centuries before the apostle Paul wrote to the Ephesians, Moses was telling the ancient Israelites, "Thou shalt remember the LORD thy God; for it is he that giveth thee power to get wealth" (Deuteronomy 8:18 KJV).

Christians walk a fine line. We are supposed to work. We are called to be strong. But the strength for our work always comes from God, and He gives that strength as we surrender to Him. Surrendering is choosing to obey or follow someone or something other than yourself. As Paul wrote elsewhere, "Don't you realize that you become the slave of whatever you choose to obey? You can be a slave to sin, which leads to death, or you can choose to obey God, which leads to righteous living" (Romans 6:16 NLT). Our strength comes from choosing to follow Christ.

A SAVED SINNER

For I am the least of the apostles, that am not meet to be called an apostle, because I persecuted the church of God. But by the grace of God I am what I am: and his grace which was bestowed upon me was not in vain; but I laboured more abundantly than they all: yet not I, but the grace of God which was with me.

1 CORINTHIANS 15:9–10 KJV

I need scarce say what new depth and intensity man's sin and God's grace give to the humility of the saints. We have only to look at a man like the apostle Paul, to see how, through his life as a ransomed and a holy man, the deep consciousness of having been a sinner lives inextinguishably.

We all know the passages in which he refers to his life as a persecutor and blasphemer. God's grace had saved him; God remembered his sins no more forever; but never, never could he forget how terribly he had sinned. The more he rejoiced in God's salvation, and the more his experience of God's grace filled him with joy unspeakable, the clearer was his consciousness that he was a saved sinner, and that salvation had no meaning or sweetness except as the sense of his being a sinner made it precious and real to him. Never for a moment could he forget that it was a sinner God had taken up in His arms and crowned with His love.

── FINISH THE ASSIGNMENT ──

*So God said to Noah, "I am going to put an end to
all people, for the earth is filled with violence because
of them. I am surely going to destroy both them and
the earth. So make yourself an ark of cypress wood;
make rooms in it and coat it with pitch inside and out."*
GENESIS 6:13–14 NIV

Put yourself in the place of Noah. Apparently, you and your family are the only God-honoring individuals currently alive. You have been given a task which will be quite public and will eventually occupy forty-three thousand days of your life. Nobody else will believe in you or your work. What do you do?

Noah, along with his three sons, rose to the challenge. They found strength in the fact that God Himself had given them this assignment. They understood that their ability to survive the coming flood was dependent on getting the job done.

Our tasks would seem to be trivial compared to what the Lord asked of Noah. But God would disagree with that assessment. The apostle Paul wrote to those who work, "Serve wholeheartedly, as if you were serving the Lord, not people, because you know that the Lord will reward each one for whatever good they do, whether they are slave or free" (Ephesians 6:7–8 NIV).

It may seem counterintuitive, but hard work begets strength. Do what God has said, in the power He gives, and you'll ultimately succeed. God will make sure you not only survive, but thrive.

HOW TO TREAT YOUR ENEMIES

*And the Lord gave them rest round about, according
to all that he sware unto their fathers: and there stood
not a man of all their enemies before them; the Lord
delivered all their enemies into their hand.*

Joshua 21:44 kjv

The Bible has a lot to say about enemies. Jesus said, "Love your enemies, bless them that curse you, do good to them that hate you, and pray for them which despitefully use you, and persecute you" (Matthew 5:44 kjv). But another time, He said, "The Lord said unto my Lord, Sit thou on my right hand, till I make thine enemies thy footstool" (Matthew 22:44 kjv, quoting from Psalm 110:1).

The implication is that you *will* have enemies in this life if you follow Christ and live out His commands. Even so, your job is to love and pray for those opponents, while turning the other cheek (see Matthew 5:39). God, however, will ultimately deliver His people's enemies into their hands, turning them into footstools. We never need to plot revenge, no matter how poorly others have treated us. We can simply obey Jesus' teachings on how to treat our enemies, then leave the rest to God.

And you may find even more than rest. It's just possible that the love you show to enemies might break through their hard hearts and usher them into the kingdom.

— WILDERNESS EXPERIENCES —

*Jesus was led by the Holy Spirit to a desert. There He was
tempted by the devil. Jesus went without food for forty
days and forty nights. After that He was hungry.*
MATTHEW 4:1–2 NLV

Immediately following His baptism, Jesus was led to the wilderness. It seems like a strange way to begin His earthly ministry: the heavens had just opened and declared Jesus to be God's Son in whom He was well pleased. Jesus could have immediately started healing the sick and cleaning out the temple, but the Holy Spirit led Him into the wastelands, where He would encounter hardship, hunger, and temptation.

Life is sometimes like that. We can experience a spiritual high on Sunday, when it feels like the heavens opened and God declared His love for us. Then Monday, back in the regular routine, we feel hungry, spiritually bereft, and tempted by the devil to lay aside our mission.

If Jesus experienced such wilderness moments, shouldn't we as His followers expect to encounter them as well? And since Jesus overcame His trials, we can claim His victory too. We can respond to temptation with God's truth. Our spiritual hunger is satisfied by His Word. Our hardships end when we follow Him home.

In this life, there's always a wilderness. But it plays a valuable role in our growth. Once we learn that the source of our strength is not in ourselves but the power of God's Word, we will be ready for the ministry God has prepared for us.

GOD IS WORTHY OF OUR TRUST

Though he slay me, yet will I trust in him.
JOB 13:15 KJV

What a sweet word is that word *trust*! But there are some things we must not trust. The reason many are in darkness is because they trust in doctrines, in creeds or ordinances, instead of in their Lord and Savior Jesus Christ.

A man said to me lately he could not trust himself. We are not required to do that, for our hearts are deceitful above all things and desperately wicked. But there is no reason why we should not trust God. God is worthy of our trust; He is always faithful. Our nearest friends may deceive us, but God never will.

God will keep them in perfect peace whose minds are stayed on Him (Isaiah 26:3). We must be able to say with Job, "Though He slay me, yet will I trust in Him." If God cannot be trusted, whom can we trust? Unbelief is more than a misfortune; it is a dreadful sin. We must learn to trust, even where we cannot see, and with all our heart. . .not a half-hearted trust. The fruits of trusting are peace, joy, happiness and mercy. Who would not trust God?

GOD'S HAND
LOCKS ONTO OURS

"So do not fear, for I am with you; do not be dismayed,
for I am your God. I will strengthen you and help you;
I will uphold you with my righteous right hand. . . .
For I am the LORD your God who takes hold of your right
hand and says to you, Do not fear; I will help you."
ISAIAH 41:10, 13 NIV

The Lord wants to take hold of your right hand in challenging, difficult, and dangerous circumstances. While God said that Job's own right hand couldn't save him (Job 40:9–14), the Lord's certainly could. From Psalm 60 to 139 we repeatedly hear that God's right hand reaches down to save those He loves and redeems. We hear a similar promise in Isaiah 41–42.

Perhaps the most thrilling picture of God's hand at work is found in Matthew 14:28–31. That's when Jesus, miraculously walking on the Sea of Galilee, is joined briefly by the impetuous Peter. When he lets his focus drift from Jesus to the storm, Peter immediately sinks. But Jesus reaches out His hand, grabs Peter's, and pulls him up and out of the water. How strong Jesus is! And how electrifying it must have felt when Jesus locked onto Peter's outstretched hand.

Why would Jesus save the impulsive apostle? To bless Peter. To rededicate him for the Lord's service. To draw Peter even closer to his Savior. To redeem Peter physically only 60 verses before his amazing confession of faith: "You [Jesus] are the Messiah, the Son of the living God" (Matthew 16:16 NIV).

Jesus is ready and willing to save us too. Just reach out your hand!

—— PROVIDER IN ADVERSITY ——

*The priests and the captain of the temple guard and the
Sadducees came up to Peter and John while they were
speaking to the people. They were greatly disturbed because
the apostles were teaching the people, proclaiming in Jesus
the resurrection of the dead. They seized Peter and John and,
because it was evening, they put them in jail until the next day.
But many who heard the message believed; so the number
of men who believed grew to about five thousand.*

ACTS 4:1–4 NIV

Before Jesus ascended to the Father, He gave His followers the
Great Commission: "Therefore go and make disciples of all nations, baptizing them in the name of the Father and of the Son
and of the Holy Spirit" (Matthew 28:19 NIV). Peter and John did
precisely what our Lord commanded them to do. The result was
immediate opposition.

Have you ever experienced that? You felt you were precisely
where God called you to be, but you faced consistent obstacles? This
might be the exact result of closely following Jesus. After all, the
Lord did tell His followers, "In this world, you will have trouble"
(John 16:33 NIV). When we share the Gospel or choose to stand with
Christ, adversity is not a possibility but an inevitability.

The good news is that the God we serve gave manna to the
Israelites in the desert (Exodus 16). He provided other miraculous bread to an exhausted Elijah (1 Kings 17:2–6). And He will
give us everything we need to accomplish our calling. As Jesus
reminds us in Matthew 28:20 (NIV), "surely I am with you always,
to the very end of the age."

SHUN THE WORLD

"But if you turn away and ally yourselves with the survivors of these nations that remain among you. . .then you may be sure that the LORD your God will no longer drive out these nations before you. Instead, they will become snares and traps for you, whips on your backs and thorns in your eyes, until you perish from this good land, which the LORD your God has given you."
JOSHUA 23:12–13 NIV

Though Israel had conquered its enemies and settled into the Promised Land, Joshua—who was an old man by now—summoned the elders, leaders, judges, and officials to give them a dire warning. If Israel turned away from God to make allies with the enemy survivors, the Lord would no longer drive those nations out of the land. In effect, He would leave the Israelites to their own devices. What a sobering thought!

We don't live in a theocracy the way Israel did. But we can certainly learn some key principles from Joshua's warning. Our culture—and this entire world—seeks to pull us away from God. It mocks our faith. It has redefined family. It values pleasure over sacrifice and sensuality over purity. It is fascinated with death and darkness. And if you don't conform, it will not tolerate you. . . despite its loud calls for tolerance.

This world will have a certain appeal to our old sin nature. But we are called to remain faithful to God and His Word. Joshua's warning is frightening, but the opposite gives us hope and strength: follow the Lord and enjoy His blessing.

TOUCH, TAKE HOLD, TAKE FAST HOLD

Take fast hold of instruction; let her not go:
keep her; for she is thy life.
PROVERBS 4:13 KJV

Faith may be well described as taking hold upon divine instruction. God has condescended to teach us, and it is ours to hear with attention and receive His words; and while we are hearing faith comes, even that faith which saves the soul.

To take "fast hold" is an exhortation which concerns the strength, the reality, the heartiness, and the truthfulness of faith, and the more of these the better. If to take hold is good, to take fast hold is better. Even a touch of the hem of Christ's garment causeth healing to come to us, but if we want the full riches which are treasured up in Christ, we must not only touch but take hold; and if we would know from day to day to the very uttermost all the fullness of His grace, we must take fast hold, and so maintain a constant and close connection between our souls and the eternal fountain of life.

It were well to give such a grip as a man gives to a plank when he seizes hold upon it for his very life—that is a fast hold indeed.

Day 34

—— THE KEY TO HAPPINESS ——

Oh, give thanks to the Lord, for He is good! For His mercy endures forever. Let Israel now say, "His mercy endures forever." Let the house of Aaron now say, "His mercy endures forever." Let those who fear the Lord now say, "His mercy endures forever." . . . This is the day the Lord has made; we will rejoice and be glad in it.
PSALM 118:1–4, 24 NKJV

Someone once said, "Never put the key to your happiness in someone else's pocket." The author of those words has been lost to time. But it's probably safe to assume that he put the key to his own happiness in someone else's pocket.

Nehemiah 8:10 says, "The joy of the Lord *is your strength.*" For many men joy seems like an unlikely source of power. But God's Word says joy is the key to our strength. It's the pivotal element necessary to get the engine started.

It's easy to allow people and things to steal our joy. Dark, low-hanging clouds can torment us day after day. But notice the intentionality of today's scripture: it is a call to consciously remember God's goodness, to consciously give Him thanks, and to consciously rejoice and be glad.

Joy is not the product of a problem-free life. It is a choice.

Are you making that choice, today and every day? You might want to check your pockets. Where are your keys?

LIVING FOR CHRIST

For to me to live is Christ, and to die is gain.
PHILIPPIANS 1:21 KJV

As he wrote his letter to the Philippians, the apostle Paul was in prison for preaching the Gospel. His survival strategy was two-pronged: sharing Jesus no matter what and anticipating the moment he would enter into glory. As long as Paul had air to breathe, nothing could stop him from preaching Christ. After that, he'd be *with* Christ.

Even in confinement he pressed on, writing letters to individual believers and to churches—"epistles" that still speak to Christians today as books of the New Testament. Paul's unwavering commitment to Jesus, even in a prison cell, stimulated other believers to share the Gospel more boldly (verse 14). In some of the most difficult situations imaginable, Paul never stopped living for Christ, knowing that one day he would see Jesus face-to-face.

That perspective can overcome all the disappointments, hardships, and pain of this life. No matter how daunting or lengthy our challenges may be—and some are incredibly heavy—a focus on Jesus will provide the strength we need to get through.

As long as there's breath in your lungs, live for Christ. Death just means you'll be alive in His presence.

—DO WE SERVE GOD IN VAIN?—

But I said, "I have labored in vain; I have spent my strength for nothing at all. Yet what is due me is in the Lord's hand, and my reward is with my God."
Isaiah 49:4 NIV

Isaiah 40–66 divides into three equal sections of nine chapters. The second third, Isaiah 49–57, begins with the Lord God commissioning His servant, the Messiah, whom Peter declared and whom we know is Jesus Christ. Yet who is speaking in the verse above? Is it Isaiah himself? God the Father in heaven? God's Son, Jesus, during His earthly ministry? And what is this statement all about?

First, the speaker clearly is Jesus. He is accurately describing the effect of His earthly ministry on the nation of Israel, God's chosen people, who turned away from Him to follow a manmade religion . . .and who violently reacted to Jesus' life, teachings, miracles, and the proof that He was God's Son. The people had Jesus crucified. What could be worse?

Notice that Jesus didn't despair. Instead, He looked forward to His Father's right hand raising Him from the dead, exalting Him to the highest place, and giving Him the name above every name (see Acts 2:32–36; Romans 8:34; Ephesians 1:19–21; Philippians 2:9–11; Colossians 3:1; Hebrews 1:3, 1:13, 8:1, and 10:12).

No wonder the apostle Peter robustly affirmed these truths (1 Peter 3:21–22). He said, in effect, "Knowing what Jesus suffered in the flesh, be done with sin and dedicate your life to obeying the will of God" (see 1 Peter 4:1–2; Romans 12:1–2; Hebrews 12:1–2). As we obey God, He sends us even more strength. Nobody serves God in vain.

—— TIME OF SECRET WORSHIP ——

For by the last words of David the Levites were numbered
from twenty years old and above. . .to stand every morning
to thank and praise the LORD, and likewise at even.
1 CHRONICLES 23:27, 30 KJV

How gracious the provision suggested by so many types and examples of the Old Testament, by which a morning hour at the opening of the day can enable us to secure a blessing for all its work and give us the assurance of power for victory over every temptation. How unspeakably gracious that in the morning hour the bond that unites us with God can be so firmly tied that during hours when we have to move amid the rush of men or duties and can scarce think of God, the soul can be kept safe and pure; that the soul can so give itself away in the time of secret worship, into His keeping, that temptation shall only help to unite it closer with Him.

What cause for praise and joy that the morning watch can so each day renew and strengthen the surrender to Jesus and the faith in Him that the life of obedience can not only be maintained in fresh vigor, but can indeed go on from strength to strength.

JUST GO

So Abram went, as the Lord had told him.
GENESIS 12:4 NIV

In terms of its wording, today's verse is simple enough for a beginning reader. But many of us would find the calling of Abram an incredible challenge.

As a seventy-five-year-old man, Abram got a visit from God along with a command: "Go from your country, your people and your father's household to the land I will show you" (Genesis 12:1 NIV). And, just like that, Abram obeyed.

God's call and Abram's response bookend a remarkable promise the Lord made. "I will make you into a great nation, and I will bless you," God said. "I will make your name great, and you will be a blessing. I will bless those who bless you, and whoever curses you I will curse; and all peoples on earth will be blessed through you" (Genesis 12:2–3 NIV).

As He did with Abram, the Lord calls us to various tasks—in our homes, our churches, and our communities. And He makes us remarkable promises as well, including this one: "Never will I leave you; never will I forsake you" (Hebrews 13:5 NIV).

The key for us is to obey. When God's will is clear, whether through a teaching of scripture or a specific call on our lives (which will always align with the teaching of scripture), we must be like Abraham and just go. God will take care of the rest.

CRY OUT FOR MERCY

When the Lord gave them special men to judge them, the Lord
was with the judge. And He saved them from those who hated
them. For the Lord showed them pity because of their pain.
JUDGES 2:18 NLV

Judges 2 contains one of the saddest verses in the Bible. Following the death of Joshua and all his contemporaries, "The children who came after them did not know the Lord. They did not know about the things He had done for Israel" (verse 10 NLV). Apparently, the stories of God's faithfulness had not been passed down, so the people did what came naturally. They served other gods and they faced God's punishment.

But in their ignorance and weakness and trouble, God showed the Israelites pity by saving them from their enemies. Judgment is in God's nature, but so is mercy—especially when He sees His chosen ones suffering, even when it's of their own doing.

Perhaps you're going through a dry period in your spiritual walk. When you avoid God, you become easy pickings for Satan. But if you cry out to God for mercy, He'll grant it quickly.

If, like the prodigal son, you ever find yourself in a pigpen of your own making, don't hesitate to call out to the Father. He will lift you up, clean you off, and embrace you in love.

BLESSED WITH PERSECUTION?

"Blessed are you when people insult you, persecute you and falsely say all kinds of evil against you because of me. Rejoice and be glad, because great is your reward in heaven, for in the same way they persecuted the prophets who were before you."
MATTHEW 5:11–12 NIV

The audience on the mountainside listened as Jesus described "blessed" people. They must have wondered if He knew what the word meant. Blessed are the poor in spirit? Blessed are those who mourn? Really?

Crowds were following Jesus because of His miracles. He obviously had power, but His view of blessing seemed very different than the world's. For one thing, Jesus' "blessed" people looked a lot like themselves. His early disciples were society's rejects—rough-cut fishermen and a hated tax collector. The people Jesus sought were poor, unpopular, broken—how could these be the blessed people?

Jesus knew they were blessed because He saw them through eternal eyes. People "blessed" with good looks or money or connections in this world are blessed only for a short time. But people who love God and value the things He values, people who are willing to endure the persecution Jesus endured, are blessed both now and forever.

How can you rejoice in hardship and persecution? By focusing on the reward ahead and knowing you are not alone in your suffering. If you are suffering for the Savior, the Savior is right there with you.

CLASSICS: *D. L. MOODY*

— MINDS STAYED ON JESUS —

But let all those that put their trust in thee rejoice:
let them ever shout for joy, because thou defendest them:
let them also that love thy name be joyful in thee.
PSALM 5:11 KJV

When it is dark and stormy here, strive to rise higher and higher, near to Christ, and you will find it all calm there. You know that it is the highest mountain peaks that catch the first rays of the sun. So those who rise highest catch the first news from heaven.

It is those sunny Christians who go through the world with smiles on their faces that win souls. And, on the other hand, it is those Christians who go through the world hanging their heads like bulrushes, that scare people away from religion. Why, it's a libel on Christianity for a religious man to go about with such a downcast look.

What does the Master say? "My joy I leave with you, my joy I give unto you" (see John 15:11). Depend upon it, if our minds were stayed upon Him, we should have perfect peace, and with perfect peace we should have perfect joy.

BOAST ONLY ABOUT THE LORD

This is what the Lord says: "Let not the wise boast of their wisdom or the strong boast of their strength or the rich boast of their riches, but let the one who boasts boast about this: that they have the understanding to know me, that I am the Lord, who exercises kindness, justice and righteousness on earth, for in these I delight," declares the Lord.
JEREMIAH 9:23–24 NIV

The best commentary on the Old Testament is the New Testament—and one of the best commentaries on this passage from Jeremiah is James 3:13–18.

First, James, the Lord's half-brother, writes: "Who is *wise* and *understanding* among you? Let them show it by their good life, by deeds done in the humility that comes from wisdom" (verse 13 NIV, emphasis added). James describes two practical implications of the scripture above: have a good heart and do good deeds in humility—clearly for God's glory, not our own boasting.

Second, James describes some of the terrible works of the flesh (see verses 14–16). Bitter envy, selfish ambition, and the like contrast greatly with the Lord's works described in today's passage. They also contrast greatly with the Lord's works through us that James mentions: "The wisdom that comes from heaven is first of all pure; then peace-loving, considerate, submissive, full of mercy. . ." (vv. 17–18 NIV). Jeremiah and James agree that the Lord exercises His good works on earth *through us*.

The prerequisite to this strength is humility. And that's something any of us can pursue.

— SURRENDER THE SITUATION —

"Therefore, in the present case I advise you: Leave these men alone! Let them go! For if their purpose or activity is of human origin, it will fail. But if it is from God, you will not be able to stop these men; you will only find yourselves fighting against God."
ACTS 5:38–39 NIV

Gamaliel had seen this before: Theudas and then Judas the Galilean claimed to be men of significance. They were killed and their followers scattered.

But with Jesus' apostles it was different. Long after Jesus' death on a cross, His followers were bolder than ever. This prompted Gamaliel, a Pharisee and "a teacher of the law who was honored by all the people" (Acts 5:34 NIV), to advise the Sanhedrin to leave Peter and the apostles alone. If God was with these men, they would prevail no matter what the Sanhedrin wanted to do about them.

Gamaliel is mentioned only briefly in scripture, but his message is profound, even in our day. Instead of taking matters into our own hands, using whatever social, political, or spiritual clout we think we have, trust that God knows best.

This is an act of surrender and deep trust in our heavenly Father. Whatever we might think we can do to get out of a difficult situation, it's best to simply give it over to God to do with as He wills. As the apostle Paul said, "when I am weak, then I am strong" (2 Corinthians 12:10 NIV). It is only in trusting God's strength that we truly find ours.

"BUT, LORD. . ."

But the Lord said to him, "For sure I will be with you.
You will destroy Midian as one man."
JUDGES 6:16 NLV

Throughout the book of Judges, the people of Israel habitually turned from the Lord. At one point, God gave His rebellious people into the hands of Midian for seven years. The Midianites destroyed the Israelites' food supply and left no sheep, cattle, or donkeys, leaving the people "very poor" (Judges 6:6 NLV). When the Israelites cried out to the Lord, He sent a prophet, followed by an angel (identified as Jehovah Himself in 6:14) to remind the people that God was with them. And He would make Gideon their deliverer.

Gideon wasn't so sure about that. "O Lord, how can I save Israel?" he asked God. "See, my family is the least in Manasseh. And I am the youngest in my father's house" (6:15 NLV).

It's understandable why Gideon would feel that way. Our world views people's importance based on status, experience, and age. But the Lord operates differently, often choosing weak people to display His awesome power.

Has the Lord ever given you a clear command and you responded like Gideon? Maybe you don't come from money, or you're not particularly popular, or you're new in the faith. But none of that matters. God stands ready to work *through* you—to empower you to do exactly what He wants. Surrender to His will and watch Him work.

COME BACK TO GOD

*The ox knoweth his owner, and the ass his master's crib:
but Israel doth not know, my people doth not consider.*
ISAIAH 1:3 KJV

It is clear from this chapter that the Lord views the sin of mankind with intense regret. We are obliged to speak of Him after the manner of men, and in doing so we are clearly authorized to say that He does not look upon human sin merely with the eye of a judge who condemns it, but with the eye of a friend who, while He censures the offender, deeply laments that there should be such faults to condemn.

"Hear, O heavens, and give ear, O earth: . . . I have nourished and brought up children, and they have rebelled against me" (Isaiah 1:2 KJV), is not merely an exclamation of surprise, or an accusation of injured justice, but it contains a note of grief, as though the Most High represented Himself to us as mourning like an ill-treated parent, and deploring that after having dealt so well with His offspring they had made Him so base a return. God is grieved that man should sin.

That thought should encourage everyone who is conscious of having offended God to come back to Him. He will rejoice when thou dost return.

YOU DON'T HAVE TO BE A STAR

*Then Peter said unto them, Repent, and be baptized every
one of you in the name of Jesus Christ for the remission of sins,
and ye shall receive the gift of the Holy Ghost. . . . Then they
that gladly received his word were baptized: and the same day
there were added unto them about three thousand souls.*
ACTS 2:38, 41 KJV

Though Jesus taught that His followers should be "servant of all"
(Mark 9:35, 10:44), our culture encourages and celebrates stardom.
To be considered a success, you must be at the top of the mountain
with plenty of other people looking up to you.

Sometimes, this attitude even colors our Christian lives. If we
don't lead an organization, speak in front of crowds, or find ourselves in some other notable public position, we might feel like
we're failing God. Or, perhaps, failing ourselves.

But the birth of the Christian church in Acts 2 provides a good
counterbalance to these fears. Notice that Peter—who was certainly
in a notable position—preached a message that led to the salvation
of three thousand people. Though it's possible that some of their
names appear throughout the New Testament letters written in
following decades, we really know almost nothing about these
early believers. Their average, everyday Christian lives, though,
lived out in a very hostile culture, caused others to accept the Gospel message, and that pattern repeated itself down to the current
day. Your own salvation is likely part of a long chain of testimony
dating to this moment in Acts 2.

You don't have to be a star to be a good Christian. God gave us
the story of these early believers to encourage simple, everyday
obedience.

A CLEAN HEART

Create in me a clean heart, O God, and renew a right spirit within me. Cast me not away from your presence, and take not your Holy Spirit from me. Restore to me the joy of your salvation.
PSALM 51:10–12 ESV

Let's face it: there are some rooms in our "house" we don't want anyone to see. Sure, we intend to clean up our thoughts someday. And we may even do a little work on our habits now and then. But if someone showed up unannounced and asked to have a look around, we would prefer to keep the door to that one certain room tightly closed.

In the Bible, David was an adulterer, a murderer, and a liar. And yet he was known as a man after God's own heart. How could that be? Perhaps the answer resides in the passion with which he always returned to God. After his sin with Bathsheba and the killing of her husband, Uriah, he cried, "Have mercy on me, O God, according to your steadfast love; according to your abundant mercy blot out my transgressions. Wash me thoroughly from my iniquity, and cleanse me from my sin! For I know my transgressions, and my sin is ever before me. Against you, you only, have I sinned and done what is evil in your sight" (Psalm 51:1–4 ESV).

The devil knows each of us by name, but calls us by our sin. Jesus knows our sin, but calls us by our name. No matter who we are, or what we've done, we can always say, "Create in me a clean heart, O God." And He will do it.

GOD IS OUR MAKER

No one is like you, LORD; you are great, and your name is mighty in power. . . . God made the earth by his power; he founded the world by his wisdom and stretched out the heavens by his understanding. . . . "With my great power and outstretched arm I made the earth and its people and the animals that are on it, and I give it to anyone I please.". . . "He made the earth by his power; he founded the world by his wisdom and stretched out the heavens by his understanding."
JEREMIAH 10:6, 12; 27:5; 51:15 NIV

When God's Word stutters, we need to listen! Jeremiah repeatedly writes of the Lord's great power and wisdom in making the heavens and earth. Only God could have created our world with scores of precisely calibrated factors to support life in all its abundance.

While astrophysicists claim the earth is a microscopic speck of dust in the universe, earth scientists say this planet is home to potentially millions of species, each populated by billions of representatives. By some estimates, earth's life forms include 3 trillion trees, 3.5 trillion fish, 1.5 billion cattle, 900 million dogs, and 300 million common starlings. Add in bugs and microscopic organisms, and the total soars into quadrillions.

Remarkably, scientists almost universally admit they have identified only a fraction of the life forms on earth. Despite centuries of exploration, no scientist had ever observed a spade-toothed whale until this past decade.

Imagine a mind vast enough to conceive all those living things—and a will powerful enough to bring them into being. We'll never be able to understand God—but we can draw on His strength by simple trust.

GOD RULES OVER ALL

And, behold, there came a man of God out of Judah by the word of the LORD unto Bethel: and Jeroboam stood by the altar to burn incense. And he cried against the altar in the word of the LORD, and said, O altar, altar, thus saith the LORD; Behold, a child shall be born unto the house of David, Josiah by name; and upon thee shall he offer the priests of the high places that burn incense upon thee, and men's bones shall be burnt upon thee.

1 KINGS 13:1–2 KJV

Josiah: Which being done above three hundred years after this prophecy, plainly shews the absolute certainty of God's providence and foreknowledge even in the most contingent things. For this was in itself uncertain and wholly depended upon man's will, both as to the having of a child and as to the giving it this name. Therefore God can certainly and effectually overrule man's will which way He pleaseth; or else it was possible that this prediction should have been false, which is blasphemous to imagine.

Whoever is sent on God's errand must not fear the faces of men. It was above three hundred and fifty years ere this prophecy was fulfilled. Yet it is spoken of as sure and nigh at hand. For a thousand years are with God as one day.

GIVING BACK TO GOD

Then Abram gave him a tenth of everything.
GENESIS 14:20 NIV

In the book of Genesis, Moses wrote that "Abram believed the LORD, and he credited it to him as righteousness" (15:6 NIV). With only slight variations in wording, this verse is quoted three times in the New Testament (Romans 4:3; Galatians 3:6; James 2:23). But though faith is Abram's primary claim to fame—and a powerful source of strength for life's challenges—his willingness to give back to God sets another example for us to follow.

Abram (whose name God changed to Abraham) was a wealthy man. Genesis 13:6 (NIV) says his possessions "were so great" that he and his nephew Lot had to separate—the land couldn't support all their flocks together. Unfortunately, out on his own, Lot was taken captive by warring kings and Abram had to organize a rescue mission with more than three hundred men from his own household. God gave success to Abram's military excursion, and then Abram gave a tithe—one tenth of all his possessions—to Melchizedek, king of Salem and "priest of God Most High" (Genesis 14:18 NIV).

Since everything belongs to God anyway (see Psalm 50:12), we only steward what He gives us. And when we hold on loosely to things, we can cling more tightly to Him. We find strength in giving back to God.

TOO MANY WARRIORS

*The LORD said to Gideon, "You have too many warriors with you.
If I let all of you fight the Midianites, the Israelites will boast
to me that they saved themselves by their own strength."*

JUDGES 7:2 NLT

Scripture doesn't tell us how large the army of the Midianites was. But Judges 7:12 indicates that their camels were "too many to count." And we know that twenty-two thousand of Israel's thirty-two thousand soldiers were frightened enough to gladly leave when given the opportunity (verse 3).

Even so, the Lord told Gideon that he still had too many warriors. God eventually trimmed the number to just three hundred, to keep Israel from boasting that their own strength had given them victory. The tiny army's rout of the Midianites left no doubt about God's power.

When facing challenges, our natural inclination is to trust our own strength. We trust our retirement funds, our good health, our solid jobs, our family and friends, or a dozen other things. But any of those could be taken away in an instant. The Lord wants to reduce our trust in such stuff so we'll learn to trust Him.

Stop and think of God's faithfulness to you and your family in the past. How has He come through for you when you didn't stand an earthly chance? Praise the Lord for that faithfulness—and allow those memories to deepen your trust in Him.

—— STRENGTH AGAINST LUST ——

"You have heard the commandment that says, 'You must not commit adultery.' But I say, anyone who even looks at a woman with lust has already committed adultery with her in his heart."
MATTHEW 5:27–28 NLT

Defense attorneys look for legal loopholes to help their clients avoid punishment. That's a defense attorney's job—but it is something we all tend to do for ourselves. Jesus knew this, and that's why He addressed "loopholes" in His famous sermon on the mount.

While the act of adultery is clearly prohibited in Exodus 20:14, Jesus wanted His hearers to understand the spirit of the law. While some might question whether premarital sex or pornography should be considered adultery, Jesus goes to the root of the issue by prohibiting lust.

God created sexual desire as a good thing within marriage. Lust, though, is something else. Pastor John Piper defines it as "taking a perfectly good thing that God created—namely, sexual desire—and abstracting it or stripping it off from an honor toward a person and stripping it off from a supreme regard for God's holiness. You take God away, and you take the honor of man away, and what you have left in sexual desire is lust."

If you struggle with lust, stop looking for loopholes to justify sinful activity. The heart of the issue is not what your eyes see, but who has your attention. Admit your weakness to God, then keep your eyes on Him and His holiness. Commit your desires—even your sexual desires—to God's purposes and trust Him to take care of you.

WAITING ON GOD

*Rest in the LORD, and wait patiently for him: fret not thyself
because of him who prospereth in his way, because of the
man who bringeth wicked devices to pass. Cease from anger,
and forsake wrath: fret not thyself in any wise to do evil.
For evildoers shall be cut off: but those that wait
upon the LORD, they shall inherit the earth.*
PSALM 37:7–9 KJV

"In patience possess your souls" (Luke 21:19). "Ye have need of
patience" (Hebrews 10:36). "Let patience have her perfect work,
that ye may be perfect and entire" (James 1:4 KJV). Such words of
the Holy Spirit show us what an important element in the Christian
life and character patience is. And nowhere is there a better place
for cultivating or displaying it than in waiting on God.

There we discover how impatient we are and what our im-
patience means. We confess at times that we are impatient with
men and circumstances that hinder us or with ourselves and our
slow progress in the Christian life. If we truly set ourselves to wait
upon God, we shall find it is with Him we are impatient because
He does not at once, or as soon as we could wish, do our bidding.
It is in waiting upon God that our eyes are opened to believe in His
wise and sovereign will and to see that the sooner and the more
completely we yield absolutely to it, the more surely His blessing
can come to us.

NOTHING IS TOO HARD FOR GOD

*"Ah, Sovereign Lord, you have made the heavens and
the earth by your great power and outstretched
arm. Nothing is too hard for you."*
JEREMIAH 32:17 NIV

Jeremiah's prayer above is a beautiful statement of God's power. If you read all of chapter 32, however, you see that the prayer is followed by an implied *but*.

Throughout the previous two chapters, the Lord had promised to restore exiled Israel—in its homeland. Then God described how He would make a new covenant with His people—in their hearts. After the first promise, Jeremiah said, "At this I awoke and looked around. My sleep had been pleasant to me" (31:26 NIV). After the second, Jeremiah stopped dictating to his assistant, Baruch. They must have rejoiced at these wonderful promises.

But then we come to Jeremiah 32, where we find the Babylonians ready to overrun Jerusalem. Jeremiah himself is imprisoned by the wicked king of Judah. Adding insult to injury, God has commanded Jeremiah to buy property in his hometown (verses 6–8)!

In response to this command, Jeremiah praised the Lord's omnipotence (verses 17, 21), but then complained loudly about having to spend money on land he never expected to use. In reply, God told Jeremiah, "I am the Lord, the God of all mankind. Is anything too hard for me?" (verse 27 NIV). And God went on to explain why and how the Babylonians were fulfilling His own plans for His people.

Though they were being disciplined, they were always God's beloved people—a nation that He promised to restore and bless. Through Jesus, God does the same thing for us as Christians today.

—— STRENGTH IN COMMUNITY ——

*All the believers were one in heart and mind. No one
claimed that any of their possessions was their own,
but they shared everything they had. With great power
the apostles continued to testify to the resurrection of the
Lord Jesus. And God's grace was so powerfully at work in
them all that there were no needy persons among them. For
from time to time those who owned land or houses sold
them, brought the money from the sales and put it at the
apostles' feet, and it was distributed to anyone who had need.*
ACTS 4:32–35 NIV

When Jesus was arrested and crucified, the disciples were *not* of one mind and heart. They scattered into the shadows. Even Peter, the one who said he would stick with Jesus to the death, abandoned his Lord.

But at Pentecost, everything changed. God's Spirit now lived inside Jesus' followers. The Christian church began. And believers could draw a supernatural strength from each other.

"Though one may be overpowered, two can defend themselves," the writer of Ecclesiastes said. "A cord of three strands is not quickly broken" (Ecclesiastes 4:12 NIV). So it was with the early church. Though persecuted, they stuck together and by the Spirit's power were able to do wondrous works.

Likewise, when we engage in Christian community, we find strength, comfort, provision, and encouragement. The challenges of life are lessened by the companionship of our brothers and sisters in the faith. If you don't have that kind of fellowship, ask God for this incredible blessing.

GRIEVING GOD

Then the Israelites put aside their foreign gods and
served the LORD. And he was grieved by their misery.
JUDGES 10:16 NLT

Some of the challenges we face are of our own making. That was certainly the case with the ancient Israelites. As was their pattern, they were up and down, hot and cold spiritually. Prior to the occasion of today's verse, they had been cold—serving images of Baal and Ashtoreth and the false gods of Aram, Sidon, Moab, Ammon, and Philistia.

In anger, God turned His people over to the Philistines and Ammonites, who oppressed them for eighteen years. Then the people pled with the Lord, confessing their sin and throwing themselves on His mercy.

How did God respond? We learn that He was grieved by their misery. If you've ever doubted that God is personal, Judges 10:16 should change your mind. And this isn't the only time we read about the godhead being grieved by sin. Ephesians 4:28–30 says we bring sorrow to God's Holy Spirit when we steal, idle our time away, fail to give to others, use foul or abusive language—in other words, when we live inconsistently with who we are in Christ.

Think about the challenges you face right now. How many of them might be due to your own sin? Much like a human parent, God is grieved by your sinful behavior—but He also stands ready to empower you to overcome it. Galatians 5:16 puts it this way: "Let the Holy Spirit guide your lives. Then you won't be doing what your sinful nature craves" (NLT).

—CAST YOURSELF ON JESUS—

How shall we escape,
if we neglect so great salvation?
HEBREWS 2:3 KJV

When a man is born of the Spirit, he will understand the word of God, and not before.

You say, "If that is so, how am I to understand how to be saved?" A great many things in the Bible are dark and mysterious, but when it comes to the plan of salvation, God has put it so plain that anyone can understand it.

You understand what it is to come: "Come unto Me," says He, "all ye that labour" (Matthew 11:28 KJV).

To take a gift: "He came unto His own, and His own received Him not. But as many as received Him, to them gave He power to become the sons of God" (John 1:11–12 KJV). "The wages of sin is death, but the gift of God is eternal life" (Romans 6:23 KJV).

To believe in a man: "believe in the Lord Jesus Christ, and thou shalt be saved" (Acts 16:31 KJV).

To put trust and confidence in a man: now put your trust and confidence in the living God, and you are saved. You are saved by casting yourself unreservedly upon the Lord Jesus Christ.

DWELLING IN ANOTHER COUNTRY

A land which the LORD thy God careth for: the eyes of the LORD thy God are always upon it, from the beginning of the year even unto the end of the year.
DEUTERONOMY 11:12 KJV

Observe here a type of the condition of the natural and the spiritual man. In this world in temporals and in all other respects the merely carnal man has to be his own providence and to look to himself for all his needs. Hence his cares are always many, and frequently they become so heavy that they drive him to desperation. He lives a life of care, anxiety, sorrow, fretfulness and disappointment.

But the spiritual man dwells in another country; his faith makes him a citizen of another land. It is true he endures the same toils and experiences the same afflictions as the ungodly, but they deal with him after another fashion, for they come as a gracious Father's appointments, and they go at the bidding of loving wisdom. By faith the godly man casts his care upon God who careth for him, and he walks without carking care because he knows himself to be the child of heaven's loving-kindness, for whom all things work together for good.

God is his great guardian and friend, and all his concerns are safe in the hands of infinite grace.

—— STRENGTH IN NUMBERS ——

We are in this struggle together.
PHILIPPIANS 1:30 NLT

The great thing about challenges for the believer is that we don't struggle alone.

Christian men have two responsibilities in this arena: to confide in our brothers and to bear one another's burdens. By doing these things, we both give and receive strength.

"Confess your sins to each other and pray for each other so that you may be healed" (James 5:16 NLT). When we admit that we're struggling, whether with a particular sin or some spiritual, emotional, physical, or relational challenge, we are on our way toward finding help. Laying down our pride and confessing that we need help will allow God to do powerful work within our lives and the lives of those around us.

"Share each other's burdens, and in this way obey the law of Christ" (Galatians 6:2 NLT). Our second responsibility is to step up and help our fellows. If we see a brother struggling in any way, our responsibility is to lend a hand. This task requires us to put aside critical, negative thoughts and, in love, help our brother get back onto his feet—or, more specifically, back to Jesus.

Interestingly, we can fulfill our second responsibility even when we're struggling ourselves. Be ready to ask for help, and be ready to help, any time and every time. Always remember, as the apostle Paul said, "We are in this struggle together."

—— SEEKING GREAT THINGS ——

*When Baruch son of Neriah wrote on a scroll the words
Jeremiah the prophet dictated in the fourth year of Jehoiakim
son of Josiah king of Judah, Jeremiah said this to Baruch: "This
is what the LORD, the God of Israel, says to you, Baruch: You said,
'Woe to me! The LORD has added sorrow to my pain; I am worn out
with groaning and find no rest.' But the LORD has told me to say to
you, 'This is what the LORD says: I will overthrow what I have built
and uproot what I have planted, throughout the earth. Should you
then seek great things for yourself? Do not seek them. For I will
bring disaster on all people, declares the LORD, but wherever
you go I will let you escape with your life.' "*

JEREMIAH 45:1–5 NIV

What a startling experience for Baruch. He must have responded
in great surprise when Jeremiah said he was relaying a personal
message from God. What would the Lord have to say to him?

God made public a woeful declaration Baruch had spoken
in his heart (verse 3), then rebuked him: "Should you then seek
great things for yourself? Do not seek them" (verse 5).

It appears self-pity was prompting Baruch to forsake Jeremiah
and pursue a better life elsewhere. The Lord said, in essence:
"Where are you planning to find that better life, Baruch?"

If God is who He says He is (and He is!), we are always better
off with Him. There is no greater thing we could seek.

—FROM THE KING'S PALACE—

*Now because we have maintenance from the king's palace,
and it was not meet for us to see the king's dishonour,
therefore have we sent and certified the king.*
EZRA 4:14 KJV

There is no help for the child of God if his heavenly Father should shut the granary door. If out of the king's palace there came no portions of meat in due season, we might lay us down and die of despair. Who could hold us up but God? Who could guide us but God? Who could keep us from falling into perdition but God? Who could from hour to hour supply our desperate wants but God?

Is it not, then, right well for us—abundantly well—that we have had our maintenance from the king's palace? While we turn over this very sweet thought, we may remember that our maintenance from the king's palace has cost His Majesty dear. He has not fed us for nothing. It cost Him His own dear Son at the very first.

We should not have begun to live if He had spared His Son and kept Him back from us; but the choicest treasure in heaven. . .He was pleased to spend for our sakes that we might live; and ever since then we have been fed upon Jesus Christ Himself.

Day 62

GOD HEARS YOU

Early the next morning Abraham took some food and a skin of water and gave them to Hagar. He set them on her shoulders and then sent her off with the boy. . . . God heard the boy crying, and the angel of God called to Hagar from heaven and said to her, "What is the matter, Hagar? Do not be afraid; God has heard the boy crying as he lies there. Lift the boy up and take him by the hand, for I will make him into a great nation."
GENESIS 21:14, 17–18 NIV

The boy is Ishmael and the father is Abraham. God has plans to bless Ishmael and make him into a mighty nation, although the nation through which "all peoples on earth will be blessed" (Genesis 12:3 NIV) will be the offspring of Isaac, Ishmael's much younger half brother. These two sons of Abraham cannot live together, and Ishmael is banished.

His mother, Hagar, is a slave who was brought from Egypt. She had undoubtedly grown accustomed to the wealth of her master's home and the affection Abraham had for Ishmael. So it was certainly a shock to her system when she and the boy were sent away to fend for themselves.

But they weren't truly alone. As Hagar and Ishmael feared the end was near, God sensed their distress and met their need. God still does that today for those who follow His Son, Jesus. His promises remain true regardless of the circumstances of your life.

You can rely on the Lord to meet your needs. Have you cried out for His help?

JUST BE OBEDIENT

*Then Jephthah went over to fight the Ammonites,
and the LORD gave them into his hands. He devastated
twenty towns from Aroer to the vicinity of Minnith,
as far as Abel Keramim. Thus Israel subdued Ammon.*
JUDGES 11:32–33 NIV

Jephthah was born to Gilead and a prostitute. His father's wife bore Gilead other children and when they were grown, they drove Jephthah away, fearing he would take their inheritance. He fled to the land of Tob, where a gang of scoundrels badgered him. But when war with the Ammonites broke out, the elders of Gilead went to Jephthah—who was known as a warrior—promising to make him commander if he would fight with them.

After agreeing to join Israel, the Spirit of the Lord came on Jephthah (Judges 11:29) and he asked God to give him victory over the Ammonites. The Lord did so. But as a part of his request, Jephthah had made a foolish vow, which cost his daughter's life.

God uses flawed people to accomplish His will. Some of us have committed big sins, others have had big sins committed against us. Whatever your case, don't let that stop you from answering God's call on your life. He's been in control the entire time, and He will use your experiences to strengthen you. You don't need to bargain with Him or make foolish promises—just be obedient.

STRANGLED BY WORRY

*"Can all your worries add
a single moment to your life?"*
MATTHEW 6:27 NLT

This world can be a frightening place. It's full of uncertainty, from diseases to terrorism to economic upheaval. Things often seem out of control, and we feel weak. That's where worry steps in. In a strange way, worry gives us a sense of control over situations.

The word *worry* comes from an Old English term meaning "to strangle." By worrying a situation, we are trying to get our arms around it, to subdue it. But *we* are the worried ones—the problem has its arms around us. By giving into worry, we allow ourselves to be strangled.

What should we do instead? Philippians 4:6 says, "Don't worry about anything; instead, pray about everything. Tell God what you need, and thank him for all he has done" (NLT).

While worry gives an illusion of control, prayer recognizes the One who's in control. When we put our problems in God's hands, we are trusting His ability to take care of them. Pray. Commit the outcome of worrying situations to the Lord. Remember those times when God has proved Himself to be faithful.

This world can be a frightening place, but it doesn't need to be. By relinquishing our control to the One who is in control. we can overcome worry and become truly strong.

THE APPROACH OF SIN

And when the woman saw that the tree was good for food,
and that it was pleasant to the eyes, and a tree to be desired
to make one wise, she took of the fruit thereof, and did eat,
and gave also unto her husband with her; and he did eat.

GENESIS 3:6 KJV

Let us remember how it was through the body sin entered. "The woman saw that the tree was good for food," this was the temptation in the flesh; through this the soul was reached, "it was a delight to the eyes"; through the soul it then passed into the spirit, and "to be desired to make one wise."

In John's description of what is in the world (see 1 John 2:15), we find the same threefold division, "the lust of the flesh, the lust of the eyes, and the pride of life." And the three temptations of Jesus by Satan correspond exactly: he first sought to reach Him through the body, in the suggestion to satisfy His hunger by making bread; the second (see Luke 4) appealed to the soul, in the vision of the kingdoms of this world and their glory; the third to the spirit, in the call to assert and prove His divine Sonship by casting Himself down.

The first approaches of sin are made through the body: in the body the complete victory will be gained.

GREAT IS GOD'S FAITHFULNESS

Yet this I call to mind and therefore I have hope: Because of the LORD's great love we are not consumed, for his compassions never fail. They are new every morning; great is your faithfulness.
LAMENTATIONS 3:21–23 NIV

The book of Lamentations is aptly named. It contains a series of five laments written by Jeremiah after the destruction of Judah's crown jewel: Jerusalem.

These laments read like a drama, with lines given to the ravaged people's belated prayers to God (see 1:9, 1:11, 1:20–22, 2:20–22), futile cries for someone to comfort them (see 1:12–16), sorrow over their suffering children (see 2:12), and the taunts of their oppressors (see 2:16–17).

Jeremiah's own suffering can be heard throughout chapters 1 and 2, before taking center stage in chapter 3. However, a third of the way through that triple acrostic (three verses for each letter of the Hebrew alphabet), Jeremiah shines the spotlight on his enduring faith and hope in the Lord God.

If anyone had cause to lose hope—humanly speaking—it was Jeremiah. After forty years of serving the Lord, though, how could Jeremiah walk away? Centuries later, the apostle Peter said it well: "*Lord*, to whom shall we go? *You* have the words of eternal life" (John 6:68 NIV, emphasis added).

This world is broken. This life is hard. But God's faithfulness is great. He has the words—and the power—of eternal life.

THE BASICS

"Brothers and sisters, choose seven men from among you who are known to be full of the Spirit and wisdom. We will turn this responsibility over to them and will give our attention to prayer and the ministry of the word."
ACTS 6:3–4 NIV

The Christian life is not easy; it's simple. What's the difference?

Believers often find themselves in tough situations. The world, the flesh, and the devil all conspire to derail us from our true calling. Hardships—some out of the blue, some of our own creation—drag us down emotionally. The apostles who spoke the words of today's verse had just been arrested and flogged for preaching about Jesus (Acts 5:17–42).

But even though these early Christian leaders lived difficult lives, they knew their basic duties were simple: praying and studying God's Word. Knowing God more deeply and spending time in His presence were the uncomplicated things that provided strength for their challenges.

In Acts 6, the apostles prioritized their "quiet time" with God over the physical duties of the church—specifically, distributing food to the needy widows. That decision in no way implied that the church leaders were more important than the widows or above physical work. . .notice that they arranged for seven wise, godly men to oversee that distribution. But the apostles knew they needed Bible study and prayer to best serve the overall church with their spiritual leadership.

An old Sunday school song really captures the truth of the Christian life: "Read your Bible, pray every day, and you'll grow, grow, grow."

— STRONGER THAN SAMSON —

*Now [Samson] was suddenly very thirsty. He called out
to God, "You have given your servant this great victory.
Are you going to abandon me to die of thirst and fall into
the hands of the uncircumcised?" So God split open the
rock basin in Lehi; water gushed out and Samson drank.*
JUDGES 15:18–19 MSG

After taking out a group of Philistine soldiers with a makeshift
weapon, Samson sang a brief song: "With a donkey's jawbone I
made heaps of donkeys of them. With a donkey's jawbone I killed
an entire company" (Judges 15:16 MSG). Then he realized he was
thirsty, which may have been an aspect of God's discipline on the
willful judge of Israel.

Samson's thirst was "a natural effect of the great pains he had
taken," John Wesley wrote. "And perhaps there was the hand of
God therein, to chastise him for not making mention of God in his
song, and to keep him from being proud of his strength."

Even Samson's prayer above has an edge to it. He seemed ex-
asperated by his thirst and God's "abandonment" of him. In His
mercy, God miraculously provided water.

That's the amazing thing about God: He often blesses us with
good things even when we fail Him—when our hearts are cold and
distracted, when we've consciously chosen to sin. Let's be sure to
acknowledge His blessings, but also to root out the attitudes and
actions that separate us from God. If we can consistently do that,
we'll be stronger than Samson ever was.

— WORK OUT YOUR SALVATION —

Wherefore, my beloved, as ye have always obeyed, not as in my presence only, but now much more in my absence, work out your own salvation with fear and trembling. For it is God which worketh in you both to will and to do of his good pleasure.
PHILIPPIANS 2:12–13 KJV

What does that passage mean—"Work out your own salvation with fear and trembling"? Well, I want you to emphasize the word *your*: "Work out your salvation." That is most important.

You hear people talk of working out salvation, when all the time they have not got it. How can you work out what you do not possess? Paul is here writing to the Christians at Philippi. They were already saved by the grace of God. Now that they had got this wonderful gift, he says: "Go, work it out."

When you see a person working *for* salvation, you may know that he has got a false idea of the teaching of the scripture. We have salvation as a gift; and of course we cannot get it by working for it. It is our appreciation of this gift that makes us work.

FORGIVE EVERYONE

*Oh, what joy for those whose disobedience is forgiven,
whose sin is put out of sight! Yes, what joy for those
whose record the Lord has cleared of guilt.*
PSALM 32:1–2 NLT

We all know someone who absolutely refuses to forgive. The offense may be fresh or it may have happened a lifetime ago. But like a tree being strangled by a vine, that person is dying. The tree is bigger, taller, and stronger than its attacker, but it is doomed. Unless the vine is killed at the root, it will consume a little more of the tree's strength and beauty every day. The tree is going to fall—the only question is when.

For some unfortunate people, this slithering snake's-nest of unforgiveness is such an obsession they actually keep a list of offenders. Some take real pleasure in letting the worst offenders know in no uncertain terms that they are on the list.

But believers must never keep such a list—we are to forgive everyone of everything. Why? Jesus said, "If you do not forgive others their sins, your Father will not forgive your sins" (Matthew 6:15 NIV). We can all admit that the list of our own sins is more than sufficient to keep us out of God's presence for good. Yet He is willing to forgive us—and happy to help us do the same for others.

SURRENDER ALL

And the king of Israel answered and said, My lord, O king,
according to thy saying, I am thine, and all that I have.
1 KINGS 20:4 KJV

The longer we continue as Christians, the deeper will be our insight into that word: surrender to Jesus. We shall always see more clearly that we do not yet fully understand or contemplate it. The surrender must become, especially, more undivided and trustful. The language which Ahab once used must be ours: "According to thy saying, my lord, O king, I am thine, and all that I have."

This is the language of undivided dedication: I am thine, and all that I have. Keep nothing back. Keep back no single sin that you do not confess and leave off. Without conversion there can be no surrender. Keep back no single power. Let your head with all its thinking, your mouth with all its speaking, your heart with all its feeling, your hand with all its working—let your time, your name, your influence, your property, let all be laid upon the altar.

Jesus has a right to all: He demands the whole. Give yourself, with all that you have, to be guided and used and kept, sanctified and blessed.

WAIT ON THE LORD

*I say to myself, "The LORD is my portion; therefore I
will wait for him." The LORD is good to those whose
hope is in him, to the one who seeks him; it is good
to wait quietly for the salvation of the LORD.*
LAMENTATIONS 3:24–26 NIV

In today's scripture, Jeremiah makes a pair of statements with strong allusions to biblical history.

The first evokes imagery from Joshua 13–21. The earlier chapters of Joshua are all about conquest, but this latter part of the book concerns "portions." One tribe of Israel at a time was assigned its own portion of the Promised Land. Each portion was mapped and described in detail. You can imagine the people's excitement: "This is what we've been waiting for! Our portion of the Promised Land!" Sadly, before long the people forgot that their infinite, eternal portion was the Lord God Himself (see also Psalm 16:5, 73:26, 119:57, and 142:5).

Jeremiah's second statement evokes imagery from Genesis 12–24. Throughout these chapters, Abraham—the father of faith in the Lord God—did exactly what Jeremiah described. That is, Abraham hoped in the Lord, sought Him, and waited quietly for His salvation.

Abraham's faith, it turns out, is a model for all of us. The apostle Paul wrote, "Against all hope, Abraham in hope believed and so became the father of many nations" (Romans 4:18 NIV). Jesus Himself said, "Abraham rejoiced at the thought of seeing my day; he saw it and was glad" (John 8:56 NIV).

Wait on the Lord. He will provide exactly what you need, at exactly the right moment.

WE OWE OUR SUCCESSES TO THE LORD

*And to the captains over hundreds did the
priest give king David's spears and shields,
that were in the temple of the LORD.*
2 KINGS 11:10 KJV

Every genuine Christian has to fight. Every inch of the way between here and heaven we shall have to fight, for as hitherto every single step of our pilgrimage has been one prolonged conflict. Sometimes we have victories, a presage of that final victory, that perfect triumph we shall enjoy with our Great Captain forever.

When we have these victories it behooves us to be especially careful that in all good conscience we hang up the trophies thereof in the house of the Lord. The reason for this lies here: it is to the Lord that we owe any success we have ever achieved. We have been defeated when we have gone in our own strength; but when we have been victorious it has always been because the strength of the Lord was put forth for our deliverance.

GOD WILL PROVIDE

Isaac spoke up and said to his father Abraham, "Father?"
"Yes, my son?" Abraham replied. "The fire and wood are here,"
Isaac said, "but where is the lamb for the burnt offering?"
Abraham answered, "God himself will provide the lamb for the
burnt offering, my son." And the two of them went on together.
GENESIS 22:7–8 NIV

The challenge is set clearly before Abraham: Does he trust God with the life of his son Isaac?

This almost incomprehensible request for Abraham to take Isaac to the distant mountains and offer him as a sacrifice had two possible outcomes. Either Abraham would prove his love for God by slaughtering his son on an altar, or God would somehow provide an alternative. Abraham knew that God would provide.

As believers, we often face situations in which the outcome is uncertain. But when seemingly impossible choices are all we see, we can act in confident faith, following the example of Abraham.

Centuries after this incident, the New Testament writer James said, "And the scripture was fulfilled that says, 'Abraham believed God, and it was credited to him as righteousness,' and he was called God's friend" (James 2:23 NIV). In this moment of extreme challenge, Abraham trusted his long-established friendship with God. He approached his terrible task in faith—and God did provide an alternative (see Genesis 22:12–13).

Along the path of life, our simple acts of obedience to God accumulate. And, like Abraham when the crisis comes, we find that trusting God is not only possible. It's the best possible option.

—— NO SCHEMING NECESSARY ——

"The Lord bless you, my daughter," [Boaz] replied [to Ruth].
"This kindness is greater than that which you showed earlier:
You have not run after the younger men, whether rich or poor."
RUTH 3:10 NIV

The first time he saw her, it seems Boaz was taken with Ruth (Ruth 2:5). Most likely considerably older, Boaz went out of his way to accommodate Ruth—and warning his men not to lay a hand on her. Imagine his surprise when he went to sleep in the threshing floor one night and woke up to find Ruth lying at his feet! She informed Boaz that he was her guardian-redeemer.

It would have been easy for Boaz to make Ruth his wife right away. Scripture doesn't say whether he was tempted to do so, but we do see his impressive actions. Knowing he wasn't the nearest guardian-redeemer, Boaz invited the other man to step in, then trusted God for the results. You probably know the rest of the story: the closer relative said "no," so Boaz ended up marrying Ruth.

Boaz and Ruth both acted honorably, exhibiting high moral character and a humble reliance on God when it would have been easy to act on impulse. We know—from the Bible and from personal experience—that God provides exactly what we need, when we need it. Remember that truth and trust Him to take care of you. He'll often provide what you want as well.

— THOSE WHO NEED A DOCTOR —

*Jesus heard it and said to them, "People who are well
do not need a doctor. Only those who are sick need
a doctor. I have not come to call those who are right
with God. I have come to call those who are sinners."*
MARK 2:17 NLV

As a rabbi, Jesus chose unlikely followers. After taking on a group
of fishermen as His disciples, Jesus reached down to the dregs of
society to call Levi, a tax collector.

Collecting taxes was not an honorable profession in Jesus' day.
As agents of the Roman empire, tax collectors took money from
their fellow Jews to give to Caesar. Many collected more than was
necessary, then depended on the might of Rome to keep them safe
from reprisal. They were viewed as traitors and prohibited from
entering the synagogue.

And yet, here was Jesus, calling tax collectors to follow Him, din-
ing with them openly. As a rabbi, Jesus should have known better.
Religious elites like the Pharisees were more than confused—they
were angry! And in their anger, they completely missed what Jesus
said about the sick needing a doctor.

Tax collectors were undoubtedly part of the sickness Jesus
came to cure, but so were the Pharisees. Jesus came to call all to
repentance, from the bottom of society to the top. The bottom-
dwellers tend to know they are sick; those at top often have no clue.

Fortunately, Jesus is still making house calls. He is ready to heal
anyone who comes to Him in humility. The treatment will cost
everything, but the sickness leads only to death.

CLEAR PROOF OF GOD'S LOVE

Can a maid forget her ornaments, or a bride her attire?
yet my people have forgotten me days without number.
JEREMIAH 2:32 KJV

It is a clear proof of the great love of God to His people that He will not lose their love without earnest expostulation. When you do not care at all for a person, he may love you or hate you, it is all the same to you; but when you have great love for him, then you earnestly desire to possess his heart in return. This, then, is clear proof that God greatly loves His people, since, whenever their hearts wander from Him, He is greatly grieved, and He rebukes them and earnestly pleads with them setting the coldness of their hearts in a true light and striving to bring them back to warm affection towards Himself.

Not only are God's rebukes proofs of His love, but when He goes farther and deals out blows as well as words, there is love in every stroke of His hand. Most truly does He say, "As many as I love I rebuke and chasten" (Revelation 3:19 KJV), since rebukes and chastenings are proofs that He will not lose our hearts without a struggle for them.

A NEW HEART

*"I [God] will give [the returning exiled Israelites] an
undivided heart and put a new spirit in them; I will remove
from them their heart of stone and give them a heart of flesh.
Then they will follow my decrees and be careful to keep
my laws. They will be my people, and I will be their God. . . .
I will give you a new heart and put a new spirit in you;
I will remove from you your heart of stone and give you a
heart of flesh. And I will put my Spirit in you and move you
to follow my decrees and be careful to keep my laws."*
EZEKIEL 11:19–20, 36:26–27 NIV

Throughout Ezekiel's ministry, the Lord spoke of His rebellious
people having hardened hearts of stone. The imagery suggests a
catastrophic stroke, paralysis, and impending death (think of the
demise of Nabal in 1 Samuel 25:37). More importantly, it suggests
an irrational, pride-induced, resolute refusal to obey the Lord,
no matter how severe the consequences (think of the Pharaoh in
Exodus 4:21–14:8).

Yet the Lord offered to give them (and, by extension, *us*) the best
possible exchange: a new heart of flesh filled with His Spirit. Then
God's people can obey Him willingly, regularly, *gladly*.

What could provide more strength for the challenge than a
living, passionate heart for God? He will provide it as we ask.

ASK FOR HELP

*The Spirit told Philip, "Go to that chariot and stay near it."
Then Philip ran up to the chariot and heard the man reading
Isaiah the prophet. "Do you understand what you are reading?"
Philip asked. "How can I," he said, "unless someone explains
it to me?" So he invited Philip to come up and sit with him.*
ACTS 8:29–31 NIV

When an Ethiopian treasury official read the words of the prophet Isaiah, he was stumped. Philip, a deacon in the church at Jerusalem, was led by the Spirit to get close to the man's chariot. When he heard the Ethiopian official reading aloud, Philip asked a simple question: "Do you understand what you are reading?"

The man in the chariot was an important person. As such, he could have dismissed Philip's inquiry. Instead, he wisely replied with humility. The Ethiopian official received both an explanation of Isaiah's prophecy and eternal life when he surrendered his heart to Jesus.

The key through many (if not most) of our trials isn't trying harder—it's seeking wisdom from good, mature, wise believers who may have just the help we need. Often times, those around us have had similar experiences, and they can help us with firsthand information.

In Proverbs 18:15 we read, "The heart of the discerning acquires knowledge, for the ears of the wise seek it out" (NIV). No matter what challenge we face, we can ask our heavenly Father and our faithful brothers in Christ to help us get through it.

NOT FORGOTTEN

"I will keep alive the name of the dead man [Mahlon] on his land. His name will not be forgotten among his brothers or from the gate of his birth-place. You have heard this today."
RUTH 4:10 NLV

Naomi returned to Bethlehem a broken woman. She'd lost her husband, Elimelech, and her two sons, Mahlon and Chilion. And when Naomi appeared in Bethlehem with her daughter-in-law Ruth, her former neighbors weren't even sure who she was (Ruth 1:19–20). She no longer wanted to be called Naomi (meaning "beautiful" or "pleasant"), but rather Mara ("bitter"). She had lost much, and she was bitter. Worst of all, Naomi felt like God had abandoned her.

Of course, God was still with Naomi. And so was Ruth. And eventually, a guardian-redeemer in the form of Boaz. He gathered the leaders and the people together and made the proclamation you read in today's verse. Naomi's son Mahlon would not be forgotten. Neither would Naomi herself, as she would become the grandmother of Ruth's son Obed, who would have a son named Jesse, who would father David. . .whose line eventually gave us Jesus, the redeemer of humankind.

What have you lost? A career? A business? Your spouse? Your health? A dream? God is able to touch your deepest pain and redeem it. He may restore what you've lost, or He may have other plans. Either way, He hasn't forgotten you.

A PRAYERFUL SPIRIT

And when Moses was gone into the tabernacle of the congregation to speak with him, then he heard the voice of one speaking unto him from off the mercy seat that was upon the ark of testimony, from between the two cherubims: and he spake unto him.

NUMBERS 7:89 KJV

In regard to the connection between prayer and the word in our private devotion, the expression of a convert from heathenism has often been quoted: "I pray, I speak to God; I read in the Bible, God speaks to me."

There is a verse in the history of Moses, in which this thought is beautifully brought out. We read, "When Moses was gone into the tabernacle to speak with God, then he heard the voice of one speaking to him from off the mercy seat: and God spake unto him." When he went in to pray for himself or his people and to wait for instructions, he found One waiting for him.

What a lesson for our morning watch. A prayerful spirit is the spirit to which God will speak. A prayerful spirit will be a listening spirit waiting to hear what God says.

Day 82

——— REJOICE IN THE LORD ———

*Whatever happens, my dear brothers and sisters,
rejoice in the Lord. I never get tired of telling you
these things, and I do it to safeguard your faith.*
PHILIPPIANS 3:1 NLT

How are you supposed to find joy in a bad medical diagnosis? Or when a financial crisis has you scrambling? Or when an important relationship is ailing? Or when any other aspect of life is out of whack?

Rejoicing in these moments is not an easy thing. But the apostle Paul commands it. (By the way, he was in prison when he wrote those words.)

Granted, the "how" of rejoicing in the Lord is easier said than it is done. We must simply trust. Rather than questioning God's motives or the process He's ordained, just trust His plan. Allow God to take full control of the situation.

Later in the letter to the Philippians, Paul wrote, "Don't worry about anything; instead, pray about everything. Tell God what you need, and thank Him for all He has done. Then you will experience God's peace, which exceeds anything we can understand" (4:6–7 NLT). These are very practical words. When worry arises, pray. Tell God what you need. Thank Him for His faithful provision already. And wait for His peace.

In our weakest moments, Jesus shines brightest. Rejoice in the Lord always, no matter what.

NO CONTEST

*The chariots of God are tens of thousands
and thousands of thousands.*
PSALM 68:17 NIV

In the Old Testament, chariots were often the measure of an army's strength. When pursuing the Israelites fleeing their slavery in Egypt, Pharaoh sent "six hundred of his best chariots, along with all the other chariots of Egypt" (Exodus 14:7 NIV). Pagan kings opposing the Israelites' entry into the Promised Land "came out with all their troops and a large number of horses and chariots—a huge army" (Joshua 11:4 NIV). Philistines in King Saul's day massed against Israel with "three thousand chariots, six thousand charioteers, and soldiers as numerous as the sand on the seashore" (1 Samuel 13:5 NIV).

Guess what? In each case, the Israelites prevailed. But not because of their own strength and courage—every battle was won by the Lord. You probably know that God caused the Red Sea— miraculously separated for the Israelites to pass through—to inundate the Egyptian soldiers. God helped Joshua defeat the pagan kings and burn their chariots. Saul's son Jonathan bravely followed God's leading into the enemy camp, setting of a panic that had Philistine soldiers killing each other. In case there's any question, 1 Samuel 14:15 says, "It was a panic sent by God" (NIV).

If you are God's child, it doesn't matter how many enemies line up against you. He has myriads of chariots and soldiers at His disposal. Never forget the experience of Elisha's servant. The prophet prayed, "Open his eyes, LORD, so that he may see." And God did. "The LORD opened the servant's eyes, and he looked and saw the hills full of horses and chariots of fire all around Elisha" (2 Kings 6:17 NIV).

Really, it's no contest.

YOUR RESPONSIBILITY, AND NO MORE

The soul that sinneth, it shall die. The son shall not bear the iniquity of the father, neither shall the father bear the iniquity of the son: the righteousness of the righteous shall be upon him, and the wickedness of the wicked shall be upon him.

EZEKIEL 18:20 KJV

Every human being sins and is guilty before God (Romans 3:23). That is the bad news that colors our entire world. But there is good news: Every human being also has the opportunity to accept God's free gift of salvation (John 3:16). This is a personal choice that, once made, makes us much-loved members of God's family, with all the rights, privileges, and protections that new relationship offers.

Sadly, not everyone makes good choices—whether in the ultimate decision to receive Jesus or the day-by-day behaviors that define our lives. Poor choices by the people we love can create tension in our own lives, but the prophet Ezekiel offers peace and strength in the words of God Himself: each person is individually responsible before the Lord.

Your father's choices, good or bad, won't pick you up or tear you down in God's eyes (Ezekiel 18:14–18). Your children's choices, good or bad, won't help or hurt you before God either (verses 5–13). When you live a faithful Christian life, God accepts that as your "reasonable service" (Romans 12:1 KJV).

Definitely pray for your loved ones who make poor choices, and try to point them to God's better way. But don't take on more responsibility than God assigns. "The righteousness of the righteous" (*Jesus'* righteousness) will be on you.

STAND LIKE A KING

And it came to pass, when Ahab saw Elijah, that Ahab
said unto him, Art thou he that troubleth Israel? And he
answered, I have not troubled Israel; but thou, and thy
father's house, in that ye have forsaken the commandments
of the LORD, and thou hast followed Baalim. Now therefore
send, and gather to me all Israel unto mount Carmel, and the
prophets of Baal four hundred and fifty, and the prophets of
the groves four hundred, which eat at Jezebel's table.
1 KINGS 18:17–19 KJV

When Elijah stood on Mount Carmel, Ahab did not see who was
with him. Little did he know the prophet's God; little did he think
that, when Elijah walked up Mount Carmel, God walked with him.
Talk of an Alexander making the world tremble at the tread of his
armies!—of the marches and victories of a Caesar, or a Napoleon!
The man who is walking with God is greater than all the Caesars
and Napoleons and Alexanders who ever lived. Little did Ahab and
the false prophets of Baal know that Elijah was walking with the
same God with whom Enoch walked before the flood. Elijah was
nothing when out of communion with God; but when walking in
the power of God, he stood on Mount Carmel like a king.

HOLD ON

So Jacob was left alone, and a man wrestled with him till daybreak. When the man saw that he could not overpower him, he touched the socket of Jacob's hip so that his hip was wrenched as he wrestled with the man. Then the man said, "Let me go, for it is daybreak." But Jacob replied, "I will not let you go unless you bless me."
GENESIS 32:24–26 NIV

Jacob was dreading the morning. He would come face-to-face with his twin brother, Esau, the man he had cheated nearly fifteen years earlier. Jacob was obeying God's instruction to return to his homeland, but he was full of anxiety about the next day.

Apparently unable to sleep, Jacob prayed for God's protection. Then he went off alone to plot ways of appeasing Esau, to "pacify him with these gifts I am sending on ahead" (Genesis 32:20 NIV).

Late in the night, a mysterious "man" confronted Jacob. Hours of exhausting wrestling followed, but neither Jacob nor his opponent was able to prevail. As daybreak arrived, this angel of God, who Jacob identified later as God Himself (see Genesis 32:30), tried to disengage and leave. But Jacob held on longer, insisting on a blessing.

He had learned, after years of relying on his own strength and cunning, that all he truly needed to face Esau was the blessing of God. Jacob held tightly to the Lord, understanding what would later be written in Psalm 55:22: "Cast your cares on the LORD and he will sustain you; he will never let the righteous be shaken" (NIV).

— THE FIRST OPTION: PRAYER —

*Hannah said, "O, my lord! As you live, my lord, I am the woman
who stood here beside you, praying to the Lord. I prayed for
this boy, and the Lord has given me what I asked of Him."*
1 SAMUEL 1:26–27 NLV

Yes, this is a "girl's story" in a men's devotional book. But the account
of God answering Hannah's desperate prayer for a son carries a
powerful lesson for everyone.

Hannah was one of Elkanah's two wives. That fact alone would
create difficulties for the barren Hannah. But life was especially
hard because the other wife, Peninnah, had children. And she
seemed to take pleasure in reminding Hannah of their differing
motherhood status.

Elkanah seemed to love Hannah but offered only clumsy com-
ments like, "Am I not better to you than ten sons?" (1 Samuel 1:8 NLV).
At Israel's worship center at Shiloh, the priest Eli initially thought
Hannah's anguished, wordless praying was drunkenness (verse
14). When she explained, Eli wisely reconsidered, and said, "May
the God of Israel do what you have asked of Him" (verse 17 NLV).

And God did. Hannah ultimately gave birth to a baby named
Samuel, who would become one of Israel's great leaders. But that
would likely not have happened apart from her prayers.

Today, we have the same opportunity to pray that Hannah
had—and took full advantage of. Prayer should never be a last
resort, but a first option. It's the quickest and most effective way
to tap into God's strength for our daily challenges.

ARE YOU OUT OF YOUR MIND?

When his family heard what was happening, they tried to take him away. "He's out of his mind," they said.
MARK 3:21 NLT

Near the beginning of Jesus' ministry, word traveled from Capernaum—where Jesus was healing the sick and casting out demons—to his hometown of Nazareth about twenty miles away. His family heard the reports of the miracle-working rabbi who consorted with tax collectors. They determined that Jesus had gone crazy.

As loving family members, they made the twenty-mile trip to Capernaum to bring Him home. They wanted to talk some sense into Jesus. When a disciple told Jesus that His mother and brothers were outside, He replied, "Who is my mother? Who are my brothers?" Then He looked around and said, "Look, these are my mother and brothers. Anyone who does God's will is my brother and sister and mother" (Mark 3:33–35 NLT).

That wasn't going to calm His family's fears.

The reality is that following Jesus—doing what He tells us to do and seeking His Father's will more than the approval of the world—may make us seem insane. But that's okay.

Our strength does not come from the world's approval. Doing God's will makes us strong. Our family and friends may not understand what we're doing. That's okay too. In time, like Jesus' own brothers, they may come around. The important thing is that we always do what God wants first.

There's nothing crazy about that.

THE RECORD OF MERCY

*Thou drewest near in the day that I
called upon thee: thou saidst, Fear not.*
LAMENTATIONS 3:57 KJV

Brethren, if our experiences have so far exceeded our expectations and belied our doubts, let us take care that we record them. Do not let us suffer our lamentations to be written in a book, and our thanksgivings to be spoken to the wind. Write not your complaints in marble and your praises upon the sand. Let the record of mercy received be carefully made, accurately measured, distinctly worded, correctly dated and so preserved that in years to come you may turn for your encouragement to it.

Jeremiah tells us that on such a day the Lord drew near to him; David remembered God from the Hermons and the hill Mizar; time and place are elements of interest in the memory of the Lord's great goodness. Note the particulars, dwell on the details—abundantly utter the memory of the divine loving-kindness.

COMMITTED TO GOD, NO MATTER WHAT

*"If we are thrown into the blazing furnace, the God we serve
is able to deliver us from it, and he will deliver us from
Your Majesty's hand. But even if he does not, we want you
to know, Your Majesty, that we will not serve your gods
or worship the image of gold you have set up."*
DANIEL 3:17–18 NIV

The undisputed king of the world's first great superpower, Nebuchadnezzar, was a tyrant. He didn't hesitate to order an instant death for anyone who displeased him. It could be fatal to hesitate, make a mistake, or fail at a task the king demanded. Few men even wanted to be in his presence.

On the other hand, at the end of Daniel 2, "the king appointed Shadrach, Meshach and Abednego administrators over the province of Babylon" *at Daniel's request* (2:49 NIV). Up to this point, Daniel's friends had done nothing but please Nebuchadnezzar.

How quickly one's circumstances and station in life can change! Yet the more the king threatened them, the more Daniel's friends resolutely insisted they would serve and worship only the one true God.

You probably know how the story ends: a furious Nebuchadnezzar had Shadrach, Meshach, and Abednego thrown into a blazing furnace. But God brought them through the fire without a singed hair or even a smell of smoke. The Lord proved His absolute superiority to even the world's strongest, most frightening ruler.

When you commit to God, no matter what, He will also take care of you—bringing you through the fire or taking you on to heaven. Christians really can't lose.

— GOD ALWAYS HAS A PLAN —

On that day a great persecution broke out against the church in Jerusalem, and all except the apostles were scattered throughout Judea and Samaria. Godly men buried Stephen and mourned deeply for him. But Saul began to destroy the church. Going from house to house, he dragged off both men and women and put them in prison. Those who had been scattered preached the word wherever they went.

ACTS 8:1–4 NIV

After the Holy Spirit arrived at Pentecost, it was time for the disciples to go into "all the world" to preach the good news about Jesus. They met opposition everywhere, culminating in the stoning of Stephen, a deacon in the Jerusalem church.

If that was where the story of Acts stopped, we might question God's plan. After all, if *we* were writing a script for the start of the church, we would probably have included a lot less persecution.

But we don't write our own stories—not entirely. We can't fully control our own future. At some point, we will find ourselves in hard situations, difficulties similar to those early believers up in the drama of first-century Jerusalem.

Thankfully, though, God always has a plan. And in Acts 8:4, we see what it was: to spread the good news of Jesus throughout the Roman world and beyond. As you continue to read through Acts, you'll see that He even planned to use the Saul, the chief persecutor of the early church.

We don't always know what God has in store for our lives. But we can be sure that *He* does, and that His plans are for our best.

Day 92

WHO CAN STAND?

*And the people of Beth Shemesh asked, "Who can
stand in the presence of the LORD, this holy God?"*
1 SAMUEL 6:20 NIV

You probably already know that Old Testament Israel committed
many sins. Did you know they almost made an idol of the ark of
the covenant?

The ark was the single point where God would meet with the
people through their high priest—but the Israelites began to view
it as a kind of good-luck charm. They foolishly took the ark into
battle against the Philistines and lost it to their arch enemies.

After the Philistines suffered from the ark's presence, they were
happy to send it back to Israel on a cart pulled by two cows. But at
Beth Shemesh, where the cows stopped, the people's joy turned to
horror when God struck down seventy of them for looking inside
the ark. The townspeople then asked the questions you see in today's verse. They were at a loss as to how to approach a holy God.

Even today, we may try to approach God through rituals or a
moral code—but our sin nature always causes us to fall short. We
can *never* be good enough for God. But there is good news: we can
come to God on the basis of Jesus Christ's righteousness.

If your spiritual life ever grows dry, or if you feel distant from
God due to a self-inflicted hardship, don't make the same mistake Israel made. Throw yourself at the foot of the cross in humble repentance. Allow the righteousness of Christ to bring you
close to the Father.

CLASSICS: ANDREW MURRAY

— THE VOICE OF CONSCIENCE —

I say the truth in Christ, I lie not, my conscience also bearing me witness in the Holy Ghost, that I have great heaviness and continual sorrow in my heart. For I could wish that myself were accursed from Christ for my brethren, my kinsmen according to the flesh.

ROMANS 9:1–3 KJV

If the voice of conscience tells you of some course of action that is the nobler or the better, and you choose another, because it is easier or pleasing to self, you unfit yourself for the teaching of the Spirit by disobeying the voice of God in nature.

A strong will always to do the right, to do the very best, as conscience points it out, is a will to do God's will. Paul writes, "I lie not, my conscience bearing me witness in the Holy Ghost." The Holy Ghost speaks through conscience: if you disobey and hurt conscience, you make it impossible for God to speak to you.

Obedience to God's will shows itself in tender regard for the voice of conscience. This holds good with regard to eating and drinking, sleeping and resting, spending money and seeking pleasure—let everything be brought into subjection to the will of God.

GROW YOUR ROOTS

*Let your roots grow down into him, and let
your lives be built on him. Then your faith will
grow strong in the truth you were taught.*
COLOSSIANS 2:7 NLT

Without its roots, a tree would be unable to draw water from the ground for its life and health. Without roots, trees would topple over at the first strong gust of wind. For these reasons, God made a tree's roots to grow deep and wide.

The apostle Paul used roots as a word-picture for our Christian growth. "Let your roots grow down into him," Paul said, referring to Christ Jesus your Lord (see verse 6). "Let your lives be built on him." And then what? "Your faith will grow strong in the truth you were taught."

What truth were you taught? The basic doctrines—of creation, sin, Christ, and salvation. The truth of scripture, from which we learn everything we need for godly living.

When our roots go deep into God's Word, we find living water. We are nourished and strengthened for whatever comes our way, including the storms of life. We'll be able to withstand even the pummeling winds of a spiritual hurricane.

2 Timothy 3:14–16 tells us that God uses His Word to teach us, to grow us, and to equip us to live well for Him. Commit to reading the Word regularly, as well as studying and memorizing it. Let your roots grow deep into scripture, so you can find strength for the challenge.

GOD IS STILL WORKING

*Then Samuel took a stone, and set it between Mizpeh
and Shen, and called the name of it Ebenezer,
saying, Hitherto hath the LORD helped us.*
1 SAMUEL 7:12 KJV

It is certainly a very delightful thing to mark the hand of God in the lives of ancient saints. How profitable an occupation to observe God's goodness in delivering David out of the jaw of the lion and the paw of the bear; His mercy in passing by the transgression, iniquity and sin of Manasseh; His faithfulness in keeping the covenant made with Abraham; or His interposition on the behalf of the dying Hezekiah.

But, beloved, would it not be even more interesting and profitable for us to mark the hand of God in our own lives? Ought we not to look upon our own history as being at least as full of God, as full of His goodness and His truth, as much a proof of His faithfulness and veracity as the lives of any of the saints who have gone before?

I think we do our Lord an injustice when we suppose that He wrought all His mighty acts in days of yore and showed Himself strong for those in the early time, but doth not perform wonders or lay bare His arm for the saints that are now upon the earth.

STRONGER THAN THE STRONGEST

I, Nebuchadnezzar, raised my eyes toward heaven, and my sanity was restored. Then I praised the Most High; I honored and glorified him who lives forever. His dominion is an eternal dominion; his kingdom endures from generation to generation. . . . Now I, Nebuchadnezzar, praise and exalt and glorify the King of heaven, because everything he does is right and all his ways are just. And those who walk in pride he is able to humble.

DANIEL 4:34, 37 NIV

Today's verse is the end of the story of Nebuchadnezzar. The powerful, prideful king of Babylon had brought God's judgment upon himself by some ill-advised self-glory, and spent seven years in a state of insanity, living with wild animals and eating grass like an ox. But the Lord was gracious to restore the king's mind, and the last time we hear of Nebuchadnezzar in scripture, he is speaking God's praise to his kingdom and beyond.

Two generations later, Darius the Mede made a similar statement of praise to God, sending it to the people of every race and nation and language throughout his empire, which comprised at least 120 provinces (Daniel 6:25–27). And a third powerful biblical king, Cyrus the Great, issued his own statement in praise to the Lord, the God of heaven, throughout the provinces as well (2 Chronicles 36:22–23; Ezra 1:1–4).

These men, powerful as they might have been, were nothing in comparison to the one true God. In His hand, "the king's heart is a stream of water that he channels toward all who please him" (Proverbs 21:1 NIV).

And, Christian, He is on *your* side.

GOD CAN HEAR EVERY PRAYER

If my people, which are called by my name, shall humble themselves, and pray, and seek my face, and turn from their wicked ways; then will I hear from heaven, and will forgive their sin, and will heal their land.

2 CHRONICLES 7:14 KJV

God has a home, and heaven is His dwelling place. How far away that home of God, that heaven, is I do not know. But one thing I do know; it is not so far away but God can hear us when we pray.

God can hear every prayer that goes up to Him there from this sin-cursed earth. We are not so far from Him but that He can see our tears and hear the faintest whisper when we lift our hearts to Him in prayer. Do we not read, "If My people, which are called by My name, shall humble themselves, and pray, and seek My face, and turn from their wicked ways, then will I hear from heaven, and will forgive their sin, and will heal their land." That is God's own word: "I will hear from heaven," and "I will forgive their sin."

GOD IS IN CONTROL

Jacob looked up and there was Esau, coming with his four hundred men. . . . He himself went on ahead and bowed down to the ground seven times as he approached his brother. But Esau ran to meet Jacob and embraced him; he threw his arms around his neck and kissed him. And they wept.
GENESIS 33:1, 3–4 NIV

Jacob had a penchant for trusting only himself, a history of deceiving those closest to him rather than relying on God to meet his needs. But now Jacob was forced to encounter one of those he had cheated.

Jacob knew he had God's blessing. He knew he had God's favor. Still, God did not yet have Jacob's full and complete trust. Didn't he realize that God in His power could cool the anger and resentment his older brother, Esau, felt over the family blessing Jacob had stolen?

Like many of us, Jacob struggled to believe that the Lord controls the future. But He does. Centuries later, God would say to Jacob's descendants, " 'I know the plans I have for you,' declares the LORD, 'plans to prosper you and not to harm you, plans to give you hope and a future' " (Jeremiah 29:11 NIV).

Jacob's positive encounter with Esau still did not convince him to fully trust God. . .but hopefully it will convince us today. God is in control of tomorrow. Trust Him to do the right thing.

GOD EMPOWERS

Saul replied, "But I'm only from the tribe of Benjamin, the smallest tribe in Israel, and my family is the least important of all the families of that tribe! Why are you talking like this to me?"
1 SAMUEL 9:21 NLT

Saul's father, Kish, was a wealthy, influential man. And Saul was known for being the most handsome male in Israel (1 Samuel 9:1–2). But when he considered his tribe's heritage—they were the smallest tribe in Israel after being decimated in a civil war (Judges 20)—he couldn't understand why Samuel said Saul and his family were the focus of all Israel's hopes (1 Samuel 9:20).

We aren't told why Saul considered his family to be the least important in his small tribe. Maybe he was naturally humble. Maybe he was overwhelmed to think that his nation's hopes would fall on his shoulders. At this point, Saul didn't seem to understand that God was behind him—and that after Samuel anointed him as king, God would give Saul a new heart (1 Samuel 10:9).

The time may come when *you* are approached with an opportunity to serve. Will you respond like Saul, with a laundry list of reasons why you aren't able? Or will you consider the possibility that God is leading you into a new ministry? If the latter, be sure of this: God will empower you to perform the job.

SUFFERING AND PERSEVERANCE

"Whoever has will be given more; whoever does not have,
even what they have will be taken from them."
MARK 4:25 NIV

Out of context, today's verse seems not only unfair, but cruel. Why give to the one who already has something? Why take from the one who doesn't? But this verse isn't referring to money or goods. It's talking about something far more precious: perseverance.

In the parable of the sower, Jesus told His listeners what happens when God's Word falls on shallow hearts. Belief sprouts easily but falls away as soon as suffering comes. In contrast, when God's Word falls on well-tilled soil, it produces a crop many times larger than what was planted.

So how do we get from shallow ground to well-tilled soil? The simple—but not easy—answer is *suffering*. Perseverance through suffering is the thing that allows God's Word in our lives to be active and growing instead of stunted and dead.

If we have perseverance, God will add understanding to our suffering and grow in us the fruits of the spirit. If we don't persevere through suffering, we are likely to walk away from our faith, casting doubt on God's faithfulness when *we* were the ones who refused to let Him till our soil properly.

The apostle Paul elaborated in Romans 5:3–5: "Not only so, but we also glory in our sufferings, because we know that suffering produces perseverance; perseverance, character; and character, hope. And hope does not put us to shame, because God's love has been poured out into our hearts through the Holy Spirit, who has been given to us" (NIV).

WEANED FROM EARTH, WED TO HEAVEN

*But we are bound to give thanks alway to God or you,
brethren beloved of the Lord, because God hath from
the beginning chosen you to salvation through
sanctification of the Spirit and belief of the truth.*

2 THESSALONIANS 2:13 KJV

When I trust God—and I hope I do that habitually—I do not find that to give up anxiety and to trust in God is difficult now, though it used to be. Blessed be my Lord, I cannot help believing Him, for He loads me down with evidences of His truth and fidelity. Once you get really into the swim of faith and you do not need to struggle, the sacred current of grace will carry you along. Give yourself completely up to the Lord Jesus Christ and the mighty energy of the blessed Spirit, and you will find it sweet to lie passive in His hand and know no will but His.

God bring you there! If there is any unconverted person here who cannot understand all this, I pray the Lord to make him a child first, and then make him a weaned child. Regeneration must come first, and sanctification will follow. Believe in Jesus for pardon, and then you will have grace given to resign yourself to the divine will. May the Lord wean you from earth and wed you to heaven.

—— GOD EXALTS THE HUMBLE ——

*At Belshazzar's command, Daniel was clothed in purple,
a gold chain was placed around his neck, and he was
proclaimed the third highest ruler in the kingdom.*
DANIEL 5:29 NIV

During a lengthy absence of King Nabonidus, his eldest son, Belshazzar, served as coregent over the Babylonian empire. At his command, Daniel was made "the third highest ruler in the kingdom" the very night the capital fell without a battle to Darius the Mede.

Belshazzar was killed, and one could have reasonably expected the same fate for Daniel, who had originally worked for Babylon's King Nebuchadnezzar. Instead, "It pleased Darius to appoint 120 satraps to rule throughout the kingdom, with three administrators over them, one of whom was Daniel" (6:1–2 NIV). This means that—for nearly seventy years—Daniel directly served the most powerful conquerors the world had ever known. What was his secret?

First, Daniel never compromised his faith in the one true Lord, the maker of heaven and earth, whose power dwarfs the entire universe. In comparison, who is man?

Second, Daniel never traded his humility for pride, despite every human temptation to do so. He and his three friends had it all, including good looks and sharp minds (see 1:4). Nebuchadnezzar had judged them ten times better than anyone else who served him (see 1:18–20).

Humble faith makes us strong. When we know we serve the almighty God—and that we are not Him!—there's no limit to what He can do through us.

Think about it: people are *still* talking about Daniel.

ARE YOU SURE, LORD?

*The Lord told him, "Go to the house of Judas on Straight
Street and ask for a man from Tarsus named Saul, for he
is praying. In a vision he has seen a man named Ananias
come and place his hands on him to restore his sight."*
ACTS 9:11–12 NIV

The message Ananias received made no sense at all: Go and find
Saul, the man who almost singlehandedly chased the church from
Jerusalem? Tell that violent persecutor about Jesus? This sounded
less like God's direction and more like a trap. But when Jesus told
Ananias a second time, he trusted the Lord and went.

That may seem easier said than done. Ananias was originally
fearful, responding to Jesus' request by saying, "Lord. . .I have
heard many reports about this man and all the harm he has done
to your holy people in Jerusalem. And he has come here with
authority from the chief priests to arrest all who call on your name"
(verses 13–14 NIV).

But Jesus reminded Ananias (as He reminds all of us) that God's
plans are good. Saul was His "chosen instrument to proclaim my
name to the Gentiles" (verse 15 NIV). With this truth in mind, Ananias
summoned his courage and did his job—confirming a conversion
that would literally change the world.

There will be times when doing the right thing seems frightening, when we want to say, "Are You sure, Lord?" But remember
His faithfulness in the past. Study His promises in scripture. And
then just step out in obedience. He'll take care of you the way He
took care of Ananias.

—THE POWER OF THE SPIRIT—

The Spirit of God came upon Saul with power when
he heard this news, and he became very angry.
1 SAMUEL 11:6 NLV

After Saul was anointed king, Ammonites surrounded the Israelite city of Jabesh-gilead, causing great fear among the residents. They quickly offered to serve King Nahash, but he wanted to humiliate them by putting out their right eyes. The people asked for a week to solicit help from elsewhere in Israel.

Nahash may have believed that Jabesh-gilead was ripe for the taking, given that Israel had a new king. Saul, who early in his rule was still farming, returned from the field to learn of Jabesh-gilead's predicament. Then the Spirit of God came upon Saul with power, allowing him to lead Israel to victory.

As born-again Christians, we don't have to wait for the Spirit to come upon us. The Holy Spirit already lives inside us! What or who is your spiritual equivalent to King Nahash and the Ammonites? Is it a sin you've never been able to conquer, one that threatens to bring you down? Or is it perhaps a coworker or neighbor or even a family member who knows how to push all your buttons? Is it laziness or workaholism or irritability or some other difficult character trait?

The answer is God's Spirit. Allow Him to prompt and empower your next steps. He will lead you to spiritual victory.

—IN HEART AGREED WITH GOD—

Can two walk together,
except they be agreed?
AMOS 3:3 KJV

I trust that most of us who are here met in the name of Jesus, feel a deep, sincere and constant agreement with God. We have been guilty of murmuring at His will; but yet our newborn nature evermore at its core and center knoweth that the will of the Lord is wise and good; and we therefore bow our heads with reverent agreement and say, "Not as I will, but as thou wilt" (Matthew 26:39 KJV). "The will of the Lord be done" (Acts 21:14 KJV).

Our soul, when through infirmity she is tempted to rebellion, nevertheless struggles after the complete resignation of her wishes and desires to the will of the Most High. Our strength shall be perfect when we have no independent will, but move and act only as we are moved and acted on by our gracious God.

I hope that at this hour we can truly say, that notwithstanding our many sins, we do love the Lord our God; and if we could have our will this morning, we would follow His commands without the slightest departure from the narrow path. We are in heart agreed with God.

FAST OR WELL?

The heavens declare the glory of God; skies proclaim the work of his hands. Day after day they pour forth speech; night after night they reveal knowledge. They have no speech, they use no words; no sound is heard from them. Yet their voice goes out into all the earth.
PSALM 19:1–4 NIV

In our hard-driving, goal-oriented society, the ability to accomplish tasks quickly is perceived as a virtue. "How quickly can you do it?" we're asked. "That should only take five minutes," we're told. Our lives become a whirlwind of worries and cares.

Why are we in such a hurry? What is gained by doing everything as fast as humanly possible? If the heavens declare the glory of God, shouldn't we declare His glory as well? If the skies proclaim the work of His hands, shouldn't the work of *our* hands bring honor and glory to the One who made that work possible?

It's been said that people will forget how fast you did a thing, but they'll remember how well you did it. If that's true, the question we really need to ask ourselves is, are we living our lives fast, or are we living our lives well?

Slow down. Make your connection with Jesus the only real priority in life. How is that possible? Perhaps it's not as hard as we think. If the merry-go-round is making you sick to your stomach, don't just sit there and hope things turn out all right. Get off.

CLASSICS: D. L. MOODY

"COME UP HITHER"

One thing have I desired of the LORD, that will I seek after;
that I may dwell in the house of the LORD all the days of my life,
to behold the beauty of the LORD, and to enquire in his temple.
For in the time of trouble he shall hide me in his pavilion: in the
secret of his tabernacle shall he hide me; he shall set me up upon
a rock. And now shall mine head be lifted up above mine enemies
round about me: therefore will I offer in his tabernacle sacrifices
of joy; I will sing, yea, I will sing praises unto the LORD.
PSALM 27:4–6 KJV

One glimpse of Christ will pay us for all we are called upon to endure here—to see the King in His beauty, to be in the presence of the King! And then, oh! The sweet thought, we shall be like Him when we see Him! And we shall see Him in His beauty; we shall see Him high and exalted. When He was down here on earth it was the time of His humiliation, when He was cast out from the world, spit upon and rejected; but God hath exalted Him and put Him at the right hand of power, and there He is now, and there we shall see Him by and by.

A few more tears, a few more shadows, and then the voice of God shall say, "Come up hither," and into the presence of the King we shall go.

— SEEING THE EXALTED LORD —

*"In my vision at night I looked, and there before me was
one like a son of man, coming with the clouds of heaven. He
approached the Ancient of Days and was led into his presence.
He was given authority, glory and sovereign power; all nations
and peoples of every language worshiped him. His dominion
is an everlasting dominion that will not pass away, and
his kingdom is one that will never be destroyed."*

DANIEL 7:13–14 NIV

Isaiah, Jeremiah, Ezekiel, and Daniel didn't just receive verbal revelations from the Lord God. They each also had stunning visions of Him, on earth (sometimes with cherubim), in the air (often with clouds), and in heaven (usually with God's throne center stage).

In the vision related in today's reading, Daniel sees "coming with the clouds of heaven" One who is clearly divine yet called "a son of man." Eternal, infinitely powerful, and worshiped by "all nations and peoples of every language," this mysterious Person is revealed by the New Testament.

Throughout the Gospels, Jesus calls Himself "the Son of Man" dozens of times. In the book of Acts, after Jesus' resurrection and ascension, Luke describes the martyrdom of Stephen, who "looked up to heaven and saw the glory of God, and Jesus standing at the right hand of God. 'Look,' he said, 'I see heaven open and the Son of Man standing at the right hand of God' " (Acts 7:55–56 NIV).

How do you see Jesus? The more awesome He is to you, the more He can do in your life.

OBEDIENCE AS THE PATHWAY TO BLESSING

The LORD rewarded me according to my righteousness;
according to the cleanness of my hands hath he recompensed
me. For I have kept the ways of the LORD, and have not wickedly
departed from my God. For all his judgments were before me,
and I did not put away his statutes from me. I was also upright
before him, and I kept myself from mine iniquity. Therefore hath
the LORD recompensed me according to my righteousness.
PSALM 18:20–24 KJV

Mark the spirit of so many of the psalms, with their confident appeal to the integrity and righteousness of the supplicant: "The LORD rewarded me according to my righteousness; according to the cleanness of my hands hath He recompensed me. . . . I was upright before Him, and I kept myself from mine iniquity: therefore hath the LORD recompensed me according to my righteousness." If we carefully consider such utterances in the light of the New Testament, we shall find them in perfect harmony with the explicit teaching of the Savior's parting words: *"If ye keep* my commandments, ye shall abide in my love" (John 15:10 KJV).

Let us seek to enter into the spirit of what the Savior here teaches us. There is a danger in our evangelical religion of looking too much at what it offers from one side, as a certain experience to be obtained in prayer and faith. There is another side which God's Word puts very strongly, that of obedience, as the only path to blessing.

A PROPER RESPONSE

*Now Israel loved Joseph more than any of his other
sons, because he had been born to him in his old age;
and he made an ornate robe for him. When his brothers
saw that their father loved him more than any of them,
they hated him and could not speak a kind word to him.*
GENESIS 37:3–4 NIV

Family dynamics, when handled poorly, can create a myriad of problems. Israel (formerly known as Jacob) fathered more than a dozen children by four different women, and chose to show extreme favoritism to one. It was not a formula for a happy home.

Joseph, as the oldest son of Israel's favored wife was more highly regarded than his much older half brothers. Succeeding chapters of Genesis show Joseph as a successful man of God, but as a seventeen-year-old, he became an object of brotherly scorn— to the point of his being sold into slavery!

Faced with incredible obstacles, Joseph continued to serve God faithfully, believing that His blessing was more important than anything this earth could provide. God would later use Joseph to save the lives of his father and brothers during a famine. This was only possible because of his choices in moments of great difficulty.

How about us? Will we respond to our challenges with the grace Joseph showed, and allow God to work all things for good? The promise is for "those who love him, who have been called according to his purpose" (Romans 8:28 NIV).

Commit to faithful obedience and give God room to work. He will.

WALK IN CONFIDENCE

And Samuel said, How can I go? if Saul hear it,
he will kill me. And the LORD said, Take an heifer
with thee, and say, I am come to sacrifice to the LORD.
1 SAMUEL 16:2 KJV

Due to Saul's pride and disobedience, the Lord rejected him as king over Israel. When God instructed Samuel to find the next king within Jesse's family, the old priest was understandably concerned. Saul would have seen the selection of his successor as an act of treason and probably tried to kill Samuel. Was the fearful reaction in today's verse a weakness in Samuel's faith?

Perhaps. But if we're honest, we realize how fearful we can be too. "The best men are not perfect in their faith," wrote the old English Bible commentator Matthew Henry, discussing Samuel's situation. "Nor will fear be wholly cast out any where on this side of heaven."

God responded by telling Samuel to offer a sacrifice, perhaps as an atonement for his weakness and doubt. Whenever we face fears over God's calling, we can be thankful that He has already provided a sacrifice for our every failure in Jesus' shed blood on the cross. We can walk in the confidence of His provision.

There are times when being a Christian may cost us something. But obeying God is always far more important. By our obedience, we can contribute to the work of His kingdom, looking forward to the day when all fear is banished.

STORMY SEAS

Jesus was in the back part of the boat sleeping on a pillow.
They woke Him up, crying out, "Teacher, do You not care that
we are about to die?" He got up and spoke sharp words to the
wind. He said to the sea, "Be quiet! Be still." At once the wind
stopped blowing. There were no more waves. He said to His
followers, "Why are you so full of fear? Do you not have faith?"
MARK 4:38–40 NLV

The Sea of Galilee is nearly seven hundred feet below sea level, surrounded by hills and mountains that reach more than twenty-five hundred feet above sea level. Shaped like an arena, it was a perfect place for Jesus to preach while standing in a boat.

After a long day of teaching, the Lord and His disciples set sail across the sea. Jesus was so tired that He didn't wake up when the weather turned ugly. Although the Sea of Galilee is beautiful, it is subject to violent storms when wind blows cold air over the heights to the warm water below.

As the storm grew, the disciples' boat took on water. Jesus slept on. When the terrified disciples woke Him, Jesus rebuked the weather. . .and then His disciples.

Though this miracle was another proof of Jesus' authority, it only happened in response to the disciples' lack of faith. Followers of Jesus have no reason to fear any storm, no matter how violent, when Jesus is in the boat. Who knows what greater miracle may have occurred if the disciples had let Jesus sleep?

Trust that the God who shaped the land and sea, who commands the winds—and who rests in your boat—will bring you safely through.

LOOKING TO CHRIST
WITH THE EYE OF FAITH

Looking unto Jesus the author and finisher of our faith; who for the joy that was set before him endured the cross, despising the shame, and is set down at the right hand of the throne of God.
Hebrews 12:2 kjv

Abraham Lincoln issued a proclamation declaring the emancipation of three millions of slaves. On a certain day their chains were to fall off, and they were to be free. The proclamation was put up on the trees and fences wherever the Northern Army marched. A good many slaves could not read: but others read the proclamation, and most of them believed it; and on a certain day a glad shout went up, "We are free!" Some did not believe it and stayed with their old masters; but it did not alter the fact that they were free.

Christ, the Captain of our salvation, has proclaimed freedom to all who have faith in Him. Let us take Him at His word. Their feelings would not have made the slaves free. The power must come from the outside. Looking at ourselves will not make us free, but it is looking to Christ with the eye of faith.

—— CONFESSION AND PRAISE ——

*"Lord, listen! Lord, forgive! Lord, hear and act!
For your sake, my God, do not delay, because
your city and your people bear your Name."*
DANIEL 9:19 NIV

The Bible contains great prayers in the ninth chapters of the books of Ezra, Nehemiah, and Daniel. Chronologically, these prayers take place in reverse order, with Daniel's the first in time, near the end of the Babylonian exile. The other prayers follow, two or three generations after some of the Jews accept Cyrus the Great's offer to return to their homeland.

The Jews had been exiled for their sin, wickedness, and outright rebellion toward God. But *every* person is selfish and disobedient. So these prayers are entirely relevant today.

Ezra, the Levites under Nehemiah's leadership, and Daniel not only confessed the terrible sins of the Israelites, they also praised the greatness of the Lord God. In particular, they praised His grace (Ezra 9:8; Nehemiah 9:17), kindness (Ezra 9:9), and mercy (Ezra 9:13; Daniel 9:9).

They also praise the Lord's righteousness (Ezra 9:15; Nehemiah 9:8, 33; Daniel 9:7, 14), glory (Nehemiah 9:5, 32; Daniel 9:4), omnipotence (Nehemiah 9:6, 32; Daniel 9:4), forgiveness (Nehemiah 9:17, 19; Daniel 9:9), compassion (Nehemiah 9:17, 27–28), love (Nehemiah 9:17, 32; Daniel 9:4), goodness (Nehemiah 9:25, 35), and faithfulness (Nehemiah 9:33).

To the degree that we know what sinners we are and praise the Lord for all that He is, we will live good, godly, honorable, and winsome lives. Confession and praise make us stronger.

OBEY WHEN AFRAID

*Then Ananias went to the house and entered it. Placing
his hands on Saul, he said, "Brother Saul, the Lord—Jesus,
who appeared to you on the road as you were coming here—
has sent me so that you may see again and be filled with the
Holy Spirit." Immediately, something like scales fell from Saul's
eyes, and he could see again. He got up and was baptized,
and after taking some food, he regained his strength.*
Acts 9:17–19 NIV

The conversion of Saul on the road to Damascus is pivotal in church history. Soon to be called Paul, the former persecutor of Christians would go on to write much of the New Testament. These books detail the victories and defeats of the early church, explain deep truths about God and Jesus, and serve as a template for godly living.

When you consider these truths, can you imagine what might have happened had Ananias given in to fear and refused the Spirit's command to visit Saul? The Christian church and our Bibles would look much different today.

The good news is that, in God's perfect plan and will, Ananias did obey—even though he was afraid. Remember, Saul was known as the destroyer of the church, a man whose actions scattered thousands of Christians throughout the Roman world.

Fear can be paralyzing. But God is in the habit of healing paralysis! When He commands, through His Word or the nudging of His Spirit, just go. God has infinite power to take care of the rest.

A NEW CALLING

*Then Samuel took the horn of oil and poured the oil
on him in front of his brothers. The Spirit of the Lord
came upon David with strength from that day on.*
1 Samuel 16:13 nlv

In the Middle East of the Old Testament, families often assigned the youngest boy to serve as shepherd. They would lead their sheep with a rod and staff—which David described so beautifully in Psalm 23—into places of good food and water. Shepherds were also responsible for protecting their flocks from predators.

When Samuel visited Jesse to discover which of his eight sons should be Israel's next king, David—the youngest, away with the sheep—was the last to be summoned. Apparently, Jesse believed David to be an unlikely candidate. David would probably have agreed. He was simply performing his family duty when God called him to be king. At that point, the Spirit of the Lord came upon David with strength, which he certainly needed up to and after the time he took the throne.

At some point in life, each of us will be called in a different direction. God transforms ex-convicts into preachers, draws businessmen into full-time missions, and impassions lay Christians to start ministries in their circles. Or He may adjust your family situation, your finances, or your health for His own purposes. These transitions can be difficult, to be sure—but when the Spirit of the Lord is directing you, you will find strength for the challenge.

Is God leading you into some new circumstance? Remember that the Spirit of the Lord gives strength.

THE MAN FOR THE HOUR

Joseph of Arimathaea, an honourable counsellor, which also waited for the kingdom of God, came, and went in boldly unto Pilate, and craved the body of Jesus. And Pilate marvelled if he were already dead: and calling unto him the centurion, he asked him whether he had been any while dead. And when he knew it of the centurion, he gave the body to Joseph. And he bought fine linen, and took him down, and wrapped him in the linen, and laid him in a sepulchre which was hewn out of a rock, and rolled a stone unto the door of the sepulchre.

MARK 15:43–46 KJV

God hath today somewhere, I know not where, in yon obscure cottage of an English village, or in a log-hut far away in the back-woods of America, or in the slums of our back streets, or in our palaces, a man who in maturer life shall deliver Israel, fighting the battles of the Lord. The Lord hath His servant making ready, and when the time shall come, when the hour shall want the man, the man shall be found for the hour. The Lord's will shall be done, let infidels and doubters think what they please. I see in this advent of Joseph of Arimathea exactly at the needed time, a well of consolation for all who have the cause of God laid upon their hearts. We need not worry our heads about who is to succeed the pastors and evangelists of today: the apostolical succession we may safely leave with our God.

LIVE WISELY

*Live wisely among those who are not believers, and make the
most of every opportunity. Let your conversation be gracious and
attractive so that you will have the right response for everyone.*
COLOSSIANS 4:5–6 NLT

How we live serves as an outward expression of our faith. When
we desire to serve Christ above all, our lives exude wisdom. The
apostle Paul is one of history's great examples of a visibly Christ-
like life. Whether he was ill, in prison, or battling a "thorn" in his
flesh, Paul lived the example that he preached. But not in his own
strength.

It was Paul's dependence on God that enabled him to live
wisely. No doubt, he had struggles: "I don't really understand
myself, for I want to do what is right, but I don't do it. Instead, I
do what I hate" (Romans 7:15 NLT). But, somehow, Paul found his
strength and endurance in Christ.

Of course, Paul was happy to share the "somehow," as he gave
the Christians of Colosse a guide for the wise living he commanded.
They were to hold fast to their faith (2:23), put their sinful desires to
death (3:5), speak the truth to each other (3:9), do everything in the
name of the Lord Jesus, with thankfulness (3:17). By committing to
these good deeds, God would provide the strength they needed to
live well. "That's why I work and struggle so hard," Paul said, "depending on Christ's mighty power that works within me" (1:29 NLT).

DON'T WORRY

The righteous cry out, and the LORD hears them;
he delivers them from all their troubles. The LORD is
close to the broken hearted and saves those who are
crushed in spirit. The righteous person may have many
troubles, but the LORD delivers him from them all.
PSALM 34:17–19 NIV

Worry. For some it's a constant companion on the road of life. Like the proverbial backseat driver, its mouth is constantly running, offering relentless, annoying, unnecessary warnings about every twist and turn, every bump and pothole, every possible direction on the road ahead.

What does God say about worry? Phrases like "do not be afraid" and "fear not" are said to occur 365 times in the Bible, one for every day of the year. So when it comes to worry, God simply says *don't*. For the believer it just isn't necessary.

In fact, worry is actually a kind of unfaithfulness. When we stress over our lives and the things we need, we're indicating that we don't really trust God. We're questioning whether He is big enough or concerned enough to know about those things and to work them all together for our good.

But worry doesn't have power to take away our problems. The only thing it takes away is our peace.

The psalm writer assures us that God hears when we cry out to Him. So today, remember to seek first His kingdom and righteousness. Don't worry about tomorrow. Let tomorrow worry about itself—*tomorrow*. Each day has enough trouble of its own.

PEACE!

I said to the one standing before me, "I am overcome with anguish because of the vision, my lord, and I feel very weak. How can I, your servant, talk with you, my lord? My strength is gone and I can hardly breathe." Again the one who looked like a man touched me and gave me strength. "Do not be afraid, you who are highly esteemed," he said. "Peace! Be strong now; be strong." When he spoke to me, I was strengthened and said, "Speak, my lord, since you have given me strength."

DANIEL 10:16–19 NIV

At this point in his story, Daniel could easily have been ninety years old. What's more, he had been fasting for three weeks. So when he saw a vision of a man with a "body like topaz, his face like lightning, his eyes like flaming torches, his arms and legs like the gleam of burnished bronze, and his voice like the sound of a multitude" (verse 6), we can forgive him for blanching (verse 8), fainting (verse 9), trembling prostrate (verse 10), falling flat and speechless (verse 15), experiencing anguish and powerlessness (verse 16), and feeling breathless (verse 17). Abject fear has frozen many a lesser man.

Deep fear produces four responses: to freeze, flee, fight, or focus. They are not exclusive and certainly not sequential. To reach the point of focus in fear, we first need to find peace. So it's no wonder the Lord and His angels frequently say things like, "Do not be afraid," "Be strong," and "Peace!" whenever they appear.

For Christians, peace is a fruit of the Holy Spirit. The more time we spend with God in His Word and prayer, allowing His Spirit to work within us, the stronger we'll be when fearful situations arise.

Peace!

BRIGHT SEASONS OF FELLOWSHIP

Thou preparest a table before me in the presence of mine enemies: thou anointest my head with oil; my cup runneth over.

PSALM 23:5 KJV

We do not know when David wrote this psalm. There seems, however, to be no period of his life in which he could have used this expression in reference purely to his temporal circumstances. Apart from the grace of God and the choice blessings of the covenant, he could not even on the throne have been able to say, "My cup runneth over."

The troubles of his heart were enlarged even to the last, and the good old man had to say upon his deathbed that, though he rejoiced in the sure covenant of God, yet his house was not so with God as his heart could have desired. David was a man of troubles; he bore the yoke in his youth and was chastened in all his old age.

So did the spiritual outweigh the natural that the consolations of the son of Jesse exceeded his tribulation, and even in his most troublous times there were bright seasons of fellowship with the Lord, in which he joyfully said, "My cup runneth over."

DOWNTURNS IN LIFE

*Joseph's master took him and put him in prison, the place
where the king's prisoners were confined. But while Joseph
was there in the prison, the LORD was with him; he showed him
kindness and granted him favor in the eyes of the prison warden.*
GENESIS 39:20–21 NIV

Working for the Egyptian official Potiphar, Joseph always did the
right thing. He respected Potiphar's business dealings. He respected
Potiphar's possessions. He respected Potiphar's family. However,
when Joseph rejected the advances of Potiphar's wife, she falsely
accused him of assault—and Joseph found himself in prison.

Joseph could have responded to this downturn in his circumstances by complaining, crying, or casting off his trust in God. But
his faith was not shaken. As he would later tell the brothers who
had initially sold him into slavery, "God sent me ahead of you to
preserve for you a remnant on earth and to save your lives by a
great deliverance" (Genesis 45:7 NIV). We help ourselves by viewing
present-day events from God's perspective, watching for His work
even in our most difficult times.

Joseph quickly began to serve the prison warden, earning his
trust as he had Potiphar's. Since God had faithfully met his needs
in the past, Joseph knew God would provide in this situation also.

We will all face downturns in life, some minor and others overwhelming. When we do, remember that there is a God in heaven
who desires our best. Keep your focus on Him and wait for His
deliverance.

GOD IS FAITHFUL

David said to the Philistine, "You come against me with sword and spear and javelin, but I come against you in the name of the LORD Almighty, the God of the armies of Israel, whom you have defied. This day the LORD will deliver you into my hands."
1 SAMUEL 17:45–46 NIV

You've heard and read—countless times—the story of David slaying Goliath, the ten-foot-tall giant. You know that David accomplished that feat with a sling and five smooth stones. In fact, he killed the enemy with his first shot. But have you ever considered where David's confidence came from?

He didn't even wear armor in the battle. But that wasn't a chest-beating display of his own manliness. David just wanted to stand up for Israel and its soldiers (1 Samuel 17:26). He had confidence in the Lord, based on his previous experience.

As a shepherd, David had told King Saul, he had gone after lions and bears that attacked his flock, striking them and rescuing sheep from their mouths. At times, he even killed the predators. "This uncircumcised Philistine will be like one of them," David declared, "because he has defied the armies of the living God. The LORD who rescued me from the paw of the lion and the paw of the bear will rescue me from the hand of this Philistine" (verses 36–37).

When you are about to face your own Goliath, what story of God's faithfulness can you tell yourself? Take some time today to recall victories that He has given you—and you'll be armed with His confidence for the future.

——ILL EQUIPPED BUT READY——

*He told them to take nothing along with them
but a walking stick. They were not to take
a bag or food or money in their belts.*
MARK 6:8 NLV

When Jesus sent His disciples out to witness to the Jews, He gave them the authority to drive out evil spirits and heal all kinds of sicknesses. But they probably felt ill equipped for their mission.

How many times did Jesus teach the disciples, only to have them miss His point? They rarely understood His words the first time, and He often had to explain Himself.

Then, on the physical level, the Lord specifically prohibited the disciples from taking supplies for their journey. They could carry a walking stick, but that was it. For food, money, and other basic needs, they were to rely on God's provision alone.

Didn't Jesus understand what the disciples needed?

Of course He did, and His disciples went out and did what Jesus asked. If He had sent them out fully provisioned with bags of food and money, they wouldn't have depended on God's providence. If Jesus had waited to send the disciples until they felt fully knowledgeable, they would have relied on their own brains instead of allowing God to speak through them.

We will sometimes feel ill equipped for the task God has given us. But that's when we are perfectly positioned. We'll see that He can overcome our weakness with His strength.

CLASSICS: D. L. MOODY

ALL THE STRENGTH IN THE WORLD

But God hath chosen the foolish things of the world to confound the wise; and God hath chosen the weak things of the world to confound the things which are mighty; and base things of the world, and things which are despised, hath God chosen, yea, and things which are not, to bring to nought things that are: that no flesh should glory in his presence.

1 CORINTHIANS 1:27–29 KJV

How it ought to encourage us all to believe we may each have a part in building up the walls of the heavenly Zion. In all ages God has delighted to use the weak things. In his letter to the Corinthians Paul speaks of five things God uses: foolish things, weak things, base things, despised things, and things which are not. What for? "That no flesh should glory in His presence."

When we are weak then we are strong. People often think they have not strength enough; the fact is we have too much strength. It is when we feel that we have no strength of our own, that we are willing God should use us and work through us. If we are leaning on God's strength, we have more than all the strength of the world.

This world is not going to be reached by mere human intellectual power. When we realize we have no strength, then all the fulness of God will flow in upon us. Then we shall have power with God and with man.

REST AND REWARD

*"Multitudes who sleep in the dust of the earth will awake:
some to everlasting life, others to shame and everlasting
contempt. Those who are wise will shine like the brightness
of the heavens, and those who lead many to righteousness,
like the stars for ever and ever. But you, Daniel, roll up and seal
the words of the scroll until the time of the end. . . . As for you,
go your way till the end. You will rest, and then at the end of
the days you will rise to receive your allotted inheritance."*

DANIEL 12:2–4, 13 NIV

After writing down his last and longest revelation, Daniel was instructed to focus on eternity. He could confidently ponder and look forward to resurrection, everlasting life, heavenly glory, and "your allotted inheritance." The latter also can be translated "the inheritance set aside for you" (NLT).

Both "allotted" and "set aside" speak of God's preparation of specific rewards for Daniel. This builds on the Old Testament idea of "portions" assigned by the Lord Himself after the conquest of the Promised Land (see Joshua 13–21).

These ideas help us appreciate Jesus Christ's words in John 14:1–3: "Let not your heart be troubled: ye believe in God, believe also in me. In my Father's house are many mansions: if it were not so, I would have told you. I go to prepare a place for you. And if I go and prepare a place for you, I will come again, and receive you unto myself; that where I am, there ye may be also" (KJV).

When life is wearisome, focus on eternity. There will be rest and reward.

—— WHO'S YOUR BARNABAS? ——

When [Saul] came to Jerusalem, he tried to join the disciples,
but they were all afraid of him, not believing that he really was a
disciple. But Barnabas took him and brought him to the apostles.
ACTS 9:26–27 NIV

Barnabas makes for an interesting study. His real name was Joseph, and he came from the Mediterranean island of Cyprus, about 250 miles from Jerusalem. Part of the Jewish tribe of Levi, which produced Israel's priests, Joseph first appears in Acts 4 shortly after the Holy Spirit's arrival at Pentecost. Members of the early church were so unified that they sold their possessions and gave generously to any other Christians in need. Joseph sold a field and handed the proceeds over to the apostles, who gave him the nickname *Barnabas*: "son of encouragement."

The next time he appears in scripture, Barnabas is encouraging an unlikely new believer named Saul—the same Saul who had been rabidly persecuting Christians. That changed when Jesus got Saul's attention on the road to Damascus; the believers' understandable fear of Saul changed when Barnabas stood up for him, bringing the future apostle to the church leadership for a proper introduction.

God has placed Barnabases in strategic locations to encourage His people at just the right times. A Barnabas may already have helped you; there may be one coming into your life right now. Either way, be willing to accept the encouragement he provides. And always look for ways to be a Barnabas yourself.

STAND STRONG

"Was that day the first time I [Ahimelek] inquired of God for [David]? Of course not! Let not the king [Saul] accuse your servant or any of his father's family, for your servant knows nothing at all about this whole affair."
1 SAMUEL 22:15 NIV

Saul's jealously against David was nearly consuming him. The Spirit of God had left Saul (see 1 Samuel 16:14) and he was being tormented by an evil spirit. These facts help to explain why Saul reacted murderously when he discovered that Ahimelek, a priest at Nob, had inquired of the Lord for David, gave him provisions, and turned over Goliath's sword.

When Saul questioned Ahimelek, the priest wondered why he wouldn't have helped David—the young warrior was the king's most trusted servant (see 22:14). But in a fit of raging jealousy, Saul had eighty-five priests killed, in addition to women, children, and animals in the town of Nob.

In Ahimelek's mind, he was simply serving his king by inquiring of the Lord for the king's most trusted servant. And he lost his life in the process. Sometimes doing the right thing comes with a heavy cost. But God is always faithful. He will give you the backbone required to stand in the face of the harshest persecution. And if you end up paying the ultimate sacrifice, the next face you see will be that of Jesus.

—— JESUS' MODEL PRAYER ——

After this manner therefore pray ye: Our Father which art in heaven, Hallowed be thy name. Thy kingdom come, Thy will be done in earth, as it is in heaven. Give us this day our daily bread. And forgive us our debts, as we forgive our debtors. And lead us not into temptation, but deliver us from evil: For thine is the kingdom, and the power, and the glory, for ever. Amen.

MATTHEW 6:9–13 KJV

Every teacher knows the power of example. He not only tells the child what to do and how to do it, but shows him how it really can be done.

In condescension to our weakness, our heavenly Teacher has given us the very words we are to take with us as we draw near to our Father. We have in them a form of prayer in which there breathe the freshness and fullness of the eternal life. So simple that the child can lisp it, so divinely rich that it comprehends all that God can give. A form of prayer that becomes the model and inspiration for all other prayer, and yet always draws us back to itself as the deepest utterance of our souls before our God.

CLASSICS: D. L. MOODY

GOD DELIGHTS
TO ANSWER PRAYER

*And it shall come to pass, that before they call, I will
answer; and while they are yet speaking, I will hear.*
ISAIAH 65:24 KJV

The scripture is full of such answers; every page of it encourages
prayer. God will have us pray, and He will answer prayer.

Surely we have all found out that in our own experience; if
not it is our own fault. "The arm of the Lord is not shortened, that
it cannot save." It is our own prayers that are shortened and that
are weak and faithless. Oh, let us "ask in faith, nothing wavering."

Some people are like the disciples in Jerusalem praying for the
release of Peter; their prayers were answered, and Peter stood
at the door, but they could not believe it; they said it must be his
spirit. But, oh! Let us take God at His word. He says, "While they
are yet speaking, I will hear." Is not that encouragement sufficient?
He delights to hear our prayers; He will not weary with our often
coming.

—THANKFULNESS IS A CHOICE—

*Be thankful in all circumstances, for this is
God's will for you who belong to Christ Jesus.*
1 THESSALONIANS 5:18 NLT

Being thankful in good times is easy enough, but it is God's will for us to be thankful in bad times too. Since no one is immune to struggle, we all have a choice to make: Will we obey the words of 1 Thessalonians 5:18 or not?

The apostle Paul, who wrote today's scripture, lived up to his own command. Acts 16:16–34 describes his experience in Philippi, where he and his missionary companion, Silas, were jailed for casting a demon from a fortune-telling slave girl. Though unjustly imprisoned, Paul and Silas prayed and sang hymns in their cell. As a result of this obedience, their chains fell off—as did the chains of everyone in that prison! Paul and Silas even got to share the Gospel with the jailer, who gladly accepted Christ.

Would any of these positive things have happened if Paul and Silas had been complaining in their cell? Had they been bemoaning their hardships and the unfairness of life? It's doubtful.

Choose to be thankful. In doing so, you fulfill God's will for your life. And when you fulfill His will, He will certainly give you whatever strength you need—"in all circumstances."

— REMEMBER NOT TO FORGET —

*"My people are being destroyed because they don't
know me. . . . Since you have forgotten the laws
of your God, I will forget to bless your children."*
HOSEA 4:6 NLT

Reading through the Old Testament, one marvels at the patience
of God in dealing with His sinful people. But before we judge the
ancient Israelites too harshly, consider that we as Christians—with
God's Spirit living inside us—often fail Him too. And know that He
has recorded the story of Israel as an example for us today (see 1
Corinthians 10:1–11).

Through the prophet Hosea, God told His people that they
didn't even know Him. By their careless and selfish living, they
had "forgotten the laws of [their] God," and in return, God would
"forget" to bless their children. That's a heavy threat, coming from
the loving, merciful, and powerful Creator of the universe.

It's certainly a warning to us today, but also a very simple
guideline: Remember not to forget. Keep God and His laws in your
thinking. Don't wander away from Him or them. Never override
the prompting of His Spirit when He tells you to do (or not do)
some particular thing.

If we remember not to forget God, we'll keep ourselves in His
love, as Jude wrote (verse 21). Such a small effort on our part will
pay large dividends of God's blessing—and strength for our daily
challenges.

—— FIND COMFORT IN GOD ——

*And Hannah prayed, and said, My heart rejoiceth in the LORD,
mine horn is exalted in the LORD: my mouth is enlarged
over mine enemies; because I rejoice in thy salvation.*
1 SAMUEL 2:1 KJV

It is very beautiful to see how the saints of old time were accustomed to find comfort in their God. When they came into sore straits, when troubles multiplied, when helpers failed, when earthly comforts were removed, they were accustomed to look to the Lord and to the Lord alone. Thus Hannah thinks of the Lord and comforts herself in His name. By this means they were made strong and glad: they began to sing instead of sighing, and to work wonders instead of fainting under their burdens, even as here the inspired poetess sings, "My heart rejoiceth in the LORD, mine horn is exalted in the LORD." To them God was a reality, a present reality, and they looked to Him as their rock of refuge, their helper and defense, a very present help in time of trouble.

Can we not at the outset learn a valuable lesson from their example? Let us do as they did; let us lean upon our God and stay ourselves upon Him when heart and flesh are failing.

GOD DOES IT

Pharaoh said to Joseph, "I had a dream, and no one can interpret it. But I have heard it said of you that when you hear a dream you can interpret it." "I cannot do it," Joseph replied to Pharaoh, "but God will give Pharaoh the answer he desires."

GENESIS 41:15–16 NIV

It was an intense dream, and Pharaoh knew it contained significant information. He simply did not know the interpretation of the dream. The Egyptian ruler sought the advice of his best counselors, the finest minds in all the land, but they didn't understand the dream either. Thankfully, one of Pharaoh's employees knew an individual who could help.

Sometime before, Pharaoh's butler had offended his boss and spent time in prison. There he met Joseph, a Hebrew slave from the house of Potiphar. The butler had also experienced a troubling dream, and young Joseph had provided an interpretation that proved to be 100 percent accurate. In this moment of Pharaoh's need, the butler remembered Joseph.

Summoned to the palace, Joseph was indeed able to provide the interpretation of Pharaoh's dream. It was a moment in which Joseph could boast, saying, "Look at me!" Instead, he declared the glory of God. Joseph refused to take credit because he understood a simple fact: God provides His children with wisdom and strength for their time of need.

We too can count on that wisdom and strength. We too should give God the glory.

FEAR GOD, NOT MAN

*Once again David inquired of the Lord, and the
Lord answered him, "Go down to Keilah, for I
am going to give the Philistines into your hand."*
1 Samuel 23:4 niv

After learning that enemy soldiers were looting the threshing
floor in Keilah—a city in southern Judah near the border with the
Philistines—David had one question for the Lord: "Shall I go and
attack these Philistines?" (1 Samuel 23:2 niv).

Even though the Lord said yes, David's men weren't ready for
battle. They admitted that they were afraid even living in Judah.
Perhaps they feared retaliation from King Saul for aligning themselves with David. Maybe they even wondered if some among their
number were loyal to Saul. So David inquired of the Lord again
and was given the same answer. He and his men went to battle
and inflicted heavy losses on the Philistines.

We as Christians are like David's men. We will certainly face
opposition for standing with Jesus, from friends or coworkers
and maybe even our families. When the Lord sent out His twelve
disciples, He promised them opposition (see Matthew 10:23; Luke
21:12; John 15:20). But here's what He told them: "Do not be afraid
of those who kill the body but cannot kill the soul. Rather, be afraid
of the One who can destroy both soul and body in hell" (Matthew
10:28 niv).

In other words, have more reverence for God than fear of man.
God is stronger, wiser, and more loving than we can even imagine.
He'll take care of us.

DUSTY FEET

> *"But if any place refuses to welcome you or listen to you,*
> *shake its dust from your feet as you leave to show that*
> *you have abandoned those people to their fate."*
> MARK 6:11 NLT

In the years of Jesus' earthly ministry, the nation of Israel had an identity crisis.

Some groups violently opposed Roman rule over Israel. Others played political games to stay in power. And some, like the Pharisees, rooted themselves in tradition, strictly observing the Mosaic Law—and many of their own laws—to set them apart from the Gentiles.

One of the Pharisees' rules required them, as a form of ritual cleansing, to shake the dust from their feet after passing through a Gentile region.

When Jesus sent His disciples to help Israel solve its identity crisis, He turned the Pharisaical practice on its head. If a town wouldn't accept Christ's disciples, these Jews were to be treated as the Pharisees treated the Gentiles—as ritually unclean.

Today, people who have grown up in the church can easily fall into Pharisaical ways of thinking. We have traditions and rules to keep us from looking like the prevailing culture, but if we aren't loving God or our neighbors, we have our own Christian identity crisis. We need to walk according to God's love rather than "shake dust off our feet." As Isaiah 52:7 says, "How beautiful on the mountains are the feet of the messenger who brings good news, the good news of peace and salvation, the news that the God of Israel reigns!" (NLT).

The love of God—the love that sent Jesus to the cross—is good news indeed. If we've heard and accepted that good news, let's be sure to share it with others. Dusty feet are part of our identity in Christ!

— CLOTHED WITH CHRIST —

*But the Spirit of the Lord came upon Gideon, and he
blew a trumpet; and Abiezer was gathered after him.*
Judges 6:34 KJV

We read in Judges, "The Spirit of the Lord came upon Gideon."
But you know that there is in the New Testament an equally
wonderful text, where we read, "Put ye on the Lord Jesus Christ"
(Romans 13:14 KJV), that is, clothe yourself with Christ Jesus.

And what does that mean? It does not only mean, by imputation
of righteousness outside of me, but to clothe myself with the living character of the living Christ, with the living love of the living
Christ. Put on the Lord Jesus. Oh! What a work.

I cannot do it unless I believe and understand that He whom
I have to put on is as a garment covering my whole being. I have
to put on a living Christ who has said, "Lo, I am with you always"
(Matthew 28:20 KJV). Just draw the folds closer round you of that
robe of light with which Christ would array you. Just come and
acknowledge that Christ is with you, on you, in you. Oh, put Him on!

REPENTANCE AND FRUIT

Sow righteousness for yourselves, reap the fruit of unfailing love,
and break up your unplowed ground; for it is time to seek the
Lord, until he comes and showers his righteousness on you.
HOSEA 10:12 NIV

We see this important and timeless theme clearly echoed throughout the New Testament.

John the Baptist exhorted, "Produce fruit in keeping with repentance" (Matthew 3:8 and Luke 3:8 NIV). Jesus Himself said, "By their fruit you will recognize them. Do people pick grapes from thornbushes, or figs from thistles? Likewise, every good tree bears good fruit, but a bad tree bears bad fruit. A good tree cannot bear bad fruit, and a bad tree cannot bear good fruit. Every tree that does not bear good fruit is cut down and thrown into the fire. Thus, by their fruit you will recognize them. Not everyone who says to me, 'Lord, Lord,' will enter the kingdom of heaven, but only the one who does the will of my Father who is in heaven" (Matthew 7:16–21 NIV).

Jesus also said that true repentance produces good fruit—not once or twice, but regularly. It keeps bearing fruit and more fruit—"fruit that will last" (John 15:16 NIV). This speaks of the eternal value of the fruit of true repentance.

Paul said, "I preached that they should repent and turn to God and demonstrate their repentance by their deeds" (Acts 26:20 NIV), and "Let us not become weary in doing good, for at the proper time we will reap a harvest if we do not give up" (Galatians 6:9 NIV).

Is it time to "break up your unplowed ground"?

SURPRISING HELP

*Once safely on shore, we found out that the island was called
Malta. The islanders showed us unusual kindness. They built
a fire and welcomed us all because it was raining and cold.*
ACTS 28:1–2 NIV

Saul, the man who would become the apostle Paul, was converted by the direct intervention of Jesus Himself. Throughout his career as a missionary, church leader, and Bible author, Paul enjoyed fellowship with other believers, interactions with angels, and even conversations with God through heavenly visions. God had promised that Paul would suffer for His name (see Acts 9:16), but the Lord also provided strong supports for His servant.

In the last chapter of Acts, we see Paul getting support from a surprising source—the pagan inhabitants of the island of Malta. Though these people didn't know the one true God (they thought Paul himself was a god when a snakebite didn't kill him), they were compassionate to the great missionary and his traveling companions, whose ship had broken apart in a storm.

That's just like God, who can use any person or nation or situation to accomplish His will. Think of the Persian king, Cyrus, restoring the Jewish nation. Or Jonah's fish. Or even the horrible choices of Judas Iscariot that led to Jesus' death on the cross. . .and the salvation of everyone who believes.

When life is hard, as is often the case, be ready for God to help—from the expected sources or even from the surprising ones.

WORSHIP DURING PERSECUTION

David stayed in the wilderness strongholds and in the hills of the Desert of Ziph. Day after day Saul searched for him, but God did not give David into his hands.
1 SAMUEL 23:14 NIV

David was God's chosen king for Israel—but he had to await the Lord's timing to take the throne. In the meantime, King Saul kept a jealous eye on the up-and-coming David.

After David and his six hundred followers saved the town of Keilah from Philistine raiders (see 1 Samuel 23:1–6), Saul caught wind of their victory. The king began to pursue David who moved from place to place to hide. Today's verse indicates that God never gave David up to Saul. What was David thinking at this time? We can turn to the psalms to find out.

Psalm 57 is a song David wrote while Saul was chasing him. Not surprisingly, David began by asking for protection. But his next theme might be surprising: he worshipped God. "Be exalted, O God, above the heavens; let your glory be over all the earth"; "My heart, O God, is steadfast, my heart is steadfast; I will sing and make music" (Psalm 57:5, 7 NIV).

When you face hardship—whether it's persecution, health issues, financial stresses, or relational problems—what is your natural response? Is worship part of the process? If not, consciously lift praise to God. As you turn your focus from your trials to your Creator and Redeemer, your soul will begin to sense a holy calm.

SINS CAST AWAY

Behold, for peace I had great bitterness: but thou hast in love to my soul delivered it from the pit of corruption: for thou hast cast all my sins behind thy back.
ISAIAH 38:17 KJV

The terrible name of sin! How it used to haunt me in my early years! I thought all my sins would be blazed out before the Great White Throne; that every sin committed in childhood and in secret, and every secret thought, and every evil desire, would be just blazed out before the assembled universe; that everything done in the dark would be brought to light.

But thanks be to God, the gospel tells me my sins are all put away in Christ. Out of love to my soul, He has taken all my sins and cast them behind His back. That is a safe place to have our sins cast away—behind God's back. God never turns back; He always marches on. He will never see your sins if they are behind His back.

That is one of His own illustrations. Out of love to my soul, He has taken all my sins upon Him. Not a part. He takes them all out of the way. "The blood of Jesus Christ His Son cleanseth us from all sin" (1 John 1:7 KJV).

THE ROAD AHEAD

*Trust in the LORD with all your heart, and lean
not on your own understanding; in all your ways
acknowledge Him, and He shall direct your paths.*
PROVERBS 3:5–6 NKJV

Sometimes a Bible passage becomes so familiar we can miss the blessing it holds. Like a man living next to a fire station, accustomed to the constant wailing of sirens, we may become desensitized to the important message being shared.

Our daily lives are filled with countless decisions. Some have little or no consequence. Others can change our destiny. Whatever the case, the Bible says that when we trust God completely, He *will* direct our paths.

Some men love to drive, and others merely tolerate it. But when we are driving, we usually don't want anyone telling us which way to go. And we certainly aren't planning to let go of the wheel! But God has a different way for us. The road that leads to His desired destination is found not by our own power and wisdom, but by giving our hearts and our lives completely to Him. We must allow Him to drive.

That's a tall order. But the destination and the joy of the journey promise to be more incredible than we would ever dare to dream. As the apostle Paul said, "Now to him who is able to do immeasurably more than all we ask or imagine. . ." (Ephesians 3:20 NIV).

— HE WILL STRENGTHEN YOU —

*But the Lord is faithful; he will strengthen
you and guard you from the evil one.*
2 THESSALONIANS 3:3 NLT

When discussing "strength for the challenge," could there be a clearer promise than this verse?

The apostle Paul, who wrote 2 Thessalonians, also penned the letter to the Ephesians. In it, he said, "we are not fighting against flesh-and-blood enemies, but against evil rulers and authorities of the unseen world, against mighty powers in this dark world, and against evil spirits in the heavenly places" (6:12 NLT). Paul wasn't trying to scare people—he just wanted Christians to be realistic. We are not capable of winning our battles on our own.

But that's where God comes in. He is faithful, Paul said, to "strengthen" us. In the context of 2 Thessalonians 3, Paul was discussing God's help in sharing the Gospel, His protection from wicked people (verse 2), and His enabling to follow biblical commands (verse 4). If we allow Him, God will lead us "into a full understanding and expression of the love of God and the patient endurance that comes from Christ" (verse 5 NLT).

The key question is, will we allow God to do His work in our lives? Will we submit to His authority, study His Word, pray for His blessing, and serve His people? Every time we say yes, He provides the strength we need to move forward.

CHOOSE LIFE!

*The LORD thunders at the head of his army; his forces are
beyond number, and mighty is the army that obeys his command.
The day of the LORD is great; it is dreadful. Who can endure it?
"Even now," declares the LORD, "return to me with all your heart,
with fasting and weeping and mourning." Rend your heart
and not your garments. Return to the LORD your God, for he
is gracious and compassionate, slow to anger and abounding
in love, and he relents from sending calamity.*

JOEL 2:11–13 NIV

During a terrible locust plague, Joel warned God's people of even
greater judgments ahead.

The phrase "the day of the Lord" appears six times in three chapters. This important phrase speaks of God's dreadful, devastating,
and decisive judgments at various points in history: contemporary,
future, and end times.

Joel called individuals from all walks of life—including farmers,
priests, elders, and even drunkards—to humble themselves, turn
from their sins, and return to the Lord wholeheartedly. He urged
them to beg God to spare their lives and pour out His blessings
again.

First, "The LORD your God. . .is gracious and compassionate,
slow to anger and abounding in love," which is the Lord's own
description of Himself going back to the time of Moses (see
Exodus 34:6; see also Psalm 86:15 and Jonah 4:2).

Second, "He [the Lord] relents from sending calamity" (Joel
2:13; see also Jonah 4:2). This is the prophet's shorthand phrase
for saying the Lord forgives "wickedness, rebellion and sin. Yet he
does not leave the guilty unpunished" (Exodus 34:7 NIV).

In other words, repent and choose life!

OUR SUREST ROAD TO HAPPINESS

*The liberal soul shall be made fat: and he
that watereth shall be watered also himself.*
PROVERBS 11:25 KJV

The general principle is, that in living for the good of others, we shall be profited also ourselves. We must not isolate our own interests but feel that we live for others.

This teaching is sustained by the analogy of nature, for in nature there is a law that no one thing can be independent of the rest of creation, but there is a mutual action and reaction of all upon all. All the constituent parts of the universe are bound to one another by invisible chains, and there is not a single creature in it which springeth up, or flourisheth, or decayeth for itself alone. The very planets, though they float far from one another, exercise attraction; and the fixed stars, though they seem to be infinitely remote, are still linked to one another by mysterious bonds.

God has so constituted this universe that selfishness is the greatest possible offense against His law, and living for others, and ministering to others, is the strictest obedience to His will. Our surest road to our own happiness is to seek the good of our fellows.

——— GREAT RESPONSIBILITY ———

Then Pharaoh said to Joseph, "Since God has made all this
known to you, there is no one so discerning and wise as you.
You shall be in charge of my palace, and all my people are to
submit to your orders. Only with respect to the throne will I
be greater than you." So Pharaoh said to Joseph, "I hereby
put you in charge of the whole land of Egypt."
GENESIS 41:39–41 NIV

It had been quite the journey in life for Joseph. Favored son of his father. Betrayed and sold into slavery by his brothers. Prominent manager for a top Egyptian official. Falsely accused by that official's wife and thrown into prison. Now, after God gave Joseph the interpretation of Pharaoh's dream, Joseph was responsible for the entire nation.

What a challenge. God had informed Pharaoh of a seven-year time of plenty, followed by seven years of calamity. Joseph was presented with a fourteen-year-long task: conserve during the good years, provide in the bad years. That may sound like an overwhelming responsibility, but God provided Joseph with the wisdom and courage to meet the challenge.

And God will help us in the same way. Writing to the church in Ephesus, the apostle Paul said, "I keep asking that the God of our Lord Jesus Christ, the glorious Father, may give you the Spirit of wisdom and revelation, so that you may know him better" (1:17 NIV). Whatever our own responsibilities, we can ask God for wisdom. We can seek insight through His Word. We can trust the promises that He's made to us. And we will find strength for each challenge that we face.

— OVERCOME EVIL WITH GOOD —

So [David] said to his men, "May the Lord not let
me put out my hand against my leader, for he is
the Lord's chosen one." David stopped his men with
these words. He did not let them go against Saul.
1 SAMUEL 24:6–7 NLV

This was David's perfect opportunity to take out his powerful persecutor. As King Saul was pursuing David, he ducked into a cave to use the restroom. It was a cave David himself was hiding in.

David's men encouraged him to kill Saul, assuming that the Lord had arranged this opportunity. But David knew better and resisted the urge to sin.

"He not only would not do this bad thing himself, but he would not suffer those about him to do it," the old-time commentator Matthew Henry wrote. "Thus he rendered good for evil, to him from whom he received evil for good; and was herein an example to all who are called Christians, not to be overcome of evil, but to overcome evil with good."

The apostle Paul picks up this theme in Romans 12:21 (NIV): "Do not be overcome by evil, but overcome evil with good."

As Christians, we all have opportunities to sin against our enemies. But with God's Holy Spirit living inside us, we dare not give in to our baser instincts. If we submit to the Spirit, He'll provide all the strength we need to overcome evil with good.

CLEAN HANDS, CLEAN HEART

"It is not what goes into a man's mouth from the outside that makes his mind and heart sinful. It is what comes out from the inside that makes him sinful."
MARK 7:15 NLV

Washing hands is important. To keep our bodies safe from germs, it's wise to wash our hands frequently for a minimum of twenty seconds. But no amount of handwashing can clean us from the spiritual sickness within.

When the Pharisees caught Jesus' disciples eating food with unwashed hands, they asked the Lord why His disciples didn't follow the Jewish handwashing rituals. Jesus fired back, asking why the Pharisees followed the traditions of the elders instead of the Word of God.

To Jesus, having unwashed hands was a physical issue, not a spiritual one. The Pharisees were so concerned about their outward ritual cleanliness that they ignored the spiritual filth corrupting their hearts.

To be physically healthy, washing our hands is a good idea. To be spiritually healthy, we must ask the Lord to cleanse us from the inside out. As Jesus said, "It is from within, out of a person's heart, that evil thoughts come—sexual immorality, theft, murder, adultery, greed, malice, deceit, lewdness, envy, slander, arrogance and folly" (Mark 7:21–22 NIV).

And Jesus is ready and able to do the job. According to 1 John 1:9, "If we confess our sins, he is faithful and just and will forgive us our sins and purify us from all unrighteousness" (NIV).

— BE SINGLE-MINDED FOR GOD —

*So they feared the LORD, and made unto themselves of the
lowest of them priests of the high places, which sacrificed
for them in the houses of the high places. They feared the
LORD, and served their own gods, after the manner of
the nations whom they carried away from thence.*
2 KINGS 17:32–33 KJV

It is recorded of the nations whom the King of Assyria, after he had carried Israel away into captivity, placed in the cities of Samaria, that "they feared the Lord, and served their own gods." "These nations," saith the inspired writer, "feared the Lord," performed an outward service to Him, "and served their graven images, both their children and their children's children."

How nearly does the practice of most modern Christians resemble this of the ancient heathens! "They fear the Lord"; they also perform an outward service to Him and hereby show they have some fear of God; but they likewise "serve their own gods." They have not laid aside the outward form of worshipping Him; but "they serve their graven images," silver and gold, the work of men's hands: Money, pleasure and praise, the gods of this world, more than divide their service with the God of Israel.

GOD IS ALWAYS TRUE

*"And afterward, I will pour out my Spirit on all people. Your sons
and daughters will prophesy, your old men will dream dreams,
your young men will see visions. Even on my servants, both
men and women, I will pour out my Spirit in those days."*
JOEL 2:28–29 NIV

Joel's prophecies address events in his day, events during the
founding of the early church, and still other events at the climax
of history.

Today's verses figure prominently on the church's birthday, the
Day of Pentecost, shortly after Jesus Christ's ascension to God the
Father's right hand.

As promised (Acts 1:4–5), Jesus sent the Holy Spirit (2:4) upon
His 120 followers (1:15, 2:1). The Spirit's arrival was accompanied
by the sound of a mighty rushing wind (2:2). His filling of the first
Christians was marked by small flames of fire above each (2:3)
and their speaking in foreign languages they didn't previously
know (2:4).

All this commotion attracted a lot of attention. Jews from around
the known world had gathered in Jerusalem for Pentecost. An
international crowd of thousands formed (2:5–6, 41). They mar-
veled to hear Christ-followers speaking in their mother tongues
(2:7–11). They wondered what was happening.

Then Peter stood up, filled with the Spirit, and preached the
life-changing Gospel of Jesus Christ. He quickly explained that
they were all witnessing the fulfillment of Joel's prophecy quoted
above (2:16–18).

It's true, three thousand people affirmed. And they were baptized that day (Acts 2:41).

Isn't it good to know that God is always true to His Word?

— MUTUAL ENCOURAGEMENT —

I long to see you so that I may impart to you some spiritual
gift to make you strong—that is, that you and I may
be mutually encouraged by each other's faith.
ROMANS 1:11–12 NIV

The apostle Paul mentions spiritual gifts in Romans 1, then explains them in greater detail in chapter 12. These gifts hold immense value to the Christian community. The abilities bestowed by God's Spirit—things like serving, teaching, encouraging, and giving—vary from person to person. But when they are shared within the church, they create mutual benefit, blessing both the giver and the receiver.

"Iron sharpens iron," the Proverbs say, "so one person sharpens another" (27:17 NIV). There is great strength to be found in the church—the worldwide "body of Christ" that is made up of the local congregations all around us. That's one reason the writer of Hebrews tells Christian believers, "Let us not neglect our meeting together, as some people do, but encourage one another, especially now that the day of [Jesus'] return is drawing near" (Hebrews 10:25 NLT).

Paul wanted to share his gifts with the church at Rome. He knew that that would help the believers there, but also encourage him. The principle still stands today. Find strength for your challenges by being involved in a local, Bible-believing church.

STAYING AWARE

*"So now, my lord, as the Lord lives, and as your soul
lives, let the Lord keep you from being guilty of blood.
Let Him keep you from punishing with your own hand."*
1 SAMUEL 25:26 NLV

David was often the model of patience. But other times—as we see in 1 Samuel 25—he could be provoked, nearly to the point of sin. After the churlish Nabal denied David's request for provisions for him and his servants, David was ready to kill the man. But Nabal's wife, Abigail, stepped in and stopped David—uttering the words in today's verse.

Abigail appealed to who David was as a believer in God. Apparently trusting that God could restrain him, she told David, "The Lord will be sure to make my lord a family that will last. Because my lord is fighting the Lord's battles. Sin will not be found in you as long as you live" (1 Samuel 25:28 NLV). These wise words, along with a gift of provisions, stopped David from sinning.

"You have kept me this day from being guilty of blood, and from punishing with my own hand," David told Abigail. "The Lord God of Israel has kept me from hurting you" (1 Samuel 25:33–34). He knew that this woman's actions were motivated by the Lord.

At various times, in one way or another, we're all tempted to sin. How open are you to God's intervention? No matter how stirred up you may be, God stands ready to deliver: "You have never been tempted to sin in any different way than other people. God is faithful. He will not allow you to be tempted more than you can take. But when you are tempted, He will make a way for you to keep from falling into sin" (1 Corinthians 10:13 NLV).

—— LOOK FROM MAN TO GOD ——

*Thus saith the LORD; Cursed be the man that
trusteth in man, and maketh flesh his arm,
and whose heart departeth from the LORD.*
JEREMIAH 17:5 KJV

If there is going to be a great work done here, God must do the work. It is not any new gospel that is wanted; it is not any new power. It is the same old power—the power of the Holy Ghost; and it is the same old story—the story of redeeming love—nothing new.

The world is running here and there after something new, and they come and hear the old, old story, and they say, "Well, it is not anything new after all." If you have come here expecting to hear something new, you will be disappointed. We are just going to preach the same old truths your ministers before have been preaching. And not only that, but we are come in weakness; and if you are leaning upon man you will be disappointed. "Cursed is the man that maketh the arm of flesh his trust."

But if we lean upon God and all our expectations are from Him, we shall not be disappointed. What we want is to cease from man and get done with man and look right away straight from man up to God.

—— INVITATION TO RETURN ——

In those days, and in that time, saith the Lord, the children
of Israel shall come, they and the children of Judah together,
going and weeping: they shall go, and seek the Lord their God.
They shall ask the way to Zion with their faces thitherward,
saying, Come, and let us join ourselves to the Lord in a
perpetual covenant that shall not be forgotten.
JEREMIAH 50:4–5 KJV

We, too, by nature are in banishment, far off from our God and the abode of His glory. We are not what we ought to have been, for the Lord did not make us to be sinners, but to be His happy and obedient creatures: our present lost estate is not our true state; we are banished through coming under the power of our great adversary; sin has carried us into captivity; we are in the far country, away from the great Father's house.

It is a great blessing when the times come, and they have come, when there is an opportunity and an invitation to return. Today the power of the adversary is broken, and we may flee out of the Babylon of sin. A greater than Cyrus has opened the two-leaved gates and broken the bars of iron in sunder and proclaimed liberty to the captives. We may now return to our God and freely enjoy the holy and happy associations, which belong to the City of our God.

HOW TO BE STRONG

The name of the LORD is a strong tower;
the righteous run to it and are safe.
PROVERBS 18:10 NKJV

The heroes of ancient literature—as well as the mythical supermen of our day—are marked by great strength, each possessing some incredible ability far beyond that of mortals.

Their names are legendary. Their stories have been told and retold, shaping the way our children think about "being a man." But is it possible they've made a god out of strength? What does the strength of Christ look like? The answer is spelled out clearly in Philippians 2:3–11 (NIV):

> *Do nothing out of selfish ambition or vain conceit.*
> *Rather, in humility value others above yourselves. . . .*
> *Have the same mindset as Christ Jesus: Who, being in*
> *very nature God, did not consider equality with God*
> *something to be used to his own advantage; rather, he*
> *made himself nothing by taking the very nature of a*
> *servant, being made in human likeness. And being found*
> *in appearance as a man, he humbled himself by becoming*
> *obedient to death—even death on a cross! Therefore, God*
> *exalted him to the highest place and gave him the name*
> *that is above every name, that at the name of Jesus every*
> *knee should bow, in heaven and on earth and under the*
> *earth, and every tongue acknowledge that Jesus Christ*
> *is Lord, to the glory of God the Father.*

As we enjoy the epic adventures of our favorite heroes, let's remember to seek the strength of Jesus Christ. It truly is the ultimate power. It's available to all of us today. And it starts with humility.

THE GATEWAY
TO SAVING FAITH

*"And everyone who calls on the
name of the LORD will be saved."*
JOEL 2:32 NIV

The day the church began, three thousand heard Peter's Gospel sermon, believed and were saved, and were then baptized (Acts 2:41). How good that the Lord loves to save people instantly, forever!

But scripture also makes it clear that some people take longer. Just witness Peter himself. The impetuous, think-aloud disciple followed Jesus for three years and still didn't understand much of the faith life. Only after Jesus' resurrection, appearances, ascension, and sending of the Holy Spirit did Peter become the world-changing apostle we recognize.

So, is someone "who calls on the name of the LORD" saved instantly or eventually? Yes. Some have little knowledge of the Lord, but they're desperate (Joel 1:13–15, 2:15–17). Others have some knowledge and are ready to cross the line. Still others call on the Lord several times before they become real Christians.

Nobody races from 0 to 60 in their knowledge of God. In this life, we do well to keep walking in the right direction in obedience to our Lord and Savior.

Still, Peter gladly quoted today's key verse in his first evangelistic sermon (Acts 2:21) and the apostle Paul also did so in one of his most important letters (Romans 10:13).

Whatever struggles you may face in life, there is one answer: call on the name of the Lord. He will be faithful to save you.

ONE DOOR

Jesus saith unto him, I am the way, the truth, and the life:
no man cometh unto the Father, but by me.
JOHN 14:6 KJV

Never try to draw near to God in prayer or praise or meditation or scripture reading or holy service apart from Jesus Christ, or your attempt must be a failure. Through the wall of fire which surrounds the throne you can only pass by way of the one door, namely, the body and blood of our great Mediator, Sacrifice, and Substitute. Is not that door sufficient? Why should we climb up some other way?

If I am very heavy of heart, do not let me try to raise my spirits, and so come in the power of human courage; but let me come just as I am, made bold through Him whose comforts delight my soul. If I feel that I have been sinning, do not let me try to get rid of my sin by some other process and then draw near to God; but let me come, sinner as I am, in the name of the sinner's Savior, and so draw near to God, having washed my robes and made them white in the blood of the Lamb. Jesus saith, "I am the way": why should we seek another?

GOD HAS A PLAN

Then Joseph said to his brothers, "Come close to me."
When they had done so, he said, "I am your brother Joseph,
the one you sold into Egypt! And now, do not be distressed
and do not be angry with yourselves for selling me here,
because it was to save lives that God sent me ahead of you.
For two years now there has been famine in the land, and for
the next five years there will be no plowing and reaping. But
God sent me ahead of you to preserve for you a remnant on
earth and to save your lives by a great deliverance."
GENESIS 45:4–7 NIV

Even though they had hated him, betrayed him, and told their father he was dead, Joseph was very gracious to his brothers. At this reunion, he comforted them by acknowledging God's providence. This is certainly commendable, but Joseph had the blessing of hindsight. The difficulties of his challenge were past.

Where do we find strength when we're still in the middle of trouble? When times get tough—or seemingly impossible—we may wonder if God has a plan. How do we find the courage to keep following Him even when the future is bleak?

Allow God to work. His solutions to life's problems are often the result of lengthy seasons of prayer. It may take time (and certainly our willingness) for Him to adjust the hearts and minds of all involved.

Joseph was likely a teenager when he was sold into slavery. He was probably approaching forty when he reconciled with his family. God's timing may seem slow to us, but He understands the past and knows the future: "The plans of the LORD stand firm forever, the purposes of his heart through all generations" (Psalm 33:11 NIV).

A GENTLE ANSWER

Then Saul said. . ."Because you [David] considered my life
precious today, I will not try to harm you again. Surely
I have acted like a fool and have been terribly wrong."
1 SAMUEL 26:21 NIV

In 1 Samuel 26, David had a second chance to kill King Saul. And for a second time he refused to do so. Instead, David made an honest appeal to Saul and, amazingly, Saul relented. Whether Saul's repentance was genuine is open to debate, but verse 25 indicates that David went on his way and Saul returned home. At the very least, David gained a reprieve.

Scripture tells us that a gentle answer turns away wrath (Proverbs 15:1). Jesus told His disciples to love their enemies, do good to those who hate them, bless those who curse them, and pray for those who mistreat them (Luke 6:27–29). Colossians 4:6 (NIV) says, "Let your conversation be always full of grace, seasoned with salt, so that you may know how to answer everyone."

When you are faced with a volatile situation, what's your default response? Is it like David's in 1 Samuel 26? Are you obedient to Jesus' words in Luke 6? Is your conversation always "full of grace," as Paul commanded? According to the New Testament's famous "fruit of the Spirit" passage (Galatians 5:22–23), one of God's works in our lives is self-control.

There will be plenty of provocations in this life, and it's only human to want to respond in kind. But Christians are called to be superhuman in their thoughts and behaviors. Ask God to control your tongue by His Spirit. He will happily answer that prayer.

TABLE SCRAPS

*The woman was not a Jew. She was from the country
of Syrophenicia. She asked Jesus if He would put the demon
out of her daughter. Jesus said to her, "Let the children have
what they want first. It is wrong to take children's food and
throw it to the dogs." She said to Him, "Yes, Lord, but even
the dogs eat the pieces that fall from the children's table."
He said to her, "Because of what you have said, go your
way. The demon is gone out of your daughter."*
MARK 7:26–29 NLV

Jesus Christ is the Savior of the world. But when He started His
ministry, He went first to the children of Israel. Jesus showed the
Jews signs that He was the Messiah they had been waiting for.
But they rejected Jesus and handed Him over to the Romans for
execution. Israel's loss became the whole world's gain.

That is the background of today's passage. Even so, it might be
surprising to see Jesus respond to a Gentile woman's request by
essentially calling her a dog. Perhaps it was because "dog" was a
common Jewish name for Gentiles. Maybe Jesus was playing on a
stereotype of Jews to test whether the woman's faith was genuine.
Whatever the reason, her response to Jesus' rebuff showed faithful
persistence. If His slur was a test, the Syrophenician woman passed.

When we pray—whether we're asking God for a healing or anything else—we must show the same faithful persistence. We can't
let the fear of rejection keep us from making requests to the only
one strong enough to help. Since the Gospel has been opened up
to the whole world, we can confidently go to the Father any time.
We don't have to beg for table scraps!

PROVE YOURSELF

Examine yourselves, whether ye be in the faith;
prove your own selves. Know ye not your own selves,
how that Jesus Christ is in you, except ye be reprobates?
2 Corinthians 13:5 kjv

The problem of self-examination is simple. According to the apostle, there are but two conditions, either Jesus Christ is in you, or ye are reprobate: one of two. There is no third condition.

The life of Christ in you may still be weak; but if you are truly born again and a child of God, Christ is in you. And then as a child you have access to the table of the Father and a share in the children's bread.

Reader, try your own self, whether you are in the faith; prove yourself. And should it appear that you do not yet have Christ, then even today receive Him. There is still time. Without delay give yourself to Christ: in Him you have a right to the Lord's Table.

NO CONTRADICTION

*Beat your plowshares into swords and
your pruninghooks into spears.*
JOEL 3:10 KJV

When the Lord says something once, it's important. When He says it twice, it's doubly important.

In Isaiah 2:1–4, and again in Micah 4:1–3, the Lord describes life "in the last days," when He reigns on the earth. The nations will gather at the temple in Jerusalem to worship the one true God and learn more about Him. Peace will spread across the globe, and weapons of war will be converted into farm implements. The hope of the ages will finally come to pass: "Nation will not take up sword against nation, nor will they train for war anymore" (Isaiah 2:4; Micah 4:3 NIV).

What a wonderful vision!

So, what is Joel talking about in today's scripture? Is he completely contradicting what God says in Isaiah and Micah? That's the assumption of a number of atheists, agnostics, and skeptics. Despite their confident assertions, however, let's not assume that an apparent Bible contradiction is a real one. Instead, simply read Joel 3:10 in context. That is, read the whole chapter. Better yet, read the whole book (it's only three chapters, after all). Then decide for yourself.

It turns out that Joel also is speaking about the last days, but right before the Lord reigns on the earth, when the nations converge in the Valley of Jehoshaphat (3:2). They converge to oppose Jesus Christ's second coming, only to be quickly and sounded defeated and then judged in the valley of decision (3:14). In other words, it's their weapons that will be converted into farm implements.

The Lord knows what He's talking about. We can trust whatever He says.

—— GLORY IN SUFFERINGS? ——

Not only so, but we also glory in our sufferings, because we know that suffering produces perseverance; perseverance, character; and character, hope. And hope does not put us to shame, because God's love has been poured out into our hearts through the Holy Spirit, who has been given to us.
ROMANS 5:3–5 NIV

It might be hard to imagine joy in suffering. But this is what the apostle Paul discovered.

He knew all about difficulties and opposition. In becoming a follower of Jesus, Paul betrayed the Jewish sect he'd been born into. And as he became an outspoken Christian leader, Paul put himself directly in the path of the persecution he had previously dealt out.

But following Jesus' footsteps, no matter the opposition, became Paul's mission. He knew that trouble would come, but also that he was serving the living God. Paul viewed persecution as an opportunity for growth, a chance to experience the love of Christ.

As with so many aspects of the Christian life, this mindset runs counter to our human expectations. Glory in suffering? Yes, it is possible. And, even more than possible, it is a promise to faithful believers. As Paul wrote, "we also glory in our sufferings, because we know that suffering produces perseverance; perseverance, character; and character, hope. And hope does not put us to shame, because God's love has been poured out into our hearts through the Holy Spirit, who has been given to us."

Hard times are certain. But so is God's ability to use them for your good.

REMEMBER HIS FAITHFULNESS

*David said to himself, "Some day Saul will kill me.
There is nothing better for me than to run to the
land of the Philistines. Then Saul will become tired
of looking for me any more in the land of Israel."*
1 SAMUEL 27:1 NLV

When we've been in a long spiritual battle, we're prone to become weary—maybe even doubtful of God's provision and protection. That seems to be the case with David in today's passage. On the run from the jealous king, David had enjoyed God's protection time and time again. In 1 Samuel 26, we even see Saul withdrawing from David, parting with a blessing (verse 25).

David was understandably skeptical of Saul. But he shouldn't have been so with God. Weariness, fear, and doubt caused David to do the unthinkable: seek refuge among the Philistines, the implacable enemies of God's people.

This world abounds with hardships—some of our own creation and others that are imposed upon us. Whatever the case, Satan is happy to use our trials to keep us from God. Like David, though, we know that God has often brought us through difficulties in the past. Remembering His faithfulness will give us strength to overcome whatever trials we're currently facing.

Classics: D. L. Moody

FULL OF LOVE

*Though I speak with the tongues of men and of angels,
and have not charity, I am become as sounding brass, or a
tinkling cymbal. And though I have the gift of prophecy,
and understand all mysteries, and all knowledge; and though
I have all faith, so that I could remove mountains, and have
not charity, I am nothing. And though I bestow all my goods
to feed the poor, and though I give my body to be burned,
and have not charity, it profiteth me nothing.*
1 Corinthians 13:1–3 kjv

Let me call your attention to Paul's first letter to the Corinthians, thirteenth chapter: In reading this passage let us use the word love instead of charity: "Though I speak with the tongues of men and of angels, and have not love, I am become as sounding brass, or a tinkling cymbal. And though I have the gift of prophecy, and understand all mysteries, and all knowledge: and though I have all faith, so that I could remove mountains, and have not love, I am nothing. And though I bestow all my goods to feed the poor, and though I give my body to be burned, and have not love, it profiteth me nothing."

It is a great thing to be a prophet like Daniel or Isaiah or Elijah or Elisha; but it is a greater thing, we are told here, to be full of love than to be filled with the spirit of prophecy. Mary of Bethany, who was so full of love, held a higher position than these great prophets did.

Day 166

— STRENGTH IN CONFESSION —

*I thank Christ Jesus our Lord, who has given me strength
to do his work. He considered me trustworthy and appointed
me to serve him, even though I used to blaspheme the name
of Christ. In my insolence, I persecuted his people. But God
had mercy on me because I did it in ignorance and unbelief.
Oh, how generous and gracious our Lord was! He filled me
with the faith and love that come from Christ Jesus.*

1 TIMOTHY 1:12–14 NLT

Confession is a difficult thing. Telling people about our sin means we have to admit we were wrong. And for men, admitting any kind of failure is tough. Showing weakness is not something we naturally enjoy, but it is essential to growing as a man of God.

The apostle Paul's confession in today's scripture is really a great sign of strength, both in his walk with Christ and his ministry to the people around him. Paul admitted his own weakness and failure but gave thanks to Jesus Christ for calling him to serve in spite of his past. Though he was a highly-educated, God-chosen leader of the early church, Paul emphasized his own weakness over any success he'd had. In fact, in another passage he said he took pleasure in his weakness and trouble since those things allowed God to be strong in him (see 2 Corinthians 12:10).

Like Paul, let's speak more of Christ than ourselves. If we ever boast, let it be in our own weakness and the strength that only Jesus gives.

"CAST ME NOT AWAY"

*Oh how great is thy goodness, which thou hast laid up for them
that fear thee; which thou hast wrought for them that trust in
thee before the sons of men! Thou shalt hide them in the secret of
thy presence from the pride of man: thou shalt keep them secretly
in a pavilion from the strife of tongues. Blessed be the Lord: for
he hath shewed me his marvellous kindness in a strong city.*
Psalm 31:19–21 kjv

Begin every morning with this steadfast purpose and seal it in believing prayer that God may keep you from everything that might
cast you away from His presence. Let this be indeed your will,
because it is also the will of God, and you shall obtain the blessing.

You shall experience that grace will also do this for you, namely,
will hear your prayer: "Cast me not away from thy presence" (Psalm
51:11 kjv). And in this blessed experience you shall be able to say
with rejoicing: "O how great is Thy goodness which Thou hast laid
up for them that fear Thee; which Thou has wrought for them that
put their trust in Thee before the sons of men. In the covert of Thy
presence shalt Thou hide them. Blessed be the Lord, for He hath
shown me His marvellous lovingkindness."

OVERFLOW WITH JUSTICE AND RIGHTEOUSNESS

*"But let justice roll on like a river,
righteousness like a never-failing stream!"*
AMOS 5:24 NIV

The prophet Amos urged people to pursue justice and righteousness. . .or face God's judgment.

Many citizens of the northern kingdom of Israel probably applauded Amos when he warned of coming judgment against neighboring nations (1:1–2:3), including the southern Jewish kingdom of Judah (2:4–5), where Amos was a farmer.

But Israelites probably hissed when their country cousin prophesied against *them* (2:6–6:14), proclaiming five visions confirming the Lord's decision to destroy them within a generation (7:1–9:10). Their sins included the torture of prisoners of war, inhumane treatment of fellow citizens, enslavement of enemies, slaughter of innocents, desecration of tombs, rejection of God's revelation, and corruption of what should be holy.

What should they do instead? Today's scripture says it all.

Justice is the fulfillment of the Ten Commandment's second tablet. It's doing what is right by others, rather than taking advantage of them (Jeremiah 22:3, 16; Ezekiel 45:9). Righteousness is the fulfillment of the first tablet. It's seeing the Lord God for who He is and actively doing His will (Micah 6:8–9).

What would it take for both to overflow? Jesus provides the best answer: "Whoever believes in me, as Scripture has said, rivers of living water will flow from within them" (John 7:38 NIV). The Gospel writer John explained: "By this he meant the Spirit, whom those who believed in him were later to receive" (verse 39 NIV; see also John 4:10; Matthew 5:6; and Isaiah 55:1). And God's Spirit is ours for the asking (see Luke 11:13).

—— GOD IS MOVED BY MISERY ——

*And she called the name of the LORD that
spake unto her, Thou God seest me: for she said,
Have I also here looked after him that seeth me?*
GENESIS 16:13 KJV

Although there was no prayer of Hagar's for God to hear, another voice spake in His ear. The angel who suddenly appeared to her said, "The Lord hath heard thy affliction." That is a very beautiful sentence. Thou hast not prayed: thou hast been willful, reckless, and at last despairing, and therefore thou hast not cried unto the Lord. But thy deep sorrow has cried to Him.

Thou art oppressed, and the Lord has undertaken for thee. Thou art suffering heavily, and God, the All-pitiful, has heard thy affliction. Grief has an eloquent voice when mercy is the listener. Woe has a plea which goodness cannot resist. Though sorrow and woe ought to be attended with prayer, yet even when supplication is not offered, the heart of God is moved by misery itself.

In Hagar's case, the Lord heard her affliction: He looked forth from His glory upon that lone Egyptian woman who was in the deepest distress in which a woman could well be placed, and He came speedily to her help.

EXACT INSTRUCTIONS

*Then Moses summoned all the elders of Israel and said
to them, "Go at once and select the animals for your families
and slaughter the Passover lamb. Take a bunch of hyssop,
dip it into the blood in the basin and put some of the blood on
the top and on both sides of the doorframe. None of you
shall go out of the door of your house until morning. When
the LORD goes through the land to strike down the Egyptians,
he will see the blood on the top and sides of the doorframe
and will pass over that doorway, and he will not permit the
destroyer to enter your houses and strike you down."*

EXODUS 12:21–23 NIV

Most people enjoy the freedom to come and go as they please and
the opportunity to express themselves. But there are times in life
when a specific and deliberate course must be followed, when
there is no opportunity for individualism.

The command of God in Exodus 12 was specific: Select a specific
animal for sacrifice. Smear the blood in a specific manner in a
specific place. Stay in a specific location. Following these specific
rules would lead to a specific outcome.

Like the ancient Israelites leaving their long years of slavery in
Egypt, we will face events that excite, confuse, or frighten us. But
God has given us specific instructions for receiving His blessing: we
read and study His Word (2 Timothy 2:15), we "pray continually"
(1 Thessalonians 5:17 NIV), and we "give thanks in all circumstances"
(1 Thessalonians 5:18 NIV).

Simple ideas, it is true—but the vehicle by which God delivers
strength for our challenges.

WALK BY FAITH

"You [David] go out and come in with me [Philistine king Achish] in the army and it is good in my eyes. I have found nothing wrong in you from the day you came to me until this day. But you are not pleasing in the eyes of the leaders."
1 SAMUEL 29:6 NLV

David found himself in a real dilemma when the Philistine king, Achish, called him to fight against Israel. David and his men, on the run from King Saul, had found refuge with the enemy Philistines. Now it was time to show David's true allegiance.

Bible commentator Adam Clarke points out that if David had gone into battle, he would have had his choice between two sins: fight for the Philistines (thereby opposing God's chosen people) or deceive and oppose Achish (who had treated David hospitably).

Other Philistine leaders, knowing that David was a celebrated warrior of Israel, objected. So Achish ultimately sent David away from the battlefield.

"God, therefore, so ordered it in His mercy that he was not permitted to go to a battle in which he was sure to be disgraced, whatever side he took, or with what success so ever he might be crowned," Clarke wrote.

David was in a pickle of his own making, but God still delivered him.

The lesson isn't to behave recklessly and wait for God to sort things out. But know that, even when we sin, He is gracious and ready to forgive. Whatever dilemmas you may face, trust God to show you the way as you walk by faith.

— A FRIGHTENING EXPERIENCE —

A young man, wearing nothing but a linen garment,
was following Jesus. When they seized him,
he fled naked, leaving his garment behind.
MARK 14:51–52 NIV

The place: Gethsemane. The situation: Jesus is being arrested. Mark records a character unmentioned by the other Gospel writers: a naked man.

Imagine the setting: Judas has given his infamous kiss. Soldiers stand with representatives of the high priest. Peter whips out a sword and cuts off someone's ear. Jesus is seized, taken away for judgment and execution.

The moment of Jesus' arrest must have filled His disciples with terror. The center of their universe, the strongest man among them, had just showed weakness. He could have said a word to stop the whole thing, but He didn't. Now He was being led away by soldiers.

When a young follower of Christ followed a little too closely, soldiers seized him too. He only got away by shrugging out of his clothes, more willing to face the shame of public nudity than to share Jesus' fate.

After all, if Jesus was too weak for the soldiers, what chance did any of the disciples have?

But Jesus wasn't being weak. He was applying His awesome strength to one of hardest things for anyone: self-sacrifice. The naked man in the garden sacrificed his clothes to save his life. Jesus would sacrifice His life to save the world from sin.

We are not called to save the world, but we are expected to stand for and with Jesus. Unlike the disciples of Gethsemane, we who follow Jesus today have the strength of the Holy Spirit in our lives. He will help us through every frightening experience.

ONE THING OR THE OTHER

*Now therefore fear the LORD, and serve him in sincerity
and in truth: and put away the gods which your fathers
served on the other side of the flood, and in Egypt; and serve
ye the LORD. And if it seem evil unto you to serve the LORD,
choose you this day whom ye will serve; whether the gods
which your fathers served that were on the other side of the
flood, or the gods of the Amorites, in whose land ye dwell:
but as for me and my house, we will serve the LORD.*
JOSHUA 24:14–15 KJV

Being a thorough-going, decided, downright man, Joshua could not
endure doublemindedness, and therefore he pushed the people
to decision, urging them to serve the Lord with sincerity, and, if
they did so, to put away altogether all their graven images. He
demanded from them a determination for one thing or the other
and cried, "If it seem evil unto you to serve Jehovah, choose you
this day whom ye will serve; whether the gods which your fathers
served that were on the other side of the flood, or the gods of the
Amorites among whom ye dwell." He shut them up to a present
choice, between the true God and the idols, and gave them no rest
in their half-heartedness.

DISPENSE WITH PRIDE

*"The pride of your heart has deceived you, you who live in
the clefts of the rocks and make your home on the heights, you
who say to yourself, 'Who can bring me down to the ground?'
Though you soar like the eagle and make your nest among the
stars, from there I will bring you down," declares the LORD.*

OBADIAH 4 NIV

The shortest prophetic book, Obadiah, warns of the Lord's judgment
on Edom. The Edomites were descendants of Esau, twin brother
of Jacob—father of the twelve tribes of Israel. Despite the close
family connection, the Edomites despised God and rejected His
chosen people.

Sometime after the fall of Jerusalem, Obadiah received a brief
but stirring message from the Lord that Edom was next in line for
destruction (1–14, 18).

The sins of Edom included acting arrogantly, deserting the
southern kingdom of Judah, plundering Judah's wealth, killing
those who tried to escape, and handing over survivors to the
dreaded Babylonians.

Obadiah's brevity wasn't all the Lord had to say about Edom's
judgment. Jeremiah, Ezekiel, and Amos all prophesied trouble as
well, and the recurring theme was Edom's confidence in its own
invincibility. Humanly speaking, there is no such thing.

That's why we as Christians are wise to dispense with pride.
God "opposes the proud but shows favor to the humble" (James 4:6;
1 Peter 5:5 NIV). No foundation is weaker than our own perceived
strength. None is greater than God's favor. The choice is yours.

UNAFRAID

Who shall separate us from the love of Christ? Shall trouble or hardship or persecution or famine or nakedness or danger or sword? As it is written: "For your sake we face death all day long; we are considered as sheep to be slaughtered." No, in all these things we are more than conquerors through him who loved us.
ROMANS 8:35–37 NIV

Most of us have shelter. In the west, at least, famine is not one of our great fears. Nor are we generally afraid of being attacked in the places we frequent. In the times of the early church, however, these were legitimate fears. Persecution sometimes chased believers from their homes. Drought could affect crops and finances and even one's ability to eat. And a trip down a remote lane could result in danger from robbers lying in wait.

Today, our hardships typically take different forms. But fear—of our future and our fate—often remains, just as it did for the people of Paul's day.

That's why the apostle wanted believers to know, with absolute certainty, that the love of Christ can obliterate all fear. Through our Lord Jesus, we are free to live without fear and able to weather any challenge life throws at us.

Life comes with great uncertainty. But take comfort in the fact that nothing we experience can ever remove the deep and strengthening love of Jesus.

STRENGTH FROM GOD

*And David was very troubled because the people talked
about killing him with stones. For all the people were
very angry in their sorrow for their sons and daughters.
But David got his strength from the Lord his God.*
1 SAMUEL 30:6 NLV

Israel's future king, David, had a strange sojourn in Philistine territory. As King Saul sought the younger man's life, David and his band of men hid out among Israel's enemies. David even developed a friendly relationship with the Philistine leader Achish.

Achish wanted David to accompany his army in battle against Israel, but other Philistine leaders demanded he return to Ziklag, a Philistine town Achish had given David. Before he and his men arrived, though, the Amalekites—a nomadic tribe who were also enemies of Israel—invaded. They carried away all the wives and children of David's band, including his wives, Ahinoam and Abigail. Then the Amalekites burned the city.

David's men were furious with him for exposing their families to such an attack. But as they talked about stoning him, today's verse says David found strength from the Lord. What did that look like, practically speaking?

For David, it meant prayer. He went straight to God to ask what his next steps should be. God answered with good news: David would recover all the kidnapped women and children.

In times of stress and upheaval, we can (and should) turn to God. "He is working in you," Philippians 2:13 (NLV) says. "God is helping you obey Him. God is doing what He wants done in you."

There's no better strength than that.

LIBERTY IN PRAYER

And Abraham drew near, and said, Wilt thou
also destroy the righteous with the wicked?
GENESIS 18:23 KJV

There is a two-fold use of prayer: the one, to obtain strength and blessing for our own life; the other, the higher, the true glory of prayer, for which Christ has taken us into His fellowship and teaching, is intercession, where prayer is the royal power a child of God exercises in heaven on behalf of others and even of the kingdom.

We see it in scripture, how it was in intercession for others that Abraham and Moses, Samuel and Elijah, with all the holy men of old, proved that they had power with God and prevailed. It is when we give ourselves to be a blessing that we can specially count on the blessing of God. It is when we draw near to God as the friend of the poor and the perishing that we may count on His friendliness; the righteous man who is the friend of the poor is very specially the friend of God. This gives wonderful liberty in prayer.

—— NEVER STOP LEARNING ——

*A wise man will hear and increase learning, and a
man of understanding will attain wise counsel.*
PROVERBS 1:5 NKJV

"It is not that I'm so smart," Albert Einstein is quoted as saying, "but I stay with the questions much longer."

Some of us are simply not willing to live with questions. In a world where the answer to every trivial question is right beneath our fingertips, finding the time or the desire to go deeper has become a lost art.

Yet the Christian life is all about "deeper." Packed schedules and a constant flood of activities have given the concept of quiet contemplation a bad name. For many men, rest has turned into a four-letter word. But rest is not laziness. When it comes to finding strength for the challenges of life, real rest—a desire to linger over the Word of God—is the only way to go.

Answers to the questions that live in the deepest, darkest places in our hearts—the questions we won't share with anyone—are all found in God's Word. But we must make up our minds that we're going to stop passing the buck to others and begin feeding ourselves. A lack of knowledge and real connection with Jesus Christ is nobody's fault but our own.

Can we honestly say we've heard it all before, especially when it comes to God's Word?

CRY TO GOD

For the people shall dwell in Zion at Jerusalem: thou shalt weep no more: he will be very gracious unto thee at the voice of thy cry; when he shall hear it, he will answer thee.
ISAIAH 30:19 KJV

I desire at this time to set forth the graciousness of God and His readiness to listen to the cry of the needy, with the hope that some here present who may have forgotten this, to whom it may be a time of need, may hear it and be encouraged to say, "I will arise and go to my Father."

It is joy to me to hope that it will be so, but I remember with sadness that if I should be helped to set this forth clearly, and if any of you who are in trouble should afterwards refuse to trust in the Lord, your alienation will be aggravated, your sin will become still more crying.

He who will not trust when he knows that the Lord will be gracious to him sins against his own soul and plunges himself in sevenfold wrath. If the Lord saith that he will be very gracious at the voice of your cry, what must be your doom if you will not cry?

FEAR THE LORD

[Jonah] said unto them, I am an Hebrew; and I fear the LORD, the God of heaven, which hath made the sea and the dry land. Then were the men exceedingly afraid, and said unto him. Why hast thou done this? For the men knew that he fled from the presence of the LORD.
JONAH 1:9–10 KJV

It's possible to say good things about God without really meaning them. Such is the case with Jonah's statement to the pagan sailors manning the ship he was on.

Jonah told the truth about his nationality, but he lied about fearing the Lord God, creator of heaven and earth and seas. At that moment, Jonah was arrogantly, defiantly disobeying God by taking a ship in the opposite direction from the place he was called to.

Still, Jonah's acknowledgement of a "fear of the Lord" offers useful insights to our strength and success today. Recognizing God's awesome power, knowledge, and holiness should cause a certain amount of fear in us—the kind a mouse undoubtedly feels in the presence of a human being. But biblical fear is also a reverent respect, a desire to know and honor and, ultimately, enjoy an eternal relationship with this awesome God, who is also love—demonstrated by the sacrificial death of His Son, Jesus Christ (Romans 5:8).

As sinful human beings, we're pulled in many directions by our own emotions, temptations, companions, and culture. But when we truly acknowledge and "fear" the Lord, He will happily guide and strengthen us in His will.

— CONSTANTLY GIVING THANKS —

*Be careful for nothing; but in every thing by prayer
and supplication with thanksgiving let your requests
be made known unto God. And the peace of God,
which passeth all understanding, shall keep your
hearts and minds through Christ Jesus.*
PHILIPPIANS 4:6–7 KJV

Among all the apostles none suffered so much as Paul; but none of them do we find so often giving thanks as he.

Take his letter to the Philippians. Remember what he suffered at Philippi; how they laid many stripes upon him and cast him into prison. Yet every chapter in that Epistle speaks of rejoicing and giving thanks. There is that well-known passage: "Be careful for nothing, but in everything, by prayer and supplication, with thanksgiving, let your requests be made known unto God." As someone has said, there are here three precious ideas: "Careful for nothing; prayerful for everything; and thankful for anything."

We always get more by being thankful for what God has done for us. Paul says again: "We give thanks to God and the Father of our Lord Jesus Christ, praying always for you" (Colossians 1:3 KJV). So he was constantly giving thanks. Take up any one of his Epistles, and you will find them full of praise to God.

THE PATH TO VICTORY

*Moses answered the people, "Do not be afraid. Stand firm
and you will see the deliverance the Lord will bring you
today. The Egyptians you see today you will never see again.
The Lord will fight for you; you need only to be still."*
EXODUS 14:13–14 NIV

The nation of Israel was finally leaving its captivity in Egypt. But now the people found themselves pursued by the Egyptian army. In front of them lay the Red Sea, a seemingly impenetrable obstacle. Their dream of freedom appeared to be ending badly.

What the people forgot was that the Lord of heaven, the God of Abraham, was more powerful than the armies of Egypt. They had yet to understand that their God, the God of Moses, was able to overcome the obstacle of the Red Sea. In just a few short hours, the people would walk across dry ground after God performed a spectacular miracle. And soon after that, the army of Egypt would be annihilated in another spectacular miracle.

The Lord was ready to fight for Israel, just as He is ready to fight for believers in Christ today. The apostle John gives us this specific encouragement: "Everyone born of God overcomes the world. This is the victory that has overcome the world, even our faith" (1 John 5:4 NIV).

This promise is our path to victory. Faith will cause us to overcome, regardless of the obstacles we face.

STILL NEED TO FIGHT

That was the beginning of a long war between those who were loyal to Saul and those loyal to David. As time passed David became stronger and stronger, while Saul's dynasty became weaker and weaker.

2 SAMUEL 3:1 NLT

Saul and his son Jonathan—David's beloved friend—were killed by the Philistines. Saul's death led to David being anointed king of Judah. But Saul's men in the northern sections of Israel were faithful to him, going so far as to anoint Ishbosheth, another son of Saul, as king. War ensued.

David was God's chosen king for Israel, but he still had to fight for his realm.

We as Christians are given a kingdom too (see Luke 12:32). But there will be a fight—in fact plenty of battles—before we find peace and comfort. We'll face many hardships, but the apostle Paul assured us that they will be worth it: "Since we are [God's] children, we are his heirs. In fact, together with Christ we are heirs of God's glory. But if we are to share his glory, we must also share his suffering. Yet what we suffer now is nothing compared to the glory he will reveal to us later" (Romans 8:17–18 NLT).

If God calls us to "share" in Jesus' suffering, He will provide the power to do so. And He promises rewards we can hardly imagine. You still need to fight, so step up to the battle lines.

—— STRENGTH IN ANXIETY ——

*For God has not given us a spirit of fear and timidity,
but of power, love, and self-discipline.*
2 TIMOTHY 1:7 NLT

Does it help you to realize that some key Bible characters dealt with anxiety and fear?

Notice how the apostle Paul speaks to Timothy in today's verse. This follows Paul describing Timothy as "my dear son" (1:2), a phrase he would repeat in 2:1, and noting Timothy's tears when he and the apostle had last parted (1:4). We get the impression that Timothy was a gentle and loving man, which is a positive thing. But because of his tenderness, Timothy might have struggled with the demands of leading the church in Ephesus.

So Paul encouraged the younger man with the words of 2 Timothy 1:7. When we are feeling the effects of anxiety on our lives, this verse is a wonderful reminder of God's provision. Fear, anxiety, and depression are not things that the Lord gives us. He may allow us to experience them for our growth. but if He does, there's a good reason.

In those moments, return to this scripture. Know for sure that God has given you a spirit of power, of love, and of self-discipline. Use this reminder to give yourself strength.

GOD IS PACIFIED

*And I will establish my covenant with thee; and thou shalt
know that I am the LORD: that thou mayest remember,
and be confounded, and never open thy mouth any more
because of thy shame, when I am pacified toward thee
for all that thou hast done, saith the Lord GOD.*
EZEKIEL 16:62–63 KJV

O believer, God is pacified towards you, for your sin is covered;
it is put away, all of it, and altogether. Since you have believed
in Jesus Christ your sin has not become dimly visible, neither by
searching may it be seen as a shadow in the distance; but God
seeth it no more forever.

And you may say, "O God, I will praise thee, for though thou wast
angry with me, thine anger is turned away, and thou comfortedest
me" (Isaiah 12:1 KJV). The many, the countless hosts of sin that you
have committed since your childhood are all scattered as a cloud,
and the one black sin, which cost you more regret than many
scores of others, has been removed as a thick cloud. They are all
gone—no enemy remaineth. They cannot rise against you from
the grave; no, not one of them, while sun and moon endure, nay,
while God endureth, for, He saith, "They shall not be mentioned
against thee anymore, forever."

God is pacified towards His people for all that they have done,
altogether pacified, for their sins have ceased to be.

FOXHOLE PRAYERS
AND REAL REPENTANCE

When my soul fainted within me I remembered the LORD:
and my prayer came in unto thee, into thine holy temple.
JONAH 2:7 KJV

After Jonah was thrown into the sea, he immediately cried out to
the Lord for mercy (2:1–9). The prayer he wrote afterward is quite
stirring. First, Jonah described his urgent pleas as he descended
below the waves, through seaweed, toward the bottom.

Second, Jonah continued his pleas from the stomach of a great
fish. Like other desperate men, he made a deal—if the Lord would
only spare his life. In the middle of that deal, Jonah thanked God
that he wasn't like some pagan idol worshipper. What a guy!

Finally, Jonah thanked the Lord for saving him from otherwise
certain death.

After the fish vomited Jonah onto dry land, the prophet headed
straight to Nineveh. Undoubtedly a terrible sight himself, Jonah
preached a stirring message of God's pending judgment (3:1–4).
Amazingly, the entire city humbled itself before the Lord and repented (3:5–9). God decided against carrying out the destruction
He had threatened (3:10).

Good news, right? Except it made Jonah angry with God (4:1–3).
So much for his promise to "pay that that I have vowed" (2:9 KJV).

It appears, however, that Jonah later repented for real, writing
the book that bears his name. In a sense, it's his confessions, a
public way of humbling himself as part of his repentance. And as
he downplayed his own goodness, he highlighted God's. That's the
fruit of real repentance in any man's life.

How are you doing on that score?

— YOU CAN'T OUT-SIN GRACE —

For I am convinced that neither death nor life, neither angels nor demons, neither the present nor the future, nor any powers, neither height nor depth, nor anything else in all creation, will be able to separate us from the love of God that is in Christ Jesus our Lord.
ROMANS 8:38–39 NIV

Jesus often visited people's homes to eat dinner and teach on the kingdom of God. One such visit, at the home of Simon the Pharisee, is recorded in Luke 7. During the meal, a "sinful woman" poured perfume on His feet, wept over them, and wiped them dry with her hair.

As Simon grumbled to himself, Jesus told him a parable: "Two people owed money to a certain moneylender. One owed him five hundred denarii, and the other fifty. Neither of them had the money to pay him back, so he forgave the debts of both. Now which of them will love him more?" (Luke 7:41–42 NIV). Simon suggested the one with the larger debt. Jesus agreed.

Then Jesus turned to the woman. Instead of saying thank you, He told her that her sins were forgiven. The audience was stunned, and her life was changed.

At times, we all need forgiveness. Perhaps we've drifted away from God, or some overwhelming life experience breaks our fellowship with Him. But no matter where we've been or how much we've sinned, we can't out-sin God's grace through Jesus Christ. As the apostle Paul put it in Romans 8, nothing can pry us away from God's love. Like the prodigal son, you can always return to His home.

—— OUR TRUSTWORTHY GOD ——

"I have been with you wherever you have gone, and I have destroyed all your enemies before your eyes. Now I will make your name as famous as anyone who has ever lived on the earth!"
2 SAMUEL 7:9 NLT

Israel had a long history of conflict. But now that David was established as king, the Lord gave the nation rest from its enemies. David began to dream of building a permanent house for the ark of God, which at that time was kept in a tent. But God told David that one of his offspring would build the temple. David could trust this promise because of God's faithfulness in the past.

The Lord reminded David how "I took you from tending sheep in the pasture and selected you to be the leader of my people Israel" (verse 8 NLT). And then God spoke the words of today's scripture, making sure David knew that he'd always had the divine presence and protection with him.

Though our calling is far different than David's, we can also claim God's power and provision in our lives. Through His Holy Spirit, God actually lives within us—which is why He can say, "I will never abandon you" (Hebrews 13:5 NLT). Jesus has encouraged us to ask His Father for our daily bread, protection from temptation, and forgiveness from sin (Matthew 6:9–13). And we who follow Jesus are assured of ultimate success: "I know the one in whom I trust, and I am sure that he is able to guard what I have entrusted to him until the day of his return" (2 Timothy 1:12 NLT). Our God is trustworthy!

KNOWLEDGE AS MEANS OF BLESSING

For the invisible things of him from the creation of the world are clearly seen, being understood by the things that are made, even his eternal power and Godhead; so that they are without excuse: because that, when they knew God, they glorified him not as God, neither were thankful; but became vain in their imaginations, and their foolish heart was darkened.
ROMANS 1:20–21 KJV

Those who boast of their knowledge betray their ignorance. Knowledge is not a possession to be proud of, since it brings with it so great a responsibility that a nurse might as well be proud of watching over a life in peril.

Knowledge may become good or ill according to the use which is made of it. If men know God, for instance, and then glorify Him as God and are thankful, their knowledge has become the means of great blessing to them; but if they know God and fail to glorify Him, their knowledge turns to their condemnation. There is a knowledge which does not puff up the mind but builds up the soul, being joined with holy love. Did not our Lord say, "And this is life eternal, that they might know thee the only true God, and Jesus Christ, whom thou hast sent" (John 17:3 KJV)?

But for men to know God and not to glorify Him as God and to be unthankful is, according to our text, no benefit to them: on the contrary, it becomes a savor of death unto them, because it leaves them without excuse.

CLASSICS: D. L. MOODY

YOU ARE JUSTIFIED

If we believe on him that raised up Jesus our Lord
from the dead; who was delivered for our offences,
and was raised again for our justification.
ROMANS 4:24-25 KJV

Christ was raised from the grave for the justification of all who put their trust in Him, and such are not only pardoned men but justified men. Justification is more than pardon.

It is said of an emperor of Russia that he sent on one occasion for two noblemen who were charged with some conspiracy, and one he found to be perfectly innocent, so he sent him home justified; but the other was proved guilty, yet was pardoned. They both returned to their homes; but ever afterwards they would stand very differently in the estimation of their Sovereign and neighbors. From that may be seen the difference between pardon and justification.

When a man is justified, he can go through the world with his head erect. Satan may come to him and say, "You are a sinner"; but the reply would be, "I know that, but God has forgiven me through Christ."

SEEK GOD, FIND GOD

*If you call out for insight and cry aloud for understanding,
if you look for it as for silver and search for it as for
hidden treasure, then you will understand the fear
of the LORD and find the knowledge of God.*
PROVERBS 2:3–5 NIV

In a world where we can have pretty much whatever we want, whenever we want it, it's easy to allow our desires to distract us from the pursuit of the things we truly need. What do we really need? Our hearts and Proverbs 2:5 say, "the knowledge of God."

God created man to have fellowship with Himself. He said, "Let us make man in our image, after our likeness. . . . And God saw every thing that he had made and, behold, it was very good" (Genesis 1:26, 31 KJV).

Our days are filled with many good things. But we often overlook the one most important thing: fellowship, time spent alone with God and His Word. He says that if we seek Him as we would search for silver—if we make Him the real driving force behind everything—*we will find Him*. And when we do, our spiritual bank account will be filled to overflowing.

Jesus doesn't hide from us. In fact, He's standing at the door to your heart right now. In those moments when we feel alone, let's put down what we're doing, give up the selfish ambitions that consume our lives, and open the door to Him.

Day 192

WHOLEHEARTED
FOR THE LORD

*And [Jonah] prayed unto the LORD, and said, I pray thee,
O LORD, was not this my saying, when I was yet in my
country? Therefore I fled before unto Tarshish: for I knew
that thou art a gracious God, and merciful, slow to anger,
and of great kindness, and repentest thee of the evil.*

JONAH 4:2 KJV

In hindsight, Jonah's prayers are pathetic, almost laughable. Apparently it was okay for the Lord to change His mind and spare Jonah's life. But somehow it wasn't all right for God to change His mind and spare the repentant Ninevites. . . .

Granted, Nineveh was wicked. It was the capital of the vicious Assyrian empire, whose soldiers gleefully cut down their enemies. They were even more gleeful and sadistic in torturing their prisoners of war.

Nevertheless, at Jonah's warning, the Assyrian king and his capital city's entire population repented with earnest prayer and serious fasting. How serious? Not even the animals were allowed to eat or drink (Jonah 3:7). And the Lord noticed (Jonah 4:11).

It's ironic that God turned around and used the Assyrians to bring judgment on His own people, the wicked northern kingdom of Israel, a few decades later (2 Kings 15:19–17:23). But not long after that, the Assyrians were more pagan than ever and God was compelled to pronounce a final judgment on Nineveh (see the book of Nahum).

It's been said that God has no grandchildren. Every individual must decide for or against the Lord. Some people choose him halfheartedly, out of fear or social pressure. But those whose hearts are whole find their daily strength in Him.

CLASSICS: ANDREW MURRAY

THE SECRET OF TRUE OBEDIENCE

And the LORD heard the voice of your words, when ye spake unto me; and the LORD said unto me, I have heard the voice of the words of this people, which they have spoken unto thee: they have well said all that they have spoken. O that there were such an heart in them, that they would fear me, and keep all my commandments always, that it might be well with them, and with their children for ever!
DEUTERONOMY 5:28–29 KJV

The secret of true obedience—let me say at once what I believe it to be—the clear and close personal relationship to God. All our attempts after full obedience will be failures until we get access to His abiding fellowship. *It is God's holy presence, consciously abiding with us, that keeps us from disobeying Him.*

Defective obedience is always the result of a defective life. To rouse and spur on that defective life by arguments and motives has its use, but their chief blessing must be that they make us feel the need of a different life, a life so entirely under the power of God that obedience will be its natural outcome. The defective life, the life of broken and irregular fellowship with God, must be healed and make way for a full and healthy life; then full obedience will become possible.

The secret of a true obedience is *the return to close and continual fellowship with God.*

A TEAM EFFORT

So Joshua fought the Amalekites as Moses had ordered, and Moses, Aaron and Hur went to the top of the hill. As long as Moses held up his hands, the Israelites were winning, but whenever he lowered his hands, the Amalekites were winning. When Moses' hands grew tired, they took a stone and put it under him and he sat on it. Aaron and Hur held his hands up—one on one side, one on the other—so that his hands remained steady till sunset. So Joshua overcame the Amalekite army with the sword.
EXODUS 17:10–13 NIV

Joshua could not complete his task without the work of Moses. Moses could not support Joshua in his task without the work of Aaron and Hur. The work was a full day, and in the end, the task was accomplished. Many times, we find strength for the challenge by relying on the help of others.

This was not the first time these men had worked together. They knew each other's strengths and weaknesses and were ready to assist when the moment called.

When we encourage our family, coworkers, or fellow citizens, we more effectively complete tasks and accomplish goals. And the receiving of strength from these same individuals can help us get past our challenges.

Who is on your team? Or who should be? Reach out to them, offering and receiving encouragement in Jesus' name.

— VICTORY BELONGS TO GOD —

So the LORD made David victorious wherever he went.
2 SAMUEL 8:6 NLT

Saul's dislike of David began shortly after the king appointed the young man as a military commander. Once, as the army returned from a battle victory, women from the towns of Israel came out to meet King Saul, dancing and singing. That was good. But their song elevated David over the king: "Saul has killed his thousands, and David his ten thousands!" (1 Samuel 18:7 NLT). Saul was not happy.

What the king failed to realize was that David's successes on the battlefield had little to do with David himself—but everything to do with God. The Lord was with David, making him victorious wherever he went. The words of today's scripture are repeated in 2 Samuel 8:14.

We know that David wasn't perfect. In fact, later in life, he would commit adultery and ultimately arrange the death of the woman's husband. But he'd been chosen by God to be king, and was described as a man after God's own heart (1 Samuel 13:14; Acts 13:22).

All of us have flaws, but God still chooses to work through us. And He empowers us to accomplish what He wills. Keep your focus on the Lord, through prayer and time in His Word. Deny yourself and take up your cross each day (Matthew 16:24). Humbly wait on the Lord, and His victory—whatever form that takes.

Day 196

— HOSPITALITY AND HEALING —

After leaving the synagogue that day, Jesus went to Simon's home, where he found Simon's mother-in-law very sick with a high fever. "Please heal her," everyone begged. Standing at her bedside, he rebuked the fever, and it left her. And she got up at once and prepared a meal for them.
LUKE 4:38–39 NLT

In the Jewish culture of Jesus' day, hospitality was more than good manners. It was a moral institution with spiritual implications. By offering hospitality to Jesus, Peter was seeking to bless his new rabbi—and perhaps even gain favor in Jesus' eyes.

But when the Lord arrived at Peter's house, He noticed His disciple's mother-in-law lying sick with a fever. So, Jesus healed her, and the woman—unnamed in scripture—immediately started serving. What could have been a social faux pas for Peter provided Jesus with a chance to show grace. . .and Peter's mother-in-law a chance to serve.

As followers of Christ, we too have invited Him into our "home." He sees where we need healing and He extends us grace. Our response should be the same as Peter's mother-in-law: to serve Him.

True strength isn't looking for opportunities to gain favor in Jesus' eyes. It receives His healing and grace with gratitude, looking then for ways to serve.

Classics: D. L. Moody

CHARACTER WINS

*Then the presidents and princes sought to find occasion
against Daniel concerning the kingdom; but they could find
none occasion nor fault; forasmuch as he was faithful, neither
was there any error or fault found in him. Then said these men,
We shall not find any occasion against this Daniel, except
we find it against him concerning the law of his God.*

Daniel 6:4–5 kjv

One of the highest eulogies ever paid to a man on earth was pro-
nounced upon Daniel, by his enemies. These men who were connected with the various parts of the kingdom could "find no occasion
against this Daniel, except they found it against him concerning
the law of his God." What a testimony from his bitterest enemies!
Would that it could be said of all of us!

Ah, how his name shines! He had commenced to shine in his
early manhood; and he shone right along. Now he is an old man,
an old statesman; and yet this is their testimony. There had been
no sacrifice of principle to catch votes; no buying up of men's votes
or men's consciences. He had walked right straight along.

Character is worth more than anything else in the wide world.

FILLED WITH POWER

*But as for me, I am filled with power, with the Spirit
of the LORD, and with justice and might, to declare
to Jacob his transgression, to Israel his sin.*
MICAH 3:8 NIV

Micah urged his readers to pay attention to the Lord's warnings of pending judgment. Like his contemporary Isaiah and several other prophets who would come later, Micah repeatedly told God's people to listen. Why? Because their sins were many and their judgment sure.

Like Isaiah, Micah didn't hesitate to denounce the godless rulers, corrupt priests, false prophets, and degenerate people who filled the kingdoms of Israel and Judah (chapters 1–3). Like Isaiah, Micah spoke of days far into the future (chapters 4–5). Like Isaiah, Micah pictured the Lord putting His people on trial (chapter 6). And like Isaiah, Micah contrasted the godlessness of his day with the glorious future ahead (chapter 7).

What inspired Micah to speak out so boldly against the sins of his people? The verse above makes it clear that the Spirit of the Lord gave him the strength.

If God's Spirit lives in us, we too will have the power to speak boldly against injustice and sin—and we'll have the power to deny those sins first in our own lives. We'll be "filled with power" to do whatever it is that God calls us to do.

The key is the indwelling Spirit, which every true Christian possesses, and our conscious, minute-by-minute decision to allow Him to control our lives.

FINDING THE GOOD LIFE

*Therefore, I urge you, brothers and sisters, in view of
God's mercy, to offer your bodies as a living sacrifice, holy and
pleasing to God—this is your true and proper worship. Do not
conform to the pattern of this world, but be transformed by the
renewing of your mind. Then you will be able to test and approve
what God's will is—his good, pleasing and perfect will.*

ROMANS 12:1–2 NIV

"You only live once." "Do what feels right." "Find yourself." These
are the popular philosophies of our world.

It's very common to find people pursuing what they think is
best for themselves. But Jesus taught and exemplified a much
different way.

His life and ministry changed everything. Not only did Jesus
open the pathway to God and eternal life, by His selfless example
He challenged the way we live this life. "For even the Son of Man
did not come to be served, but to serve," Jesus said, "and to give
his life as a ransom for many" (Mark 10:45 NIV).

In the book of Romans, the apostle Paul likewise urged Christians
to get beyond themselves. Though human nature is to do whatever
feels right in the moment, we help ourselves by sacrificing our
desires to God—serving Him by building up others, attending to people's needs, looking after those who cannot look after themselves.

We find the good life by denying our own desires.

THE MORE YOU STUDY SCRIPTURE. . .

And when he was alone, they that were about him with the twelve
asked of him the parable. And he said unto them, Unto you it is
given to know the mystery of the kingdom of God: but unto them
that are without, all these things are done in parables.
MARK 4:10–11 KJV

The Word of God tells us plainly that the natural man cannot understand spiritual things. It is a spiritual book and speaks of spiritual things, and a man must be born of the Spirit before he can understand the Bible. What seems very dark and mysterious to you now will all be light and clear when you are born of the Spirit.

I can remember some portions of scripture that were very dark and mysterious to me when I was converted, but now they are very clear. I can remember things that ten years ago were very dark and mysterious, but as I have gone on I understand them better, and the more we know of God, and the more we study the Word, the plainer it will become.

CLASSICS: CHARLES SPURGEON

WE SHALL BE RICHER

So the LORD blessed the latter end of Job more than his beginning:
for he had fourteen thousand sheep, and six thousand camels,
and a thousand yoke of oxen, and a thousand she asses.
He had also seven sons and three daughters.
JOB 42:12–13 KJV

We are not all like Job, but we all have Job's God. Though we have neither risen to Job's wealth, nor will, probably, ever sink to Job's poverty, yet there is the same God above us if we be high, and the same God with His everlasting arms beneath us if we be brought low; and what the Lord did for Job He will do for us, not precisely in the same form, but in the same spirit, and with like design.

If, therefore, we are brought low tonight, let us be encouraged with the thought that God will turn again our captivity; and let us entertain the hope that after the time of trial shall be over, we shall be richer, especially in spiritual things, than ever we were before.

—— HELP WHEN CORNERED ——

But Abishai son of Zeruiah came to David's rescue and killed the Philistine. Then David's men declared, "You are not going out to battle with us again! Why risk snuffing out the light of Israel?"
2 SAMUEL 21:17 NLT

As David neared the end of his life, he was still going out to battle with his men. He even fought Philistine giants, just as he had battled Goliath in his youth. But on one occasion, David became weak and exhausted from the fight (2 Samuel 21:15). Ishbi-benob, a descendant of the giants, carrying a spear with a seven-pound bronze point, cornered David and was about to kill him. Happily for the king, help arrived in the form of an Israelite soldier named Abishai, son of Zeruiah.

We all become battle-weary at times. And in some cases, God doesn't strengthen us personally. Instead, He helps us face our challenge by summoning other believers to our rescue. Perhaps God does this to humble us—a reminder of our own frailty will encourage our dependence on Him. Or maybe He's preparing our rescuer for some even bigger task in the future.

Are you willing to accept aid from a fellow believer for the challenges you face? When moments of weariness and weakness come, don't consider yourself a failure—those times happen to us all. Instead, thank God for His perfect wisdom and timing in sending a willing soldier to help when you're cornered.

THE PRAYER OF FAITH

*Then Jesus answered and said unto her, O woman,
great is thy faith: be it unto thee even as thou wilt.
And her daughter was made whole from that very hour.*
MATTHEW 15:28 KJV

Alas! How many prayers are wishes, sent up for a short time and then forgotten, or sent up year after year as matter of duty, while we rest content with the prayer without the answer.

But, it may be asked, is it not best to make our wishes known to God and then to leave it to Him to decide what is best, without seeking to assert our will? By no means. This is the very essence of the prayer of faith, to which Jesus sought to train His disciples, that it does not only make known its desire and then leave the decision to God. That would be the prayer of submission, for cases in which we cannot know God's will.

But the prayer of faith, finding God's will in some promise of the Word, pleads for that till it come. Jesus said to the Syrophenician woman: "Great is thy faith; be it unto thee even as thou wilt." Faith is nothing but the purpose of the will resting on God's word and saying: I must have it. To believe truly is to will firmly.

CONSIDER THE
WHOLE PICTURE

*"But you, Bethlehem Ephrathah, though you are small
among the clans of Judah, out of you will come for me one
who will be ruler over Israel, whose origins are from of old,
from ancient times." . . . He will stand and shepherd his flock
in the strength of the Lord, in the majesty of the name of
the Lord his God. And they will live securely, for then his
greatness will reach to the ends of the earth.*
MICAH 5:2, 4 NIV

The first Old Testament prophecy quoted in the New Testament has
proved especially popular thanks to Matthew's oft-repeated Christmas story. It's so familiar that we sometimes miss the biggest point.

When wise men arrived in Jerusalem from the east asking,
"Where is he that is born King of the Jews?" (Matthew 2:2 KJV), Herod
the Great quickly decided to slaughter this threat to his kingship.
But he needed to know where, so he asked the Jewish religious
leaders who replied with a misquoting of today's scripture. In the
first sentence, they stopped at "ruler," borrowed "shepherd" from
the following verse, and inserted "my people" before Israel.

The chief priests and teachers of the law deliberately avoided
the most important messianic portions of today's scripture. Let's
not do the same.

First, the Messiah's "origins are from of old, from ancient times."
Second, everything He does is "in the strength of the Lord, in the
majesty of the Lord his God." Third, "his greatness will reach to
the ends of the earth."

We must fully know who we serve to fully enjoy the blessing
of His strength.

THE TIME FOR ACTION

And the LORD said unto Moses, Wherefore
criest thou unto me? speak unto the
children of Israel, that they go forward.
EXODUS 14:15 KJV

Spiritual men, in their distresses, turn at once to prayer, even as the stag when hunted takes to flight. Prayer is a never-failing resort; it is sure to bring a blessing with it. The very exercise of prayer is healthy to the man engaged in it. Far be it from me ever to say a word in disparagement of the holy, happy, heavenly exercise of prayer. But, beloved, there are times when prayer is not enough—when prayer itself is out of season.

You will think that a hard saying. Moses prayed that God would deliver His people; but the Lord said to him, "Wherefore criest thou unto me?" As much as to say this is not the time for prayer; it is the time for action.

When we have prayed over a matter to a certain degree, it then becomes sinful to tarry any longer; our plain duty is to carry our desires into action, and having asked God's guidance, and having received divine power from on high, to go at once to our duty without any longer deliberation or delay.

STORIES TOLD

*Moses told his father-in-law about everything the Lord
had done to Pharaoh and the Egyptians for Israel's sake
and about all the hardships they had met along the way and
how the Lord had saved them. Jethro was delighted to hear
about all the good things the Lord had done for Israel in
rescuing them from the hand of the Egyptians.*
EXODUS 18:8–9 NIV

Moses had followed God's command to confront Pharaoh over
his enslavement of Israel. He had gotten strength from the Lord
to complete this task, and now it was time to share what God had
accomplished through him.

It's not surprising that Moses spoke with his father-in-law soon
after the events of the Exodus. Years before, when Moses had fled a
murder charge in Egypt, he worked as a shepherd for Jethro, even
marrying his daughter. Moses was in Jethro's household when
God spoke to him from a burning bush. Now, after the Israelites'
miraculous escape from Egypt, Jethro was one of the first individuals Moses spoke to.

Jethro was truly blessed to hear how God was working in the life
of Moses and the nation of Israel. The news caused him to break
out in praise and present a sacrifice to the Lord.

God gives us strength through the stories of other believers'
experiences. So be sure you're around faithful people who can
share encouraging accounts of the Lord's faithfulness. If you're
not finding those people, pray and ask God to direct you to them.
He is happy to answer such prayers.

— SUPERNATURAL STRENGTH —

"In your strength I [David] can crush an army;
with my God I can scale any wall."
2 SAMUEL 22:30 NLT

David was a bundle of contradictions. He was a great sinner who was also a man after God's own heart. He was a man who could be patient but sometimes acted in haste. He showed great mercy—as he did with Jonathan's disabled son, Mephibosheth—or he could be utterly ruthless. He was a warrior as well as a poet. The latter may have made him especially sensitive to understanding who he was before a holy God: a weak vessel.

Three times in in 2 Samuel 22, David's song of praise to the Lord, David mentioned that God strengthened him. He sang about God as his rock, his fortress, and his savior. But David didn't stop there. God was his shield, the power that saved him, his place of safety, his refuge, and more.

If the man who killed the giant Goliath recognized his dependence on such a God, how much more should we? We too are bundles of contradictions. We sin much while also chasing after God. We are impatient with others but also try to show compassion. We can only do the good, though, as God works in us.

And once we've tasted of His power, how can we do anything else but praise Him like David did?

FORWARD ON FAITH

When he had finished speaking, he said to Simon, "Now go out
where it is deeper, and let down your nets to catch some fish."
"Master," Simon replied, "we worked hard all last night and didn't
catch a thing. But if you say so, I'll let the nets down again."
Luke 5:4–5 NLT

Simon, also known as Peter, wasn't a rabbi—he was a fisherman.
He didn't tell Jesus how to teach or heal, and he didn't expect Jesus
to tell him how to fish. But when Jesus gave him an order, Peter
knew enough to listen.

He was about to be schooled.

After following Jesus' instructions, the fish that evaded Peter
the night before were now lured miraculously into his nets. Soon,
Peter and his brother Andrew had to signal another boat to help
them with the catch, lest the haul of fish sink their boat. The Gospel
writer Luke reports, "When Simon Peter realized what had happened, he fell to his knees before Jesus and said, 'Oh, Lord, please
leave me—I'm such a sinful man' " (5:8 NLT).

Peter learned the limits of his own expertise and the faith required to follow the One who called him to fish for men.

When we rely on our own expertise—whether we're fishermen,
plumbers, businessmen, or evangelists—we aren't depending on
God to provide what we truly need. Like Peter, let's admit our own
sinfulness and move forward on faith alone.

Classics: D. L. Moody

— GET IN LOVE WITH THE BIBLE —

I am afflicted very much: quicken me,
O Lord, according unto thy word.
PSALM 119:107 KJV

A quickening that will last must come through the Word of God. The more you love the scriptures, the firmer will be your faith. There is little backsliding when people love the scriptures. If you come into closer contact with the Word, you will gain something that will last, because the Word of God is going to endure.

In Psalm 119 David prayed nine times that God would quicken him—according to His word, His law, His judgment, His precepts, etc. If I could say something that would induce Christians to have a deeper love for the Word of God, I should feel this to be the most important service that could be rendered to them.

Do you ask: How can I get in love with the Bible? Well, if you will only arouse yourself to the study of it and ask God's assistance, He will assuredly help you.

DO WHAT'S GOOD

He hath shewed thee, O man, what is good; and what doth the LORD require of thee, but to do justly, and to love mercy, and to walk humbly with thy God?
MICAH 6:8 KJV

Is it true that God has showed mankind what is good? Yes. Much of the Old Testament—whether by the rules given to Israel or in the examples of people's lives—clearly shows what God wants and the danger of doing otherwise.

In the New Testament, did Jesus exhort His listeners "to do justly, and to love mercy, and to walk humbly with thy God"? Yes. We can't read far into the Gospels without seeing things like this: "Love your enemies, bless them that curse you, do good to them that hate you" (Matthew 5:44 KJV; see also Luke 6:27, 35), and, "Is it lawful to do good on the sabbath days, or to do evil? to save life, or to kill?" (Mark 3:4 KJV; see also Luke 6:9).

Did the apostles say similar things? Yes. Paul taught, "As we have therefore opportunity, let us do good unto all men, especially unto them who are of the household of faith" (Galatians 6:10 KJV). And Peter wrote, "He that will love life, and see good days, let him refrain his tongue from evil, and his lips that they speak no guile: let him eschew evil, and do good; let him seek peace, and ensue it" (1 Peter 3:10–11 KJV).

God's expectations are clear: do what's good. He provides both the desire and the power, which grow as we exercise each.

GOD'S WEAKNESS?

For the foolishness of God is wiser than human wisdom,
and the weakness of God is stronger than human strength.
1 CORINTHIANS 1:25 NIV

In the Old Testament, the twelve Israelite spies who explored Canaan agreed that the land was just as God had described. It flowed with milk and honey (Numbers 13:27).

But there was disagreement on how to proceed. Ten of the spies said there was no chance of Israel conquering the land. The people of Canaan were giants and much stronger than the Israelites, who were like grasshoppers in comparison.

Two of the spies, though, insisted that God had promised Canaan to Israel, and that made all the difference. "We should go up and take possession of the land," Caleb and Joshua said, "for we can certainly do it" (Numbers 13:30 NIV).

The ten fearful spies had forgotten the most significant thing. God had committed this land to His people, just as He had committed Himself to them. As the Creator of everything, as the power behind the plagues on Egypt and the parting of the Red Sea, He could certainly handle the inhabitants of Canaan.

God is stronger than any obstacle we could ever face. In fact, the apostle Paul says God's weakness is stronger than any human power. His foolishness is wiser than any human scheming. When we are in God's hands, nothing should ever frighten us.

THE PATIENCE OF JOB

*There was a man in the land of Uz, whose name
was Job; and that man was blameless and upright,
and one who feared God and shunned evil.*

JOB 1:1 NKJV

Job was "blameless and upright." He loved God, turning his back
on the wickedness all around him. Job's tender, heaven-bent heart
brought blessing to his family and work. And yet his godliness
didn't protect him from the trials of life. How can this be? How
can God be fair and just if He allows calamity to befall the children
He claims to love?

Read further and see that, "There was a day when the sons of
God came to present themselves before the LORD, and Satan also
came among them. . . . Then the LORD said to Satan, *'Have you considered my servant Job, that there is none like him on the earth?'* "
(verses 6, 8 NKJV, emphasis added).

The devil was furious that Job truly loved God. And Satan hated
God for protecting Job and his family. Take away that protection,
Satan argued, and Job will deny God to His face.

But God knew how much Job loved Him. He knew Job's heart
was completely His. So, what did God say to Satan? Take away Job's
earthly possessions and watch what happens!

God knew exactly how Job's story would end. Perhaps the lesson
He was attempting to teach wasn't meant only for Job.

THE "MAN OF GOD"

And this is the blessing, wherewith Moses the man
of God blessed the children of Israel before his death.
DEUTERONOMY 33:1 KJV

The man of God! How much the name means! A man who comes from God, chosen and sent of Him. A man who walks with God, lives in His fellowship and carries the mark of His presence. A man who lives for God and His will; whose whole being is pervaded and ruled by the glory of God; who involuntarily and unceasingly leads men to think of God. A man in whose heart and life God has taken the right place as the All in All, and who has only one desire, that He should have that place throughout the world. Such men of God are what the world needs; such are what God seeks, that He may fill them with Himself and send them into the world to help others to know Him. Such a man Moses was so distinctly that men naturally spoke of him thus—Moses, the man of God! Such a man every servant of God ought to aim at being—a living witness and proof of what God is to him in heaven and is to him on earth and what He claims to be in all.

— AN UNDERSTANDING HEART —

"Give me [Solomon] an understanding heart so that I can govern your people well and know the difference between right and wrong. For who by himself is able to govern this great people of yours?"

1 KINGS 3:9 NLT

At this stage in Solomon's reign, the kingdom was firmly in his grip (1 Kings 2:46). His half brother Adonijah's attempt to steal the throne had been foiled, and one of his father's enemies, Shimei, had been killed for foolishly presuming on Solomon's kindness.

Yet in prayer Solomon referred to himself as a "little child who doesn't know his way around" (1 Kings 3:7 NLT). So he asked God for an understanding heart to be able to govern well. The Lord was pleased with Solomon's request and not only gave him wisdom, but also riches and fame (1 Kings 3:10–13).

Solomon, like all of us, was a flawed man. The book of Ecclesiastes chronicles his many personal failures. But he had enough self-awareness to recognize that he wasn't ready to lead God's people. Solomon turned to the Lord, who supplied everything he needed and much of what he wanted.

Our situations vary, but every man is a leader in some sense, whether on the job or in our churches or homes or communities. Leadership is difficult and often thankless work. But like Solomon, we can always ask God for an understanding heart to know how to serve those He has given us to lead. Such prayers are pleasing to the Lord, and He's happy to honor them.

LIKE A GOOD SOLDIER

*Endure suffering along with me,
as a good soldier of Christ Jesus.*
2 TIMOTHY 2:3 NLT

Soldiers go through rigorous training to become battle-ready warriors. They are torn down physically, mentally, and emotionally, then rebuilt into the kind of fighters their country requires. When the actual battle comes, soldiers must endure—it's literally the difference between life and death.

As Christians, we undergo a similar process of training, remaking, and enduring. We were one way before salvation, but we are rebuilt into "good soldiers of Christ Jesus." When our spiritual battles come, we—like the apostle Paul—must endure to the end. But where do we get the strength to endure?

In verse 1 (NKJV), Paul tells his protégé Timothy to "be strong in the grace that is in Christ Jesus." We find strength in God's grace, His generous blessing on undeserving people. Grace shows itself in a million ways, but the clearest, most obvious example is Jesus' death on the cross.

If the God of the universe sent His beloved Son as a sacrifice for you, you must be very important to Him. If you are important to God, you can trust that He will take care of you in any and every battle. God's grace allows you to be a "good soldier of Christ Jesus."

—— WISDOM AND STRENGTH ——

To fear [the Lord's] name is wisdom.
MICAH 6:9 NIV

Who speaks today's key verse? Obviously, Micah the prophet does, through the inspiration of the Holy Spirit (see 2 Peter 1:21). Job also speaks this truth (Job 28:28). So does the psalmist (Psalm 111:10). In the Proverbs, Solomon says it three times (1:7, 9:10, 15:33). Isaiah puts his own twist on the teaching (Isaiah 11:2, 33:6). In other words, Micah isn't coining a new idea. . .it's a very old and very important truth. So we had best understand and heed it!

There's only one way to be truly wise, and that's by "fearing" the Lord's name. Most people are what the Bible calls "fools," because they have decided they're smart enough to go through life without God. They forget (or choose to ignore the fact) that the Lord is omniscient. . .the reality is that even the most brilliant human being knows only a tiny fraction of what God knows. We can understand only a tiny fraction of His ways.

But today's key verse doesn't only focus on God's omniscience. Notice the mention of His "name"—that is, all of who the Lord is. So our wisdom begins by fearing everything about God, including His omnipotence, His omnipresence, His utter holiness, and His providence and love. The less we know about the Lord, the more we sin. Conversely, the more we know and fear who the Lord is, the wiser we are.

And the wiser we are, the stronger we are—because we'll be strong in His infinite power.

MORE PRAYING, MORE REJOICING

Pray without ceasing.
1 Thessalonians 5:17 kjv

The position of our text is very suggestive. Observe what it follows. It comes immediately after the precept, "Rejoice evermore"; as if that command had somewhat staggered the reader and made him ask, "How can I always rejoice?" and, therefore, the apostle appended as answer, "Always pray." The more praying, the more rejoicing.

Prayer gives a channel to the pent-up sorrows of the soul; they flow away, and in their stead streams of sacred delight pour into the heart. At the same time the more rejoicing the more praying; when the heart is in a quiet condition and full of joy in the Lord, then also will it be sure to draw nigh unto the Lord in worship.

Holy joy and prayer act and react upon each other.

REST

"Remember the Sabbath day by keeping it holy.
Six days you shall labor and do all your work, but
the seventh day is a sabbath to the Lord your God."
EXODUS 20:8–10 NIV

There are times when the most important thing you can do to find strength for the challenge is simply to rest. Take a break. Relax and recharge and reset.

The Bible offers many examples of men who rested to their benefit, including Jesus Himself. The Lord would sometimes move away from the crowds—even from His closest associates—to spend time alone in prayer. He would also retreat to the homes of friends like Mary, Martha, and Lazarus for a meal and quiet conversation.

Many Jews today observe a Sabbath from sundown Friday to sundown Saturday. While a part of the regular life of Israel, this specific command is not repeated in "church age" of the New Testament. Yet rest is essential to our thriving as believers in Christ. His words from Matthew 11 are significant: "Come to me, all you who are weary and burdened, and I will give you rest. . . . My yoke is easy and my burden is light" (verses 28, 30 NIV).

Find strength through rest. Allow the Lord to share your challenges. Allow yourself the opportunity to recharge and reset.

—— SPEAK WITH AUTHORITY ——

God gave Solomon very great wisdom and understanding,
and knowledge as vast as the sands of the seashore. . . . He
could speak with authority about all kinds of plants, from
the great cedar of Lebanon to the tiny hyssop that grows from
cracks in a wall. He could also speak about animals, birds,
small creatures, and fish. And kings from every nation sent
their ambassadors to listen to the wisdom of Solomon.
1 KINGS 4:29, 33–34 NLT

The Enlightenment period of the seventeenth and eighteenth centuries was grounded in intellectualism. According to *Encyclopedia Britannica*, human reason was heralded as the power "by which humans understand the universe and improve their own condition." But the thinkers of that era had nothing on King Solomon. He received his wisdom from God.

Today, we often hear of highly educated people who don't believe in the triune God. Many argue that Christianity has no place in the public square—that religion is acceptable only if it is kept within the church walls on Sunday mornings. But God cannot be contained like that.

By God's design and grace, Solomon spoke intelligently about the natural sciences. He oversaw the politics, economic policies, and trade of a great nation. He excelled in matters of the mind and the written word.

Sometimes we feel intimidated by the academics, politicians, and business leaders of our world, intelligent and well-educated people who often completely disagree with our biblical morality. But followers of Jesus have "the mind of Christ" (1 Corinthians 2:16 NLT) and the power of the Spirit (Romans 15:13). We can speak with authority on anything God gives us to say.

— LOVE WITHOUT EXPECTATION —

*"But to you who are listening I say: Love your enemies,
do good to those who hate you, bless those who
curse you, pray for those who mistreat you."*
LUKE 6:27–28 NIV

Most everyone knows the Golden Rule: "In everything, do to others what you would have them do to you, for this sums up the Law and the Prophets" (Matthew 7:12 NIV).

The problem with using the Golden Rule as a basis for Christian love is its inherent reciprocity. Too often, it becomes a social contract fraught with expectations. We think, "If I treat him like this, he'd better treat me like that."

But that isn't what Jesus wants for His disciples. We are to live and love without expectations.

In Luke 6:32–35 (NIV), Jesus says, "If you love those who love you, what credit is that to you? Even sinners love those who love them. And if you do good to those who are good to you, what credit is that to you? Even sinners do that. And if you lend to those from whom you expect repayment, what credit is that to you? Even sinners lend to sinners, expecting to be repaid in full. But love your enemies, do good to them, and lend to them without expecting to get anything back. Then your reward will be great, and you will be children of the Most High, because he is kind to the ungrateful and wicked."

It would be far easier to love others like we want to be loved—but that isn't how Jesus loved us. If we commit ourselves to loving without expectation of earthly reward, our Lord will give us the strength we need—and, ultimately, the blessing we want.

— SPEAK A WORD FOR CHRIST —

*Praying always with all prayer and supplication in the Spirit,
and watching thereunto with all perseverance and supplication
for all saints; and for me, that utterance may be given unto me,
that I may open my mouth boldly, to make known the mystery
of the gospel, for which I am an ambassador in bonds: that
therein I may speak boldly, as I ought to speak.*
EPHESIANS 6:18–20 KJV

It is a privilege to work for Jesus; I am tired of hearing about the
"duty" of so doing. Oh! If every Christian would resolve not to let
a day pass without offering to some individual a personal invitation to come to Christ, in one twelvemonth there would not be a
man or a woman in England who would not have heard such an
appeal. If Christ died for us, we ought surely to be prepared to
speak a word for Him.

I have found this practice has been a great help in keeping my
own heart warm. I have felt that my words themselves were cold
and icy when I was not working for the salvation of others. There
are some who say, "We don't have any sympathy with these special
efforts;" and I sympathize with that objection. I believe it is the
privilege of the child of God to make continuous efforts for the
salvation of others, every day throughout the year.

——— WHO IS LIKE OUR GOD? ———

Who is a God like you, who pardons sin and forgives the
transgression of the remnant of his inheritance? You do not
stay angry forever but delight to show mercy. You will again
have compassion on us; you will tread our sins underfoot
and hurl all our iniquities into the depths of the sea.
MICAH 7:18–19 NIV

From the earliest pages of scripture, we can clearly see who God is.

The book of Genesis describes Adam and Eve in the garden of Eden, the serpent's temptation, and humanity's terrible fall, and then shows us God's reaction. We see Him cursing both the serpent and the ground. We read how He prescribes hard work for men and hard labor in childbirth for women. But notice that the Lord doesn't curse Adam and Eve themselves. In His mercy, He sacrifices an animal or two to make clothing for His beloved people. In His kindness, the Lord makes it impossible for Adam and Eve to eat from the tree of life and live forever in a perpetually fallen world. Instead, He promises a future Messiah who will tread the serpent underfoot. By this promise, God is committing Himself—in the person of Jesus Christ—to die for us and for our sins.

These powerful images of the Lord God—pardoning, forgiving, showing mercy and compassion, getting rid of human sin forever—resonate throughout the rest of scripture.

Who is like our God, indeed!

— WISDOM FROM THE SOURCE —

Do not deceive yourselves. If any of you think you are wise by the standards of this age, you should become "fools" so that you may become wise. For the wisdom of this world is foolishness in God's sight. As it is written: "He catches the wise in their craftiness."
1 CORINTHIANS 3:18–19 NIV

You're probably familiar with the Old Testament character Daniel and his three friends, Hananiah, Mishael, and Azariah (better known as Shadrach, Meshach, and Abednego). "In every matter of wisdom and understanding about which the king questioned them," Daniel 1:20 reports, "he found them ten times better than all the magicians and enchanters in his whole kingdom" (NIV). The Babylonian king was very pleased with the contributions of these young Jewish exiles. But jealousy burned in the hearts of the native Babylonian "wise men."

The Babylonians consulted with each other. Daniel and his brothers consulted with God. The outcome was dramatically different: Daniel became one of the highest officials in the land, while the wise men and their families were ultimately fed to lions.

This story illustrates what the apostle Paul taught the Corinthians. Wisdom from earthly sources, even the most impressive and respected people, is no match for the wisdom of God.

Our lives are full of choices—some small and insignificant but others life altering. Don't ever think you should make every decision yourself—get your wisdom from the source by seeking God for answers. He will always provide the wisest guidance of all.

— CURSE GOD AND DIE? —

His wife said to him, "Are you still maintaining
your integrity? Curse God and die!"
JOB 2:9 NIV

There will be times when we must live our lives as if there were only two people in the entire world: ourselves and Jesus Christ.

Remember that Job was blameless and upright. The calamities that hammered him were not in any way God's judgment for moral or spiritual failure—they were purely the result of Satan's malevolence. Job 1 describes Satan asking God's permission to take the man's possessions. Job 2 shows Satan demanding Job's health. God allowed the devil to harm Job physically, though not to kill him. "He still maintains his integrity," God said of Job, "though you incited me against him to ruin him without any reason" (verse 3 NIV). Soon, Job's wife was recognizing Job's integrity too, but urging him to drop it. "Curse God and die!" she said.

Sometimes the people closest to us will say and do terrible things that are not easily undone. Words like "curse God and die" are a clear indication that a situation has pushed another person beyond their capacity to act and speak in a godly manner. In situations like this, we must be like Job, holding tightly to Christ alone, believing for ourselves *and our loved ones* that God is still good. When we do, we have the prophet Isaiah's promise: "You will keep him in perfect peace, whose mind is stayed on You, because he trusts in You" (26:3 NKJV).

FAITH FEEDS ON GOD

For I say, through the grace given unto me, to every man
that is among you, not to think of himself more highly
than he ought to think; but to think soberly, according
as God hath dealt to every man the measure of faith.
ROMANS 12:3 KJV

There can be no true prayer without faith; some measure of faith must precede prayer. And yet prayer is also the way to more faith; there can be no higher degree of faith except through much prayer. This is the lesson Jesus teaches here. There is nothing needs so much to grow as our faith.

When Jesus spoke the words, "According to your faith be it unto you" (Matthew 9:29 KJV), He announced the law of the kingdom, which tells us that all have not equal degrees of faith, that the same person has not always the same degree, and that the measure of faith must always determine the measure of power and of blessing. If we want to know where and how our faith is to grow, the Master points us to the throne of God.

It is in prayer, in the exercise of the faith I have, in fellowship with the living God, that faith can increase. Faith can only live by feeding on what is divine, on God Himself.

GOD OF THE DEAL

So the LORD gave wisdom to Solomon, just as he had promised.
And Hiram and Solomon made a formal alliance of peace.
1 KINGS 5:12 NLT

The scriptures don't indicate that Solomon and King Hiram of Tyre had any animosity toward one another. In fact, a King Hiram was said to have sent Solomon's father cedar logs, carpenters, and stonemasons to build a palace (2 Samuel 5:11). When it came time for Solomon to build the temple, Hiram was happy to supply cedar at Solomon's request. As payment, Solomon sent Hiram 100,000 bushels of wheat and 110,000 gallons of olive oil each year.

It seems like a fairly simple transaction. But today's verse indicates that the Lord provided Solomon the wisdom he needed in transacting the deal. Perhaps God allowed Solomon to form an even stronger alliance with Tyre that would benefit both countries. Whatever the case, we can conclude that the big picture mattered to God because He intervened in the process.

Likewise, God cares about the way we conduct our business. He wants a fair exchange between all parties (see Leviticus 19:35–36; Deuteronomy 25:13–16; Proverbs 11:1, 20:10; Micah 6:11; and others). So whenever we make any kind of deal, we need to keep God's righteousness in mind. Pray for wisdom before you make any transaction, whether for a used lawn mower or a multimillion-dollar business. As He did with Solomon, God will give both wisdom and peace.

IT WILL BE DONE

Paul, a servant of God, and an apostle of Jesus Christ, according to the faith of God's elect, and the acknowledging of the truth which is after godliness; in hope of eternal life, which God, that cannot lie, promised before the world began; but hath in due times manifested his word through preaching, which is committed unto me according to the commandment of God our Saviour.

TITUS 1:1–3 KJV

God is always true to what He promises to do. He made promises to Abraham, Jacob, Moses, Joshua, etc., and did He not fulfill them? He will fulfill every word of what He has promised; yet how few take Him at His word!

When I was a young man I was clerk in the establishment of a man in Chicago, whom I observed frequently occupied sorting and marking bills. He explained to me what he had been doing; on some notes he had marked B, on some D, and on others G; those marked B he told me were bad, those marked D meant they were doubtful, and those with G on them meant they were good; and, said he, you must treat all of them accordingly.

And thus people endorse God's promises, by marking some as bad and others as doubtful; whereas we ought to take all of them as good, for He has never once broken His word, and all that He says He will do, will be done in the fulness of time.

— THE LORD IS OUR STRENGTH —

The LORD is good, a refuge in times of trouble.
He cares for those who trust in him, but with an
overwhelming flood he will make an end of Nineveh.
NAHUM 1:7–8 NIV

The book of Nahum warns of God's judgment on the Assyrian capital of Nineveh.

Though the entire population of the city had repented of their sins and worshipped the Lord a century earlier (see the book of Jonah), subsequent generations rejected the truth, growing increasingly rebellious, murderous, and vile. As a result, God called the prophet Nahum to pronounce a final judgment on the city.

Its sins included arrogance over its power and wealth, plotting against the Lord God, brutally slaying people without cause, crushing the northern Jewish kingdom of Israel, scheming against the southern kingdom of Judah, and actively promoting the worship of horrid idols.

Over against this wickedness, though, we see the wonderfulness of the Lord our God. He is infinitely and eternally "good"—that's just who He is. He is "a refuge in times of trouble. He cares for those who trust in him"—that is, God is omniscient, omnipresent, and omnipotent, and He loves and protects us.

Nineveh, for all its power, didn't stand a chance against God. The conquering Babylonians so obliterated the Assyrian capital that its location was unknown for twenty-four centuries.

No matter the challenge, the Lord is our strength.

FOREWARNED AND FOREARMED

And David sware moreover, and said, Thy father certainly knoweth that I have found grace in thine eyes; and he saith, Let not Jonathan know this, lest he be grieved: but truly as the LORD liveth, and as thy soul liveth, there is but a step between me and death.
1 SAMUEL 20:3 KJV

This was David's description of his own condition. King Saul was seeking to destroy him. The bitter malice of that king would not be satisfied with anything short of the blood of his rival.

Jonathan did not know this. He could not believe so badly of his father as that he could wish to kill the champion of Israel, the brave, true-hearted young David; and so he assured David that it could not be so—that he had not heard of any plots against him.

But David, who knew better, said, "It is certainly so. Your father seeks my blood, and there is but a step between me and death." Now it was by knowing his danger that David escaped. Had he remained as ignorant of his own peril as his friend Jonathan had been, he would have walked into the lion's mouth, and he would have fallen by the hand of Saul. But to be forewarned is to be forearmed; he was, therefore, able to save his life because he perceived his danger.

A SURPRISING SOURCE OF STRENGTH

The Israelites had done all the work just as the Lord had commanded Moses. Moses inspected the work and saw that they had done it just as the Lord had commanded. So Moses blessed them.
EXODUS 39:42–43 NIV

The Lord had given Moses specific instructions for setting up Israel's corporate worship. Perhaps hundreds of skilled workers were commissioned to fashion the tabernacle, garments for the priests, and the instruments used in worship rituals. It was a monumental undertaking, and those charged with the task completed their work as commanded. Then came Moses' inspection.

The work was perfect: "The Israelites had done all the work just as the Lord had commanded Moses." There were no changes to be made or additions to be discussed. The challenge had been met and it was time to celebrate. We can imagine Moses moving from individual to individual, offering his thanks for their efforts. The Bible says specifically that "Moses blessed them."

Sometimes, a source of our own strength is the opportunity to bless another person, whether a family member, a coworker, or a fellow church member. Every day is an opportunity to brighten someone's day, which in turn lightens ours.

Every true believer hopes one day to hear the Lord say, "Well done." Why not offer that same kind of blessing to others now?

GOD STILL PROVIDES

*Then the LORD said to Elijah, "Go to the east and hide
by Kerith Brook, near where it enters the Jordan River.
Drink from the brook and eat what the ravens bring you,
for I have commanded them to bring you food."*
1 KINGS 17:2–4 NLT

After a series of evil kings had ruled in Israel, God raised up Elijah the prophet. A drought was on the way, and God told Elijah to shelter near a brook that fed into the famed Jordan River. That would provide the prophet's water. Meanwhile, the Lord was planning to provide food for Elijah in the most unusual of ways—via ravens.

"If Providence calls us to solitude and retirement, it becomes us to go: when we cannot be useful, we must be patient; and when we cannot work for God, we must sit still quietly for him," Matthew Henry wrote in his classic commentary. "The ravens were appointed to bring him meat, and did so. Let those who have but from hand to mouth, learn to live upon Providence, and trust it for the bread of the day, in the day."

Sometimes we find ourselves in situations that make no human sense. But if God calls us to stand on principle, give generously, love our enemies, or any of a hundred other things that seem impossible, know that He will provide for and in our obedience.

Don't hesitate to obey. As He did for Elijah, God still provides for His people.

FRUIT INSPECTION

"A good tree cannot have bad fruit. A bad tree cannot have good fruit. For every tree is known by its own fruit. Men do not gather figs from thorns. They do not gather grapes from thistles."
LUKE 6:43–44 NLV

In an age where anyone can send their opinion across the internet in less time than it takes to ask whether they should, false teaching has never been more readily available.

Fortunately, there's a test for false teachers. Unfortunately, it isn't as easy as retweeting or clicking share. The test requires patience: Jesus told His disciples that a tree can be recognized by its fruit, but fruit doesn't grow overnight. It takes time to see whether we are looking at an apple or a pear producer.

Once we've identified the type of tree, we must look closely at the fruit itself. Even a good-looking apple can hide bruises or worms easily enough. If the fruit isn't good, don't swallow it.

Finally, when we recognize a bad tree by its bad fruit, we must also recognize its only value: "Every tree that does not have good fruit is cut down and thrown into the fire" (Matthew 7:19 NLV).

True strength requires a healthy diet of good fruit from good trees. There's no better source for solid, healthy teaching than the Bible. When it comes to other sources, let's ask God for the wisdom to be good fruit inspectors.

AS HOLY AS A PARDONED SINNER CAN BE

*And I will sanctify my great name, which was profaned among
the heathen, which ye have profaned in the midst of them;
and the heathen shall know that I am the Lord, saith the Lord
God, when I shall be sanctified in you before their eyes.*
Ezekiel 36:23 kjv

We must learn to look upon religion, upon a life like Christ's, having the very same mind that was in Him, as the supreme object of daily life. It is only when a prayer such as that of M'Cheyne becomes ours, "Lord, make me as holy as a pardoned sinner can be," and begins to be offered by an increasing number of ministers and believers, that the promise of the New Covenant will become a matter of experience.

As the preaching of God in His holiness, of Christ as our sanctification, of the work of the Spirit as the Spirit of holiness, takes the place that it has in God's Word, God's people will have the power to do the work to which God has called them in making Christ known to every living creature. The promise will then be fulfilled: "The heathen shall know that I am the Lord, saith the Lord God, when I shall be sanctified in you before their eyes."

WHEN WE'RE DISMAYED

O LORD my God, my Holy One, you who are eternal—surely you
do not plan to wipe us out? O LORD, our Rock, you have sent
these Babylonians to correct us, to punish us for our many sins.
HABAKKUK 1:12 NLT

Habakkuk urged his readers to trust the Lord even when evil over-ran their world. The prophet captured a unique dialogue between himself—the Old Testament's "doubting Thomas"—and God.

How long, Habakkuk asked, would God allow the southern king-dom of Judah to perpetrate wickedness before He judged it (1:1–4)? The Lord replied that He was already raising up the Babylonians to carry the people of Judah into exile (1:5–11).

The answer astonished the prophet. Habakkuk asked how God could plan to use such a vile and pagan nation to judge Judah (1:12–2:1). The Lord replied that He would take care of the Babylonians later. Habakkuk must continue to place his faith in God (2:2–20).

That instruction turns out to be the most important message from the Lord to Habakkuk—and all of us. After all, consider who the Lord is. In the words of today's scripture, He is "my God." He's personal—that's why He could have a dialogue with Habakkuk in the first place. Second, the Lord is "my Holy One, you who are eternal." The Lord is eternally and infinitely holy, just, pure, and righteous. He always does what is right. Finally, He is "our Rock"—that is, to the faithful, not to the obstinate, wicked, and rebellious.

When world events dismay us (and they will), the Lord is our Rock, indeed.

BE A HARD WORKER

*We work hard with our own hands. When we are cursed,
we bless; when we are persecuted, we endure it; when we are
slandered, we answer kindly. We have become the scum of the
earth, the garbage of the world—right up to this moment.*
1 CORINTHIANS 4:12–13 NIV

Working hard is an admirable trait. Consider the apostle Paul, who worked tirelessly for the Gospel of Christ: He spent years on the mission, covering thousands of miles by foot and by boat. He started, encouraged, and corrected churches. Along the way, he wrote several books of the New Testament—much of the time while facing intense persecution.

Paul's work on behalf of the Gospel was obvious. But he also labored less visibly to shape his character to be more like Jesus. "I do not run like someone running aimlessly," he told the Corinthian Christians, "I do not fight like a boxer beating the air. No, I strike a blow to my body and make it my slave so that after I have preached to others, I myself will not be disqualified for the prize" (1 Corinthians 9:26–27 NIV).

Paul's life and teaching demand that we also work hard, not only outwardly but inwardly. When we do the "heavy lifting" to shape our hearts and minds to become more like Christ, we'll find ourselves stronger when the inevitable troubles of life come on us. We'll be able, like the apostle, to weather our trials with grace.

STRENGTH IN PURITY

Everything is pure to those whose hearts are pure. But nothing is pure to those who are corrupt and unbelieving, because their minds and consciences are corrupted. Such people claim they know God, but they deny him by the way they live. They are detestable and disobedient, worthless for doing anything good.

TITUS 1:15–16 NLT

For many men, the word *purity* refers primarily to sexual matters. But the term really covers a much wider landscape. In today's scripture, the apostle Paul is describing the rebellious people of Crete, people who "claim they know God, but. . .deny him by the way they live."

This practice of false living isn't limited to a first-century Mediterranean island. Unfortunately, it happens all the time, even in our own lives. When sin goes unchecked and unconfessed for too long, it will eventually rear its ugly head. So Paul urged Titus to encourage the people to seek purity in their thoughts and actions.

The things we allow to enter our mind bear significant weight—they will influence our behavior. So purity of mind, body, and spirit should be top priority. Identify whatever causes the corruption of your life and let those things go. Detestable, disobedient, and worthless are strong adjectives, and an obvious sign of weakness in a Christian. To turn that weakness into strength, put aside the old things that cause you to stumble (Ephesians 4:22). Consciously pursue the things that please the Lord (Romans 12:1).

A MAN IN
COMMUNION WITH GOD

And Enoch lived sixty and five years, and begat Methuselah:
and Enoch walked with God after he begat Methuselah three
hundred years, and begat sons and daughters: and all the days
of Enoch were three hundred sixty and five years: and Enoch
walked with God: and he was not; for God took him.
GENESIS 5:21–24 KJV

Enoch was one of the small number of men against whom nothing is recorded in the Bible. He lived in the midst of the world as Cain and his descendants had made it. In the midst of such a state of things, Enoch "walked with God"; and in the very same world we are also called to walk with God.

The record of his life is that he "had this testimony, that he pleased God" (Hebrews 11:5 KJV). Notice that this man accomplished nothing that men would call great, but what made him great was that he walked with God.

The faith of Enoch drew God down from heaven to walk with him. He maintained unbroken fellowship with God. A man in communion with God is one of heaven's greatest warriors. He can battle with and overcome the world, the flesh, and the devil.

AN ENDLESS SUPPLY

*For the Lord God of Israel says, "The jar of flour will not
be used up. And the jar of oil will not be empty, until
the day the Lord sends rain upon the earth."*
1 KINGS 17:14 NLV

Imagine having only enough food in the house for one small meal
with your child, knowing it will probably be the last one before
you both die of starvation. Then imagine a man that you've never
met requesting your food.

That's the scenario a new widow faced in 1 Kings 17. The prophet
Elijah arrived in Zarephath (a Gentile city) at the Lord's direction.
Also at the Lord's direction, he asked this woman for a meal. She
informed him that she didn't have bread—only a little flour and oil.

"Have no fear," Elijah told her (verse 13). Easier said than done,
to be sure—but she obeyed, and the Lord was faithful to supply
her and her son with food and oil for many days.

It would have been natural to focus on the hardship. And who
could have blamed this woman for protecting her last morsels of
food for her son? But God's ways of helping people through challenges are often much different than we would expect.

Think of an area of your life right now in which you are lacking.
Are you willing to offer up what you do have as a sacrifice to God?
Pray and ask for His guidance. You might just find that He'll meet
your need in a way you never dreamed.

WALK IN FAITH

And this is love, that we walk after his commandments.
This is the commandment, That, as ye have heard
from the beginning, ye should walk in it.
2 JOHN 6 KJV

There is in the Christian life great need of watchfulness and of prayer, of self-denial and of striving, of obedience and of diligence. But "all things are possible to him that believeth." "This is the victory that overcometh, even our faith."

It is the faith that continually closes its eyes to the weakness of the creature and finds its joy in the sufficiency of an almighty Savior that makes the soul strong and glad. It gives itself up to be led by the Holy Spirit into an ever deeper appreciation of that wonderful Savior whom God hath given us—the Infinite Immanuel. It follows the leading of the Spirit from page to page of the blessed Word, with the one desire to take each revelation of what Jesus is and what He promises as its nourishment and its life. It lives by every word that proceedeth out of the mouth of God.

And so it makes the soul strong with the strength of God, to be and to do all that is needed for abiding in Christ.

JUST BY FAITH

The just shall live by his faith.
Habakkuk 2:4 kjv

Today's scripture is quoted three times by New Testament writers, in Romans 1:17, Galatians 3:11, and Hebrews 10:38. This verse must have something important to say to us!

The word *just* speaks of someone who is humble, fully dependent on the Lord God, and living righteously according to His Word. These three characteristics cannot exist independently. You can't be humble while relying on your own strength and intelligence. Nor can you fully depend on the Lord while ignoring and disobeying the Bible. These characteristics are bound together inseparably.

The word *faith* speaks of one's belief and trust in the Lord, and his steadiness in revering and obeying Him. "Faith" isn't something in the past—it's something that directly shapes what I think, feel, say, and do today. Faith, then, is a way of life borne out of humility, wholehearted dependence on the Lord, and righteous living according to scripture.

Any of us can claim to be humble, just, and righteous, but often we're not. How can we be sure we're just, and living by faith?

Jesus said it best: "Everyone who hears these words of mine and puts them into practice is like a wise man who built his house on the rock" (Matthew 7:24 niv). Know what He wants of you, by studying His Word. Then do what it says. It's the only way to really live. . .just by faith.

NEVER GO BEFORE PROVIDENCE

*And let it be, when thou hearest the sound of a going
in the tops of the mulberry trees, that then thou shalt
bestir thyself: for then shall the LORD go out before
thee, to smite the host of the Philistines.*
2 SAMUEL 5:24 KJV

My brethren, let us learn from David to take no steps without God. The last time you moved, or went into another business, or changed your situation in life, you asked God's help and then did it, and you were blessed in the doing of it. You have been up to this time a successful man; you have always sought God, but do not think that the stream of providence necessarily runs in a continuous current; remember, you may tomorrow without seeking God's advice venture upon a step which you will regret but once, and that will be until you die.

You have been wise hitherto; it may be because you have trusted in the Lord with all your heart and have not leaned to your own understanding (Proverbs 3:5–6). If Providence tarries, tarry till Providence comes; never go before it. He goes on a fool's errand who goes before God, but he walks in a blessed path who sees the footsteps of Providence and reads the map of scripture and so discovers, "This is the way wherein I am to walk."

COMING THROUGH LOUD AND CLEAR

"If you bring a grain offering baked in an oven, it is to consist of the finest flour: either thick loaves made without yeast and with olive oil mixed in or thin loaves made without yeast and brushed with olive oil. If your grain offering is prepared on a griddle, it is to be made of the finest flour mixed with oil, and without yeast. Crumble it and pour oil on it; it is a grain offering. If your grain offering is cooked in a pan, it is to be made of the finest flour and some olive oil. . . ."

LEVITICUS 2:4–7 NIV

Honestly, the book of Leviticus is tough to read. If it seems like page after page of detailed instructions, that's because it is page after page of detailed instructions. Leviticus was the ancient Israelites' handbook for offerings to God, personal and community hygiene, dietary rules, and other things of the sort. So what does Leviticus have to say to us today, men seeking strength for the challenge?

Simply this: in Leviticus we see that our God is orderly, specific, and happy to communicate His expectations. The Lord's rules for the Israelites were definite and distinct, and came through loud and clear.

Though there will always be some mysteries in life, God has revealed everything we absolutely need to know (see Deuteronomy 29:29). As we devote ourselves to studying His Word, we'll discover both the expectations He has for us and the strength we need to fulfill them.

TAKE IT TO THE LORD

*So he got up and ate and drank. And he went
in the strength of that food forty days and
forty nights to Horeb, the mountain of God.*
1 KINGS 19:8 NLV

Living for the one true God has always been risky. It often comes with a cost. Jesus explains why: "People love darkness more than the Light because the things they do are sinful" (John 3:19 NLV).

Rather than repenting, those who love darkness often turn to persecution. Elijah experienced that after executing the 450 prophets of Baal, prompting Jezebel—the wife of King Ahab—to threaten to kill God's prophet.

Elijah ran for his life. When he came to Beersheba of Judah, he sat under a juniper tree and asked the Lord to take his life. Exhausted, Elijah fell asleep, only to be awakened and fed by an angel. Perhaps still depressed, Elijah fell back asleep until the angel repeated his actions. Elijah gained a miraculous strength that lasted forty days and forty nights.

Have you ever reached the end of your strength? Run out of resolve to serve the Lord? Sometimes the challenge is just too difficult, and everything seems to be against you. When you feel like Elijah (you just want to give up), pray like Elijah (tell the Lord exactly how you feel). Admit that you are drained, frightened, and unable to face the challenge in your own strength. This is the precise moment when God takes over, providing strength to sustain you.

FORGIVEN MUCH

*Then Jesus told him this story: "A man loaned money
to two people—500 pieces of silver to one and 50
pieces to the other. But neither of them could repay him,
so he kindly forgave them both, canceling their debts.
Who do you suppose loved him more after that?"*
LUKE 7:41–42 NLT

When Simon the Pharisee invited Jesus to a banquet, he may
not have expected Jesus to come. After all, Jesus was notoriously
antagonistic toward the Pharisees. But Jesus did attend, and Simon
learned that when we invite Jesus in, He will reveal our weaknesses.

Jewish hospitality suggested friends be greeted with a kiss.
Special occasions called for anointing the guest's head with an
inexpensive oil. When Simon received Jesus, he did neither.

During the banquet, however, Jesus was approached by a woman
of sinful reputation. The scene suggests that Jesus had interacted
with the woman previously and forgiven her sins. As He ate, the
woman wept on His feet, dried the tears with her hair, and anointed
Jesus with expensive perfume.

Simon thought to himself, "If this man were a prophet, he would
know what kind of woman is touching him. She's a sinner!" (Luke
7:39 NLT). Simon doubted Jesus, judging both Him and the woman.

Then Jesus told His parable of two debtors. The point was clear:
by neglecting hospitality to his guest, Simon proved he had little
love for Jesus. The forgiven woman showed her love in excess.

If we have received Jesus' forgiveness, we have been forgiven
much. May we never forget the debt we owed Him, and the price-
less gift of its cancellation.

GOD'S WOES ARE BETTER THAN THE DEVIL'S WELCOMES

Woe unto them that draw iniquity with cords
of vanity, and sin as it were with a cart rope.
ISAIAH 5:18 KJV

The text begins with "Woe"; but when we get a woe in this book of blessings it is sent as a warning, that we may escape from woe.

God's woes are better than the devil's welcomes. God always means man's good and only sets ill before him that he may turn from the dangers of a mistaken way and so may escape the ill which lies at the end of it. Think me not unkind at this time because my message sounds harshly and has a note in it of sorrow rather than of joy. It may be most for your pleasure for ages to come, dear friends, to be for a while displeased. It may make the bells ring in your ears forever if tonight you hear the shrill clarion startling you to thoughtfulness. Mayhap "Woe, woe, woe," though it should sound with a dreadful din in your ear, may be the means of leading you to seek and find your Savior, and then throughout eternity no woe shall ever come near to you.

May the good Spirit of all grace put power into my warning, that you may profit by it.

PRAY WISELY

The LORD is in his holy temple;
let all the earth be silent before him.
HABAKKUK 2:20 NIV

Ecclesiastes 3:7 tells us that there is "a time to be silent and a time to speak" (NIV). In Habakkuk's prophecy, we see both in action.

In 1:13, God was asked to break His silence and speak to Habakkuk. But in 2:20, Habakkuk told everyone to be silent before the Lord.

Woe to us when God doesn't speak; on the other hand, woe to us if we don't stop speaking to Him! Solomon said, "Do not be quick with your mouth, do not be hasty in your heart to utter anything before God. God is in heaven and you are on earth, so let your words be few" (Ecclesiastes 5:2 NIV). And Jesus taught, "When you pray, do not keep on babbling like pagans, for they think they will be heard because of their many words" (Matthew 6:7 NIV).

Does this mean we should never offer lengthy prayers to the Lord? No. Solomon, who encouraged "few words" in Ecclesiastes 5, also offered a substantial prayer at the dedication of God's temple (1 Kings 8:22–53; 2 Chronicles 6:12–42). And Jesus, shortly before His arrest and crucifixion, prayed the long "high priestly prayer" in Gethsemane (John 17:1–26).

The difference seems to be respect. Our unthinking babbling neither honors God nor helps us. But a reasoned prayer that acknowledges His holiness and requests His blessing will always reach God's heart. With the right frame of mind, we can "approach God's throne of grace with confidence," and "receive mercy and find grace to help us in our time of need" (Hebrews 4:16 NIV).

TRAIN HARD

Do you not know that in a race all the runners run, but only
one gets the prize? Run in such a way as to get the prize.
Everyone who competes in the games goes into strict
training. They do it to get a crown that will not last,
but we do it to get a crown that will last forever.
1 CORINTHIANS 9:24–25 NIV

Just as a marathon runner would not wait until race day to prepare, we as Christians cannot wait for adversity to strike before we make plans to deal with it. In those moments when life is going well, we can arm ourselves for future battles by spending time in prayer, memorizing scripture, and sharpening our faith in fellowship with Christian friends.

Jesus tells His twelve disciples (and, by extension, we as Christians today) that there will be trouble in life (John 16:33). The fact is that we could find ourselves engaged in a spiritual battle at any moment.

That's why we must be diligent to prepare, engaging in the training that Paul describes in 1 Corinthians 9. As we work to strengthen our relationship with God, challenging our minds and bodies to behave more like Christ, we are developing strength for our challenges. When trouble rears its ugly head, our rigorous preparation will put us in good stead—not just to survive, but to win.

WITH FRIENDS LIKE THESE. . .

*"If I were you, I would appeal to God; I would lay
my cause before him. . . . We have examined this,
and it is true. So hear it and apply it to yourself."*
JOB 5:8, 27 NIV

Job's friends, Eliphaz, Bildad, and Zophar certainly meant well.
Their hearts were in the right place—they saw their friend was in
trouble and went to him to offer help. But in each case, the help
they offered moved quickly from godly compassion to a kind of
self-absorbed religious rhetoric. You may know the kind: words that
make the speaker feel good about his own deep well of wisdom,
but don't help the unfortunate hearer at all.

It's critical to remember that scripture says Job was "blameless
and upright" (1:1 NIV). As his difficult situation spun further and
further out of control, it must have become increasingly challenging to maintain focus on God. We may find ourselves in similar
situations: surrounded by difficulties that are only made worse by
the careless words of friends and loved ones.

When the storms of life blow their hardest, take hope in the
perfect wisdom and love of God. Cling tightly to the undeniable
goodness and love of your Savior. "A bruised reed he will not break,
and a smoldering wick he will not snuff out," the prophet Isaiah
wrote. "In faithfulness he will bring forth justice" (Isaiah 42:3 NIV).

— STRONG AND SIMPLE FAITH —

And the Lord said, If ye had faith as a grain of
mustard seed, ye might say unto this sycamine
tree, Be thou plucked up by the root, and be thou
planted in the sea; and it should obey you.
LUKE 17:6 KJV

I remember when I was a boy, in the spring of the year, when the snow had melted away on the New England hills where I lived, I used to take a certain kind of glass and hold it up to the warm rays of the sun. These would strike on it, and I would set the woods on fire.

Faith is the glass that brings the fire of God out of heaven. It was faith that drew the fire down on Carmel and burned up Elijah's offering (1 Kings 18). We have the same God today and the same faith. Some people seem to think that faith is getting old and that the Bible is wearing out. But the Lord will revive his work now; and we shall be able to set the world on fire if each believer has a strong and simple faith.

OPEN EYES

Then Elisha prayed and said, "O Lord, I pray, open his eyes,
that he may see." And the Lord opened the servant's eyes,
and he saw. He saw that the mountain was full of horses
and war-wagons of fire all around Elisha.
2 KINGS 6:17 NLV

As Syria and Israel fought a war, the prophet Elisha was able to inform the king of Israel about all of Syria's movements. When the Syrian leader got wind of Elisha's actions, he sent troops to capture him in Dothan. Elisha's servant woke up the next morning and saw they were surrounded. But Elisha explained that the Syrians were outnumbered. He prayed a simple prayer and his servant's eyes were opened to see that all around them were horses and war-wagons (chariots) of fire.

Elisha's servant could only see trouble with his physical eyes, Then, in answer to the prophet's prayer, the Lord opened the servant's spiritual eyes to the larger reality. Elisha understood what the apostle Paul wrote centuries later: "Our struggle is not against flesh and blood, but against the rulers, against the authorities, against the powers of this dark world and against the spiritual forces of evil in the heavenly realms" (Ephesians 6:12 NIV).

Spiritual battles are being fought all around us. Satan wants to steer us off track, making us think that other people are our enemies—or our salvation. Pray today for the spiritual eyes to see God's reality: He has the power to protect and prevail in any danger you encounter.

WORTHY OF RESPECT

*Teach the older men to exercise self-control, to be
worthy of respect, and to live wisely. They must have
sound faith and be filled with love and patience.*
TITUS 2:2 NLT

Although this verse is addressed to "older men," the apostle Paul also urges young men to "live wisely" in verse 6. So nobody gets a free pass as it relates to that key phrase, "be worthy of respect."

It's interesting that Paul doesn't command Christian men to "be respected." That is the decision of other people; "to be worthy of respect" is a pursuit that each of us can choose for ourselves. In other words, whether or not you receive the esteem of others, live in a manner that's worthy of it.

How do we do that? The key phrase is flanked by two critical commands that will lead to worthiness of respect: if you "exercise self-control" and "live wisely," you'll achieve the goal—to be worthy of respect.

If our focus is on ourselves—to earn the attention we think we deserve or gain a following—we risk becoming our own idols. But when we choose to make the Lord famous above ourselves, we become worthy of respect. And that leaves plenty of room for God to do His work in and around us.

NO MATTER WHAT, LOOK TO GOD

*Although the fig tree shall not blossom, neither shall fruit
be in the vines; the labour of the olive shall fail, and the
fields shall yield no meat [food]; the flock shall be cut off
from the fold, and there shall be no herd in the stalls: Yet I
will rejoice in the Lord, I will joy in the God of my salvation.
The Lord God is my strength, and he will make my feet like
hinds' feet, and he will make me to walk upon mine high places.*
HABAKKUK 3:17–19 KJV

Habakkuk concludes his prophecy with a hauntingly beautiful psalm. The closing lines, quoted above, speak of terrible challenges—yet also the experience of the Lord's strength.

Like many other prophets, Habakkuk served a people who had sinned greatly against God. And when the Lord sent punishment by way of the powerful Babylonian army, Judah's orchards, vineyards, fields, flocks, and herds were wiped out. There was little food left for the poor, devasted remnant of God's people. Physically, what could be worse?

But after the shock of the invasion, Habakkuk focused his attention on the Lord. After all, God is the source of everything, from our daily physical needs to our emotional and spiritual strength to our eternal salvation. This recognition explains Habakkuk's otherwise inexplicable joy. The prophet was so energized by the Lord that he imagined himself climbing the surrounding mountains like a surefooted deer.

In this life, trials are guaranteed. But so is God's presence and strength for those willing to seek them. No matter what, look to God. You'll find Him.

MEDITATION

*My mouth shall speak of wisdom; and the
meditation of my heart shall be of understanding.*
PSALM 49:3 KJV

The true aim of education, study, reading, is to be found not in what is brought into us, but in what is brought out of us, by the awakening into active exercise of our inward power. This is as true of the study of the Bible as of any other study.

God's Word only works its true blessing when the truth it brings to us has stirred the inner life and reproduced itself in resolve, trust, love, or adoration. When the heart has received the Word through the mind and has had its spiritual powers called out and exercised on it, the Word is no longer void but has done that whereunto God has sent it. It has become part of our life and strengthened us for new purpose and effort.

It is in meditation that the heart holds and appropriates the Word. Just as in reflection the understanding grasps all the meaning and bearings of a truth, so in meditation the heart assimilates it and makes it a part of its own life.

ACCEPT HELP

*"One man from each tribe, each of them the
head of his family, is to help you. These are
the names of the men who are to assist you. . ."*
NUMBERS 1:4–5 NIV

The fourth book of the Old Testament begins with a census, hence
the name *Numbers*. In the Sinai Desert, fourteen months after the
Israelites left their slavery in Egypt, God told Moses to count the
Israelite men "who are twenty years old or more and able to
serve in the army" (Numbers 1:3 NIV). It was a big job, since that
number ultimately came out to 603,550!

But Moses didn't have to count each of these potential soldiers
himself. That would have been nearly impossible, finding each
eligible male among a nomadic nation of perhaps two million or
more people. God specifically told Moses to call on the help of twelve
men, the current heads of the various tribes of Israel: Elizur from
the tribe of Reuben, Shelumiel from the tribe of Simeon, Nahshon
from the tribe of Judah, and on down the line. Considering that, on
average, these men were counting some fifty thousand military-age
males themselves, it's safe to assume that they too called on help
to accomplish their task.

Many men hate to ask for help—or even to accept it when offered. But scripture contains many examples of people working
together, whether on a physical job or an emotional and spiritual
level. Strength for the challenges of life often comes through our
fellow believers.

THE LORD'S FAVOR

Then Jehoahaz sought the Lord's favor,
and the Lord listened to him.
2 Kings 13:4 niv

In the Old Testament, we often see the kings of both Israel and Judah failing to fully follow the Lord's commands and subsequently paying a heavy price for their sin. It's easy to wonder why they weren't more faithful. Couldn't they see that their way led to destruction? Couldn't they understand that God wanted the best for them and their people? Of course, we have the benefit of scripture and hindsight—but don't we often act in the same ways?

Jehoahaz ruled for seventeen years in Israel and he—as so many others before him—did evil. So the anger of the Lord burned against Israel, and they ended up oppressed by the Syrians. But when Jehoahaz begged for the Lord's favor, God listened to him. And the Lord saved His people from their enemy.

Sometimes we find ourselves in challenging situations of our own making, sometimes due to carelessness and sometimes due to conscious sin. When that happens, don't ever succumb to the lie that you are too far gone for the Lord. He always cares and will act on behalf of a humble heart. That's why the Bible often shows Him rescuing disobedient kings.

Of course, it's far better to walk in obedience. But if you stray and find yourself in the proverbial pigpen, never hesitate to call out to the Lord. He is ready to show favor.

—— FEEDING THE MULTITUDE ——

*Then he took the five loaves and the two fishes, and looking
up to heaven, he blessed them, and brake, and gave to
the disciples to set before the multitude. And they did
eat, and were all filled: and there was taken up of
fragments that remained to them twelve baskets.*

LUKE 9:16–17 KJV

Jesus' twelve apostles were on a mission to preach and heal in Jewish communities around the Sea of Galilee. When they returned, they inadvertently brought a crowd of thousands of people with them. While the disciples wanted to send the crowd away, Jesus had compassion on the people—and saw a teachable moment for His team.

With echoes of the forthcoming Last Supper, Jesus took the bread, blessed it, broke it, and gave it to the disciples. They distributed what He had given them, and what was originally deemed insufficient ended in twelve baskets of leftovers.

For the crowd who ate the bread, Jesus' act cast Him in the light of Moses who prayed and provided manna for God's people. This was truly a prophet!

For the disciples who doubted their resources, Jesus showed that it is not the amount of bread or fish (or human ability) that enables the feeding of a multitude, but faith in the God of infinite resources. This was truly the Messiah!

When we feel our ability insufficient for the task God has given us, He asks us to move forward in faith—not in our strength but His. Do as Jesus did: pray for blessing, break the bread, and trust in God's ability to provide.

── A PATH OF SEPARATION ──

*The righteous also shall hold on his way, and he that
hath clean hands shall be stronger and stronger.*
JOB 17:9 KJV

The man who is righteous before God has a way of his own. It is not
the way of the flesh, nor the way of the world; it is a way marked
out for him by the divine command, in which he walks by faith. It
is the King's highway of holiness, the unclean shall not pass over
it: only the ransomed of the Lord shall walk there, and these shall
find it a path of separation from the world.

Once entered upon the way of life, the pilgrim must persevere
in it or perish, for thus saith the Lord, "If any man draw back, my
soul shall have no pleasure in him" (Hebrews 10:38 KJV). Perseverance in the path of faith and holiness is a necessity of the Christian,
for only "he that endureth to the end, the same shall be saved"
(Matthew 10:22 KJV).

— GOD, THE MIGHTY WARRIOR —

The great day of the Lord is near—near and
coming quickly. The cry on the day of the Lord
is bitter; the Mighty Warrior shouts his battle cry.
ZEPHANIAH 1:14 NIV

The prophet Zephaniah described God as a "Mighty Warrior," shouting a battle cry on the "great day of the Lord." This latter phrase speaks of God's terrifying judgments both near at hand and far into the future, both on God's people and the surrounding pagan nations.

During the reign of King Josiah, Zephaniah warned of God's judgment against Judah. "At that time," God said through His prophet, "I will search Jerusalem with lamps and punish those who are complacent, who are like wine left on its dregs, who think, 'The Lord will do nothing, either good or bad.' Their wealth will be plundered, their houses demolished. Though they build houses, they will not live in them; though they plant vineyards, they will not drink the wine" (1:12–13 NIV). Judah's sins included idolatry, child sacrifice, pride, and indifference to the things of the Lord. The nations of Philistia, Moab, Ammon, Ethiopia, and Assyria would also suffer God's heavy punishment (chapter 2).

But if the people would turn from their sins, they would find the Mighty Warrior on their side. "Seek the Lord, all you humble of the land, you who do what he commands," Zephaniah told Judah. "Seek righteousness, seek humility; perhaps you will be sheltered on the day of the Lord's anger" (2:3 NIV). There would even be blessing on the other side (3:10–20).

As Christians, possessors of God's Holy Spirit, we enjoy a more intimate relationship with this powerful God than the ancient Jews did. Whatever battles we face—from outside or within—God, the Mighty Warrior, is on our side.

A WAY OUT

So, if you think you are standing firm, be careful that you don't fall! No temptation has overtaken you except what is common to mankind. And God is faithful; he will not let you be tempted beyond what you can bear. But when you are tempted, he will also provide a way out so that you can endure it.
1 Corinthians 10:12–13 niv

Some biblical principles must be extrapolated from multiple passages that only touch on a topic. Then there are biblical promises that hit you between the eyes. The thirteenth verse of 1 Corinthians 10 is one of the latter.

When we are tempted, God will provide a way of escape. Not *might*, not *could*, but *will*. That is a guarantee of strength for the challenge of sin.

What's not guaranteed is our own obedience. Will we walk away when the temptation comes? Will we tell ourselves "no" when our emotions are saying "yes"? As difficult as it may seem to resist the lure of sin, we have God's promise that we will never "be tempted beyond what [we] can bear."

Maybe it's worth memorizing these verses, so the Holy Spirit can bring them to mind at the appropriate moment. Temptation is a normal human experience. But, biblically speaking, there is no reason for it ever to lead to sin.

—— OUT OF THE WHIRLWIND ——

Then the Lord answered Job out of the whirlwind,
and said, Who is this that darkeneth counsel by
words without knowledge? Gird up now thy loins like
a man; for I will demand of thee, and answer thou me.
JOB 38:1–3 KJV

The prophet Elijah sought God's voice in a mighty wind, then in an earthquake, and finally in a raging fire. But he ultimately heard God in a whisper, His "still small voice" (1 Kings 19:12). God did not have to shout, because Elijah was listening.

Job was listening as well. But as his situation unfolded, and as his well-meaning friends pounded him with wave after wave of conflicting advice, Job began to lose grip on the unchanging love of God. He began to question God's motives and even God's right to rule in Job's life.

Few stories in the Bible make clearer our need to be and to stay intimately connected to our Creator. Job's situation caused him enormous pain, and the unhelpful input of others pushed him even farther away from the only real help available.

How about us? Are we daily listening for God's still small voice? Or have we allowed the cares of this world, and the deceitfulness of riches, or the lust for other things to overwhelm His Word? Let's not force God to speak to us out of the whirlwind.

CLASSICS: D. L. MOODY

WASHED IN THE BLOOD OF THE LAMB

For when we were yet without strength, in due time Christ died for the ungodly. For scarcely for a righteous man will one die: yet peradventure for a good man some would even dare to die. But God commendeth his love toward us, in that, while we were yet sinners, Christ died for us.
ROMANS 5:6–8 KJV

Many people try to come to Christ but think they cannot come unless they first become good. But Jesus loves His people even before their sins are washed away. He loves them and then washes them in His own blood, as it is written, "Unto him that loved us, and washed us in his own blood, and hath made us kings and priests unto God and his Father; to him be glory and dominion for ever and ever" (Revelation 1:5–6 KJV).

Oh! It is wonderful love. To think that He loves them first and then washes them in His blood free from their sins! There is no devil in hell that can pluck them out of His hand. They are perfectly safe, for they are washed in the blood of the Lamb.

A LASTING IMPACT

*Elisha said, "Get a bow and some arrows," and [Jehoash]
did so. "Take the bow in your hands," he said to the king
of Israel. When he had taken it, Elisha put his hands on the
king's hands. "Open the east window," he said, and he opened
it. "Shoot!" Elisha said, and he shot. "The LORD's arrow of
victory, the arrow of victory over Aram!" Elisha declared.
"You will completely destroy the Arameans at Aphek."*
2 KINGS 13:15–17 NIV

As Elisha was suffering with an illness that would claim his life,
Jehoash—the wicked king of Israel—did something good. He went
to visit Elisha and weep over him.

Then Elisha gave an odd instruction. He wanted Jehoash to
take up a bow and arrow. Elisha managed to put his hands on the
king's hands as he shot the arrow out the prophet's window. Elisha
declared it the Lord's "arrow of victory." This unusual little story
is really a beautiful picture of God strengthening His prophet one
final time to point others to faith.

And God provides His strength to all of His children, all the
time. We just need to accept it. No matter what you're experiencing
right now, good or bad, the Lord will strengthen you to shine for
His kingdom. Be open to any possibilities, as He leads, to leave a
lasting impact on peoples' lives.

—— BENEFITS OF FORGIVENESS ——

I appeal to you to show kindness to my child, Onesimus.
I became his father in the faith while here in prison.
Onesimus hasn't been of much use to you in the past,
but now he is very useful to both of us.
PHILEMON 10–11 NLT

Onesimus was a slave with a history. He had run away from his master, Philemon, in Colosse, and apparently met the apostle Paul in Rome. It seems that Onesimus had somehow wronged Philemon—perhaps stealing from him—because Paul wrote to the one-time slaveowner, "If he has wronged you in any way or owes you anything, charge it to me. . .I will repay it" (Philemon 18–19 NLT).

The apostle had apparently led Onesimus to faith in Jesus (verse 10), and Paul was now urging Philemon to accept his escaped slave back as "more than a slave, for he is a beloved brother" (verse 16 NLT).

Forgiveness is a distinguishing trait of the Christian faith. God forgives our sins when we ask Him to, and we are then expected to forgive the "trespasses" of the people around us (Matthew 6:14–15 KJV). Human nature often balks at extending forgiveness, but we must obey what God commands. And what God commands, He empowers.

If we make a good-faith effort to forgive, God will see us through. And then, as Paul told Philemon, we gain a "useful" relationship— one that has benefit to all involved.

Commit to taking that first step of forgiveness, and see how God uses it for bigger and better things.

MIGHTY WARRIOR, JOYFUL SINGING

*"But I will leave within you the meek and humble. The remnant
of Israel will trust in the name of the Lord. . . . The Lord your
God is with you, the Mighty Warrior who saves. He will take
great delight in you; in his love he will no longer rebuke
you, but will rejoice over you with singing."*
Zephaniah 3:12, 17 niv

Warned of God's coming judgment, Zephaniah urged the people of
Judah to repent. But the prophet then spoke of God's future blessings on the kingdom. We see this pattern throughout the prophets
from Isaiah to Malachi: after terrible judgment, future mercies.

No prophet, however, pulled the heartstrings quite as much as
Zephaniah. He described the Lord God as the ultimate David, the
Warrior King who will return from battle, gather His people, and
"rejoice over you with singing." God would do this out of His great
delight in and love for the remnant of His people—those who were
spared the devastation of His judgment.

These people are described as "meek" (possessing a gentle
strength) and "humble" (without pride), the very words Jesus used
to describe Himself in Matthew 11:29. The remnant will also "trust
in the name of the Lord," a phrase echoing Joel 2:32, Acts 2:21, and
Romans 10:13, which all say, "Everyone who calls on the name of
the Lord will be saved" (niv).

True Christians have called on the name of the Lord. They will
be saved, and truly are now saved. Their God, the Mighty Warrior,
takes great delight and rejoices over them with singing. Today, you
are (or can be) among that number.

Classics: Charles Spurgeon

—— LAY HOLD OF THE ALTAR ——

Then tidings came to Joab: for Joab had turned after Adonijah,
though he turned not after Absalom. And Joab fled unto the
tabernacle of the Lord, and caught hold on the horns of the
altar. . . . And Benaiah came to the tabernacle of the Lord, and
said unto him, Thus saith the king, Come forth. And he said,
Nay; but I will die here. And Benaiah brought the king word
again, saying, Thus said Joab, and thus he answered me.
1 Kings 2:28, 30 kjv

I have two lessons which I am anxious to teach at this time. The
first is derived from the fact that Joab found no benefit of sanctuary even though he laid hold upon the horns of the altar of God's
house, from which I gather this lesson—that outward ordinances
will avail nothing. Before the living God, who is greater and wiser
than Solomon, it will be of no avail to any man to lay hold upon
the horns of the altar.

But, second, there is an altar—a spiritual altar—whereof if a
man do but lay hold upon the horns and say, "Nay; but I will die
here," he shall never die; but he shall be safe against the sword of
justice forever; for the Lord has appointed an altar in the person
of His own dear Son, Jesus Christ, where there shall be shelter for
the very vilest of sinners if they do but come and lay hold thereon.

RIGHTING A WRONG

The LORD said to Moses, "Say to the Israelites: 'Any man or woman who wrongs another in any way and so is unfaithful to the LORD is guilty and must confess the sin they have committed. They must make full restitution for the wrong they have done, add a fifth of the value to it and give it all to the person they have wronged.' "

NUMBERS 5:5–7 NIV

Living a life of faithfulness to the Lord is a worthy goal for all of us. But even the most dedicated and talented followers of God still err, whether their sin is intentional or accidental. In today's scripture, the Lord wanted the Israelites to know that how they responded after a wrong is important.

The first step to restoration is to "confess the sin." This confession should be made to all who have been wronged. It is certainly difficult to humble yourself before someone you've mistreated. But this effort honors both them and the Lord.

The next step is "full restitution." Give back what was taken. Correct what was stated falsely. Make good what was done badly. The biblical command required an added 20 percent for restitution that involves goods.

How much better life would be—in our families, our workplaces, or our churches—if we followed this basic rule. Have I wronged someone? Go to them and confess it as sin. Has someone wronged me? Give them the opportunity to make it right. God often gives strength as a direct result of our obedience to scripture.

DELIVER US!

*"Now, LORD our God, deliver us from his hand,
so that all the kingdoms of the earth may
know that you alone, LORD, are God."*
2 KINGS 19:19 NIV

Sennacherib, king of Assyria, couldn't imagine that Israel's God was any stronger than the gods of the other nations he'd conquered.

"Has the god of any nation ever delivered his land from the hand of the king of Assyria?" Sennacherib taunted. "Where are the gods of Hamath and Arpad? Where are the gods of Sepharvaim, Hena and Ivvah? Have they rescued Samaria from my hand? Who of all the gods of these countries has been able to save his land from me? How then can the LORD deliver Jerusalem from my hand?" (2 Kings 18:33–35 NIV).

Sennacherib soon found out how wrong he was. An angel of the Lord killed 185,000 Assyrians (2 Kings 19:35). God did so for His name's sake (2 Kings 19:34).

Who or what is your Assyria? It probably seems insurmountable in your own strength. But, praise God, you don't have to rely on your own strength. Like King Hezekiah in today's scripture, go to the Lord in prayer. If He delivers you, praise Him publicly, so everyone else can know God's power and strength. If He allows you to go through a trial, praise Him anyway, and rely on His strength to endure. Either way, God is worthy of your worship.

REWARD TO COME

*"If anyone wants to keep his own life safe, he must lose it.
If anyone gives up his life because of Me, he will save it."*
LUKE 9:24 NLV

The apostles knew that Jesus was the Messiah. He taught with power. He performed miracles like the prophets of old. But the twelve didn't understand the kind of messiah Jesus was to be.

Everyone in Israel was waiting and hoping for the Son of Man promised in Daniel 7:13–14 (NLV): "I kept looking in the night dream and saw One like a Son of Man coming with the clouds of heaven. He came to the One Who has lived forever, and was brought before Him. And He was given power and shining-greatness, and was made King, so that all the people of every nation and language would serve Him. His rule lasts forever. It will never pass away. And His nation will never be destroyed."

When Jesus came to earth, Israel was subject to Roman authority. Jews longed for the Messiah to come in power and might, to be King over every nation, to throw off the chains of Roman rule. But Jesus was a different kind of messiah.

To save the world, He had to die. His coronation would be with a crown of thorns. And everyone who followed Him could expect the same treatment. If we want to live, we must lay aside our selfish desires—even our instinct for self-preservation. We must die to this life to be filled with Christ's life.

Jesus never promised wealth or power for His followers in this life. The reward is in the eternal life to follow.

—— WALK CLOSELY WITH GOD ——

*And when Abram was ninety years old and nine,
the LORD appeared to Abram, and said unto him, I am
the Almighty God; walk before me, and be thou perfect.*
GENESIS 17:1 KJV

Walk before Me, and be thou perfect. It is in the life fellowship with God, in His realized presence and favor, that it becomes possible to be perfect with Him. Walk before Me: Abraham had been doing this; God's Word calls him to a clearer and more conscious apprehension of this as his life calling.

It is easy for us to study what scripture says of perfection, to form our ideas of it and argue for them. But let us remember that it is only as we are walking closely with God, seeking and in some measure attaining, uninterrupted communion with Him, that the divine command will come to us in its divine power and unfold to us its divine meaning.

Walk before Me, and be thou perfect. God's realized presence is the school, is the secret, of perfection. It is only he who studies what perfection is *in the full light of God's presence* to whom its hidden glory will be opened up.

—————— "I AM WITH YOU" ——————

*Then Zerubbabel son of Shealtiel, Joshua son of Jozadak,
the high priest, and the whole remnant of the people obeyed
the voice of the Lord their God and the message of the
prophet Haggai, because the Lord their God had sent him.
And the people feared the Lord. Then Haggai, the Lord's
messenger, gave this message of the Lord to the people:
"I am with you," declares the Lord.*
HAGGAI 1:12–13 NIV

The prophet Haggai urged his readers to repent of their misplaced priorities. He was the first of three prophets to rebuke God's people after the Babylonian captivity. Although more than fifty thousand had forsaken their idolatrous ways, returned to the land of Judah, and started to rebuild the temple, they had not wholeheartedly committed themselves to serving God.

Eventually, their work on the temple foundation stopped. Years went by with no progress. Meanwhile, drought crippled their agriculture. "You have planted much, but harvested little," God told them. "You eat, but never have enough" (1:6 NIV).

The Lord exhorted the people and their leaders to consider their miserable plight and get back to work on the temple, and the people listened. And when they heard and obeyed, God made one of the most beautiful promises in all of scripture: "I am with you."

Though in one sense, God is always "with us" (that's the idea behind His omnipresence), He is truly with us when we—like the ancient Israelites—do what He says. Come near to Him, and He will come near to you, James wrote (4:8 NIV). How do we draw near to God? Read the rest of that verse from James: "Wash your hands, you sinners, and purify your hearts, you double-minded." Do right, and He will reward you with His presence.

YOU MATTER

If the foot says, "I am not a part of the body because I am
not a hand," that does not make it any less a part of the body.
And if the ear says, "I am not part of the body because I am
not an eye," would that make it any less a part of the body? If
the whole body were an eye, how would you hear? Or if your
whole body were an ear, how would you smell anything?
1 CORINTHIANS 12:15–17 NLT

Herding the Corinthian Christians into one cohesive group was
a significant challenge for the apostle Paul. There was pride and
prejudice in the congregation, with various factions claiming to
follow Paul, Apollos, Peter, and (the really spiritual ones) Jesus. Some
church members were taking others to court. People in the church
were allowing one particular member to live in gross sexual sin.

Toward the end of his first letter to Corinth, what we now call
1 Corinthians 12, Paul tried to explain how every member played
an important—really, indispensable—role in the church, the "body
of Christ." Whether they were eyes or ears or feet or hands, each
Christian in Corinth had God-given responsibilities and privileges.
Each one of them mattered, both to God and to their fellow believers.

Wherever this scripture finds you today, remember that there
are no spare parts in the body of Christ. No one is more important
than another, and no one is insignificant. You matter—so do the
job God gave you!

Day 272

CLASSICS: *D. L. MOODY*

—— JOINT HEIRS WITH JESUS ——

And he that sat upon the throne said, Behold, I make all things new. And he said unto me, Write: for these words are true and faithful. And he said unto me, It is done. I am Alpha and Omega, the beginning and the end. I will give unto him that is athirst of the fountain of the water of life freely. He that overcometh shall inherit all things; and I will be his God, and he shall be my son.

REVELATION 21:5–7 KJV

After the Chicago fire a man came up to me and said in a sympathizing tone, "I understand you lost everything, Moody, in the Chicago fire."

"Well, then," said I, "someone has misinformed you."

"Indeed! Why I was certainly told you had lost all."

"No; it is a mistake," I said, "quite a mistake."

"Have you got much left, then?" asked my friend.

"Yes," I replied, "I have got much more left than I lost; though I cannot tell how much I have lost."

"Well, I am glad of it, Moody; I did not know you were that rich before the fire."

"Yes," said I, "I am a good deal richer than you could conceive; and here is my title-deed: 'He that overcometh shall inherit all things.'" They say the Rothschilds cannot tell how much they are worth; and that is just my case. All things in the world are mine; I am joint heir with Jesus the Son of God.

SO SIMPLE A THING

And his servants came near, and spake unto him, and said,
My father, if the prophet had bid thee do some great thing,
wouldest thou not have done it? how much rather then,
when he saith to thee, Wash, and be clean?
2 KINGS 5:13 KJV

I honestly confess that before I knew Christ and the way of salvation by His finished work, I would have done anything in order to be saved. Such was my sense of guilt, and such my fear of the wrath to come, that no pilgrimage would have been too wearisome, no pain too intense, no slavery too severe, to appease my troubled conscience. I would gladly have laid down my life if I might have saved my soul thereby. Times without number have I thought I wished I had never been born; and could there have been put before me any possible form of penance, though it might have consisted of excruciating agony, I am sure I would gladly have accepted it if I might be saved.

Little did I think that it was done for me by another, and that what I had to do was to accept what had been done, and not to do anything but to trust in Christ. We cannot conceive it possible that so simple a thing as relying and trusting upon Christ can save our souls. . .nothing else can.

DEATH ISN'T THE END

"Go back and tell Hezekiah, the ruler of my people, 'This is what the LORD, the God of your father David, says: I have heard your prayer and seen your tears; I will heal you.' "
2 KINGS 20:5 NIV

King Hezekiah's illness seemed to come out of the blue. . .and it was terminal. The Lord told the faithful king to put his house in order because he wasn't going to recover. Hezekiah did what any of us would do: he prayed. Oddly, though, he didn't pray directly for healing.

"Remember, LORD," he said, "how I have walked before you faithfully and with wholehearted devotion and have done what is good in your eyes" (2 Kings 20:3 NIV). In other words, Hezekiah "reminded" God that he had lived in a way that seemed worthy of a *longer* life. He'd been as faithful to God as a man could be. The Lord graciously heard Hezekiah's prayer and granted him an additional fifteen years.

Hezekiah was facing what we will all face someday—mortality. Most of us don't really want to think about our own deaths, but when we follow Jesus, our mortality should hold no terror. No matter how long we live, we are destined to die, and for believers, the Lord alone is our goal (see Psalm 16:5). Do not fear. Death isn't the end for us as believers—it's simply the beginning of a perfect, sinless, everlasting life.

—— ACCEPT THE INVITATION ——

For I say unto you, That none of those men
which were bidden shall taste of my supper.
LUKE 14:24 KJV

Glorious invitation! With adoration I receive it and prepare myself to make use of it. I have read of those who hold themselves excused because they are hindered—one by his merchandise, another by his work, and a third by his domestic happiness. I have heard the voice which has said, "I say unto you, that none of these men which were bidden shall taste of My supper." Under the conviction that He who so cordially invites me is the Holy One, who will not suffer Himself to be mocked, I will prepare myself to lay aside all thoughtlessness, to withdraw myself from the seductions of the world; and with all earnestness to yield obedience to the voice of the heavenly love. I will remain in quiet meditation and in fellowship with the children of God, to keep myself free from all needless anxiety about the world, and as an invited guest, to meet my God with real hunger and quiet joy.

He Himself will not withhold from me His help in this work.

THE LORD'S ALMIGHTY, SO BE STRONG

> " 'Now be strong, Zerubbabel,' declares the LORD. 'Be strong,
> Joshua son of Jozadak, the high priest. Be strong, all you people
> of the land,' declares the LORD, 'and work. For I am with you,'
> declares the LORD Almighty. . . . 'The glory of this present
> house will be greater than the glory of the former house,'
> says the LORD Almighty. 'And in this place I will grant
> peace,' declares the LORD Almighty."
>
> HAGGAI 2:4, 9 NIV

God gave the prophet Haggai several messages for the leaders and people of Judah. In Haggai 2, the Lord urged them to be strong even though their task of rebuilding the Jerusalem temple was arduous (verses 1–9).

In today's key verses, we can't miss the threefold repetition of one of God's favorite names: "the LORD Almighty." He is the omnipotent and all-powerful God! And still that is only a part of His infinite personality.

We also can't miss the threefold repetition of the command, "be strong." Through Haggai, God told His people to be courageous and brave. This is the same command the Lord gave to Joshua and many other heroes of the faith in both the Old and New Testaments. The Lord even told the normally fearless apostle Paul, "Do not be afraid; keep on speaking, do not be silent. For I am with you" (Acts 18:9–10 NIV). That final phrase is yet another biblical favorite, as we see in Haggai 2:4 above.

What does all this mean to us? If we forget that the Lord is almighty, we won't be strong. When we acknowledge God's immense power, we can accomplish whatever He calls us to do.

TREAT OTHERS AS YOUR MASTER WOULD

*Therefore if any man be in Christ, he is a
new creature: old things are passed away;
behold, all things are become new.*
2 CORINTHIANS 5:17 KJV

In the frontier, when a man goes out hunting he takes a hatchet with him and cuts off pieces from the bark of the trees as he goes along through the forest: this is called "blazing the way." He does it that he may know the way back, as there is no pathway through these thick forests.

Christ has come down to this earth; He has "blazed the Way," and now that He has gone up on high, if we will but follow Him, we shall be kept in the right path. I will tell you how you may know if you are following Christ or not. If someone has slandered you or misjudged you, do you treat them as your Master would have done? If you do not bear these things in a loving and forgiving spirit, all the churches and ministers in the world cannot make you right. "If any man have not the Spirit of Christ, he is none of his" (Romans 8:9 KJV). "If any man be in Christ, he is a new creature: old things are passed away; behold, all things are become new."

STOP AND REMEMBER

*And the L<small>ORD</small> spake unto Moses in the wilderness of Sinai,
in the first month of the second year after they were come
out of the land of Egypt, saying, Let the children of Israel
also keep the passover at his appointed season.*
N<small>UMBERS</small> 9:1–2 <small>KJV</small>

One year removed from their miraculous escape from Egypt, God told the Israelites to observe the Passover, "according to all the rites of it, and according to all the ceremonies thereof" (Numbers 9:3). Those rites and ceremonies are explained in Exodus 12, which also describes the death of the Egyptian firstborn, the ultimate plague that caused Pharaoh to let God's people go.

Now in the wilderness, on their way to the promised land of Canaan, the people were to stop and remember how God had rescued them from their slavery. Ideally, this recollection would strengthen them for the challenges of their journey and the settlement of Canaan. Sadly, from our perspective, we realize the people were only *one fortieth* of their way home. The Israelites complained and feared and distrusted God, and nearly every one died in the wilderness. Different generations, decades later, would enter the promised land.

As Christians, we have an advantage the ancient Israelites lacked: God's Spirit living within us. But we're still prone to complain and fear and distrust God, so the directive to Israel is a good one for us too: stop and remember.

What good things has God done in your life? What miracles, even? How can the memories of His goodness and strength help you through today's challenges?

START FRESH

Go ye, enquire of the LORD for me [Josiah], and for the people, and for all Judah, concerning the words of this book that is found: for great is the wrath of the LORD that is kindled against us, because our fathers have not hearkened unto the words of this book, to do according unto all that which is written concerning us.
2 KINGS 22:13 KJV

Much had changed since good King Hezekiah's reign. His son, Manasseh, did evil in the Lord's sight. So did Manasseh's son, Amon. By the time Amon's son, Josiah, became king at age eight, the book of the Law had long since faded from Judah's memory. It wasn't till the eighteenth year of Josiah's reign that the high priest stumbled across the Law in the temple. He took it to the king.

After hearing the Law read, Josiah tore his clothes in mourning. He realized that God's wrath was on the nation because it had neglected His Word. But because Josiah's heart was responsive, God relented—at least for a while.

If your Bible has been gathering dust, change that today. Crack it open and begin to read. Praise God, Christians today are under the covenant of grace—one that is far superior to the rules of the Old Testament. But there's a principle in Josiah's story that still applies to us today: As we stray from the Word, we're sowing troubled seeds that yield a difficult harvest. As we return to scripture, it will mold and shape us into the image of Christ. How could we be more blessed?

FREEDOM IN CHRIST

To the Jews who had believed him, Jesus said, "If you hold to my teaching, you are really my disciples. Then you will know the truth, and the truth will set you free."
JOHN 8:31–32 NIV

Everyone serves a master. We are all slaves to someone (or something). The implications of this teaching were uncomfortable to the Jews Jesus originally addressed. They're uncomfortable to us today.

When Jesus told a crowd how they could be free, they balked. "We are Abraham's descendants and have never been slaves of anyone," they argued. "How can you say that we shall be set free?" (John 8:33 NIV).

They apparently forgot the Jews' slavery experience in Egypt; how Israel had been conquered by Assyrian, Babylonian, Persian, and Syrian armies; and how they were currently subject to Roman authority. Long-term slavery had seemingly convinced them that they had never been slaves at all. Who was Jesus to offer them freedom?

But Jesus was qualified to offer freedom, because He was the only One who never served an earthly master!

Today, we are faced with the same proposition of freedom. By holding to Jesus' teachings—including the hard ones like self-sacrifice and loving our neighbors—we prove ourselves to be His disciples. When Jesus is our Master, we are free from the world's slavery.

Freedom in Christ does not mean we can do whatever we want. We are free to do what *God* wants—and given the strength to accomplish His tasks.

CLASSICS: JOHN WESLEY

DON'T ENVY THE WICKED

Surely thou didst set them in slippery places: thou castedst them down into destruction. How are they brought into desolation, as in a moment! they are utterly consumed with terrors. As a dream when one awaketh; so, O Lord, when thou awakest, thou shalt despise their image.

PSALM 73:18–20 KJV

Anyone that considers the foregoing verses will easily observe that the psalmist is speaking directly of the wicked that prosper in their wickedness. It is very common for these utterly to forget that they are creatures of a day; to live as if they were never to die; as if their present state was to endure forever; or, at least as if they were indisputably sure that they "had much goods laid up for many years." So that they might safely say, "Soul, take thine ease; eat, drink, and be merry."

But how miserable a mistake is this! How often does God say to such a one, "Thou fool! this night shall thy soul be required of thee!" Well, then, may it be said of them, "O, how suddenly do they consume!"—perish, and come to a fearful end. Yea, "even like as a dream when one awaketh; so shalt thou make their image to vanish out of the city."

RETURN TO GOD

*"Therefore tell the people: This is what the L*ORD* Almighty says: 'Return to me,' declares the L*ORD* Almighty, 'and I will return to you,' says the L*ORD* Almighty."*
ZECHARIAH 1:3 NIV

One mystery of the Christian life is why followers of Jesus would ever stray away from God. And yet that's not only possible, but common. Even the great apostle Paul said, "I do not understand what I do. For what I want to do I do not do, but what I hate I do. . . . The evil I do not want to do—this I keep on doing" (Romans 7:15, 19 NIV). Paul blamed the problem on the "sin living in me" (verse 20 NIV).

As Christians, most of us know the promise of 1 John 1:9—"If we confess our sins, he is faithful and just and will forgive us our sins and purify us from all unrighteousness" (NIV). Or, to paraphrase Zechariah, "Return to God and He will return to you."

Sin weakens us. It makes us slaves to Satan, a power far less than God but far greater than ourselves. When we continue in sin, we're like shackled prisoners being marched down a road not of our own choosing.

But like the father in Jesus' story of the prodigal son, God is waiting for us to come to our senses (Luke 15:17). When we decide to turn away from sin and back to God, He comes running to meet us. And there's no more powerful place to be than in His will.

— BETTER DAYS ARE COMING —

Our earthly bodies are planted in the ground when we die, but they will be raised to live forever. Our bodies are buried in brokenness, but they will be raised in glory. They are buried in weakness, but they will be raised in strength. They are buried as natural human bodies, but they will be raised as spiritual bodies.
1 CORINTHIANS 15:42–44 NLT

No matter how hard this life becomes, Christians can look forward to better days ahead.

In this world, our bodies become weary, old, and sick. Our emotions can swing from joy to misery with a quick turn of circumstances. Whether we always realize it or not, we are engaged in a cosmic spiritual battle against the sworn enemy of God. "People are born for trouble," the Old Testament character Job noted, "as readily as sparks fly up from a fire" (5:7 NLT).

That's the bad news. But God is the author of good news, the meaning of the word *Gospel.* When we believe in the work of His Son, Jesus Christ, we are placed on an upward path. There will still be aches and pains and sorrows and tears in this world, ending in the decline and death of our bodies. But the apostle Paul promises that death is only the gateway to real life.

When life is hard—when it's tough to get out of bed, when there seems to be no light at the end of the proverbial tunnel—remember that better days are coming. Someday, you'll be "raised to live forever. . .in glory. . .in strength." If you follow Jesus Christ, this is your eternal destiny.

NOT LOOKING AT OUR FAULTS

So the LORD blessed the latter end of Job more than his beginning. . . . After this lived Job an hundred and forty years, and saw his sons, and his sons' sons, even four generations. So Job died, being old and full of days.
JOB 42:12, 16–17 KJV

The story of Job has a happy ending. Skeptics may dismiss the entire narrative, but for those who know—beyond a shadow of a doubt—that every word of God is true, this ending is confirmation of the true nature of God and the faithfulness of Jesus Christ.

There are no easy answers to the question of why bad things happen to good people. But the Bible says *no one* is good, really. We have all sinned and fall short of the glory of God. These things were true of Job as well. But still, God said of Job, "There is none like him on the earth, a blameless and upright man, one who fears God and shuns evil" (Job 1:8 NKJV).

As shocking as it may seem, God is not looking at our faults. Are they there? Of course. But when we say yes to Jesus Christ, when we ask Him to come and make our heart His home, those sins are cast as far away as the east is from the west (see Psalm 103:12).

Job was blessed at the end of his life because God loved him just as He loves us. And God's promise is to bless us and provide for all of our needs as well—when we love and trust Him with all our heart.

AFTER GOD'S HEART

*But now thy kingdom shall not continue: the LORD hath
sought him a man after his own heart, and the LORD hath
commanded him to be captain over his people, because thou
hast not kept that which the LORD commanded thee.*
1 SAMUEL 13:14 KJV

Of the two expressions God uses here of David, we often hear the
former: "a man after Mine own heart." The use of the latter, "who
shall do all My will," is much less frequent. And yet it is no less
important than the other.

A man after Mine own heart: that speaks of the deep unseen
mystery of the pleasure a man can give to God in heaven. *Who shall
do all My will*: that deals with the life down here on earth which
can be seen and judged by men. Let us seek and get full hold of
the truth that it is *the man who does all God's will* who is the man
after His own heart.

Such men God seeks: when He finds them He rejoices over
them with great joy: they are the very men He needs, men He
can trust and use. His heart, with its hidden divine perfections,
reveals itself in His will: he that seeks and loves *and does all His
will* is a man altogether after His own heart: the man of absolute
surrender to God's will.

—— GOD'S PROMISES ——

He [the Lord our God] remembers his covenant forever,
the promise he made, for a thousand generations.
1 CHRONICLES 16:15 NIV

Charles Spurgeon once preached a sermon titled "All the Promises," based on 2 Corinthians 1:20 (KJV): "For all the promises of God in him are yea, and in him Amen, unto the glory of God by us." In the sermon, Spurgeon made this observation: "We sometimes read, or hear, or speak of the promises written in God's Word, but do not give them as much credit as if they were the promises of a friend, or of our father, or our brother. If we valued them more, we should believe them better."

The fact is that scripture is packed with promises from God. There are scores of prophecies which are both stated and fulfilled within the Bible's pages. There are countless offers of help and hope that we as Christians have all partaken of. There are incredible promises of future glory that we can know by faith will one day be fulfilled, because of God's inherent trustworthiness.

At least we should take all of God's promises in confident faith. When you see biblical assurances of God's goodness, as in today's scripture, or hear the words of a wise believer like Charles Spurgeon, take them to heart. Know that God always keeps His promises, and among them is this: "He who began a good work in you will carry it on to completion until the day of Christ Jesus" (Philippians 1:6 NIV). If that isn't strength for the challenges of life, what is?

—COMMIT TO GOD'S TRUTH—

*But you, dear friends, by building yourselves up in your
most holy faith and praying in the Holy Spirit, keep
yourselves in God's love as you wait for the mercy of
our Lord Jesus Christ to bring you to eternal life.*
JUDE 20–21 NIV

The New Testament letter of Jude bears some striking similarities
to 2 Peter. Jude—believed by many to be a half brother of Jesus
(see Matthew 13:55 and Mark 6:3)—actually quoted Peter in verses
17 and 18: "But, dear friends, remember what the apostles of our
Lord Jesus Christ foretold. They said to you, 'In the last times there
will be scoffers who will follow their own ungodly desires' " (see
2 Peter 3:3). And Jude made several other allusions found in the
second chapter of 2 Peter: about the imprisonment of fallen angels;
the destruction of Sodom and Gomorrah; proud sinners who speak
evil of "celestial beings," and false teachers and their condemnation.
Jude even echoed some of Peter's descriptions of false teachers:
compare "mists driven by a storm" (2 Peter 2:17) and "clouds
without rain, blown along by the wind" (Jude 12).

In today's world, some might accuse Jude of plagiarism. But we
can assume that God was simply directing Jude to confirm and
fortify the important message Peter had shared.

False teaching destroys lives. Careful study, good doctrine,
and obedience to God's Word makes us strong, ready for any and
every attack of the world, the flesh, and the devil. We can, as Jude
urges in today's scripture, build ourselves up in the faith and keep
ourselves in God's love. But to do so, we must commit ourselves
to God's truth.

ONE OF GOD'S PEOPLE

"Shout and be glad, Daughter Zion. For I am coming, and I will live among you," declares the LORD. "Many nations will be joined with the LORD in that day and will become my people."
ZECHARIAH 2:10–11 NIV

Chances are, most people reading this devotional do not have a Jewish heritage. God's historic people make up only a tiny percentage of the world population.

But even though the Old Testament is largely the story of God choosing a man (Abraham) and making a special nation of his family (Israel), there are also indicators that one day everyone will have an opportunity to become one of God's people. Today's scripture, from the prophet Zechariah, is a case in point.

While the recently exiled Jews were rebuilding the temple in Jerusalem, God promised His presence and protection, saying, "whoever touches you touches the apple of [My] eye" (verse 8). The Lord told the people that He was coming to live among them, making Jerusalem and Judah his "portion in the holy land" (verse 12).

That's a beautiful promise to an ancient people, but there's also good news for Gentiles today. A time would come when many other people would be joined to the Lord and become His own. Though the ultimate fulfillment of the prophecy remains to be seen, we know that "if anyone acknowledges that Jesus is the Son of God, God lives in them and they in God" (1 John 4:15 NIV).

Today, enjoy all the power and privilege that being one of God's people implies.

CLASSICS: D. L. MOODY

NOT FINDING FAULT

Do all things without murmurings and disputings: that ye may be blameless and harmless, the sons of God, without rebuke, in the midst of a crooked and perverse nation, among whom ye shine as lights in the world.
PHILIPPIANS 2:14–15 KJV

I remember hearing of a Sunday school in our country where the teacher had got into ruts. A young man was placed in charge as superintendent, and he wanted to rearrange the seats. Some of the older members said the seats had been in their present position for so many years that they could not be moved!

There is a good deal of that kind of spirit nowadays. It seems to me that if one method is not successful we ought to give it up and try some other plan that may be more likely to succeed. If the people will not come to the regular "means of grace," let us adopt some means that will reach them and win them. Do not let us be finding fault because things are not done exactly as they have been done in the past, and as we think they ought to be done.

But let us go forward with the work that God has given us to do.

HOW MUCH IS ENOUGH?

*The rabble with them began to crave other food,
and again the Israelites started wailing and said,
"If only we had meat to eat! . . . Now we have lost
our appetite; we never see anything but this manna!"*
NUMBERS 11:4, 6 NIV

Moses had brought the Hebrew people out of Egypt. They were moving toward the land that God had promised to Abraham many years earlier. The journey was arduous, and food and water were scarce. At various times, the people—who numbered in the hundreds of thousands—became upset. They took out their frustrations on Moses.

The people began to look back on their captivity with nostalgia, longing for the small pleasures from that time: "the fish we ate in Egypt at no cost—also the cucumbers, melons, leeks, onions and garlic" (Numbers 11:5 NIV). Because of the hardships of the transition, they couldn't see that God was moving them on to a much more wonderful existence. The Israelites wanted more when they should have been content with what they had.

Overcoming discontentment is a challenge for all of us. But the fact is that God has provided enough for each of us today. Impressive job titles, larger homes, and fancier cars are temporary at best, idolatrous at worst. Contentment is a choice, as the apostle Paul indicated: "If we have food and clothing, we will be content with that" (1 Timothy 6:8 NIV). And as we choose to say, "I have enough," we find strength for the challenges we face.

WHY DO BAD THINGS HAPPEN?

As Jesus was walking along, he saw a man who had been blind from birth. "Rabbi," his disciples asked him, "why was this man born blind? Was it because of his own sins or his parents' sins?" "It was not because of his sins or his parents' sins," Jesus answered. "This happened so the power of God could be seen in him."
JOHN 9:1–3 NLT

At the Feast of the Tabernacles in Jerusalem, when Jesus encountered a man born blind, the disciples assumed the man's condition was due to sin. But was it the man's own sin or the sin of his parents?

Before we look at Jesus' answer, let's add context to the miracle that followed.

The Feast of the Tabernacles commemorated the Israelites' wilderness experience with people building *sukkot*—frail huts—as they would have had in the wilderness. The feast also featured the drawing of water from the Pool of Siloam and the lighting of lamps at the temple.

After declaring Himself the living water (John 7:37–38) and the light of the world (John 8:12), Jesus was about to heal a man born in darkness with water from Siloam.

Why was this man born blind? So God's power could be shown, testifying the truth about Jesus. He is the living water and the light of the world—a Savior who loves and heals the weak.

When we ask why bad things happen, our focus is in the wrong place. We should ask what God is seeking to do in our troubles. Let's simply believe in His power and rely on His strength to bring us into light and life everlasting.

A PERSONAL STAKE

*And king David said to Ornan, Nay; but I will verily buy it
for the full price: for I will not take that which is thine
for the Lord, nor offer burnt offerings without cost.*
1 Chronicles 21:24 kjv

In 1 Chronicles 21, we find examples of David's willful sin and of
his careful response.

First the sin: In an apparent act of pride, David commanded Joab
to count the number of Israelites. Joab tried to dissuade the king,
but "the king's word prevailed" (verse 4 kjv). God was angered by
David's decision, and offered him a choice of punishments: three
years of famine in the land, three months of enemy oppression, or
three days of pestilence sent by God. David chose the third option,
trusting that God's mercy would limit the pain. Still, seventy thousand Israelites died. As David begged for mercy on his people, God
sent a prophet to tell the king to set up an altar at the threshing
floor of a farmer named Ornan.

Now, the response: When David requested Ornan's land for
the altar, the farmer immediately offered to give it to David without cost—along with the materials for the sacrifice itself. But
David wisely declined the offer, saying "I will not take for the Lord
what is yours, or sacrifice a burnt offering that costs me nothing"
(verse 24 niv).

The king paid Ornan and set up an altar, and God relented from
His punishment. David realized that his own choice had created
the problem, and he needed a personal stake in the solution. May
we always do the same.

Classics: Charles Spurgeon

THEY NEED NOT FEAR

For the Lord God is a sun and shield: the Lord will give grace and glory: no good thing will he withhold from them that walk uprightly. O Lord of hosts, blessed is the man that trusteth in thee.
Psalm 84:11–12 kjv

Have you fears about the future? I need not stay to tell you how sweetly the text will lull them all to sleep. Yet suffer me these few sentences.

Do you fear the darkness of future trial? The Lord God is your sun. Do you fear dangers which lie before you in some new sphere upon which you are just entering? The Lord will be your shield. Are there difficulties in your way? Will you need great wisdom and strength? God's grace will be sufficient for you, and His strength will be glorified in your weakness. Do you fear failure? Do you dread final apostasy? It shall not be. He who gives you grace will, without fail, give you glory.

Between here and heaven there is provender for all the flock of God, so that they need not fear famishing on the road. He that leads them shall guide them into pastures that never wither and to fountains that are never dried up, for "no good thing will he withhold from them that walk uprightly."

STRENGTH FOR THE CHALLENGE, INDEED!

*Not by might, nor by power, but by
my spirit, saith the Lord of hosts.*
ZECHARIAH 4:6 KJV

God isn't against us having might and power. Just the opposite. But the only source of true and lasting strength is the Lord's Holy Spirit indwelling and filling us. Another Old Testament prophet put it like this: "Truly I am full of power by the spirit of the Lord, and of judgment, and of might, to declare unto Jacob his transgression, and to Israel his sin" (Micah 3:8 KJV).

The Old Testament couldn't be more clear that God is the only source of true strength. "Great is our Lord, and of great power" (Psalm 147:5 KJV). "Behold, the Lord God will come with strong hand, and his arm shall rule for him" (Isaiah 40:10 KJV, see also verse 26). "There is none like unto thee, O Lord; thou art great, and thy name is great in might" (Jeremiah 10:6 KJV, see also 16:21).

Why is the Lord the only source of might and power? Think about who He is: the One who could simply speak the word and create the entire universe out of nothing. All the power and might in the universe is a speck compared to His. The Lord God is omnipotent, indeed.

This God knows every challenge you face—and He won't even break a sweat to give you strength.

YES, YOU CAN

Be on guard. Stand firm in the faith.
Be courageous. Be strong.
1 CORINTHIANS 16:13–14 NLT

Don't believe anyone who tells you the Christian life is easy. In the same way, don't believe anyone who says the Christian life is impossible.

Throughout scripture, we see that God empowers us for His purposes. But He also expect us to do our part. As the apostle Paul said in 1 Corinthians 15:10, "I worked harder than any of the other apostles; yet it was not I but God who was working through me by his grace" (NLT). Paul did his human part, and God did His divine part. Paul stepped out in faith, and God gave the grace to accomplish tremendous things.

That's why, in today's Bible reading, Paul could issue a string of commands to the Christians of Corinth—and, by extension, to all of us who follow Jesus nearly two thousand years later. "Be on guard. Stand firm in the faith. Be courageous. Be strong." Are those things easy? No. Are they impossible? Absolutely not. Our job is to obey. God's promise is to empower. He will empower as we obey.

Paul's teaching is simply an elaboration of something Jesus Himself said: "All who love me will do what I say. My Father will love them, and we will come and make our home with each of them" (John 14:23 NLT).

If the Trinity is making its home with you, you'll have strength for every challenge.

Yes, you can.

EMPTINESS

"Meaningless! Meaningless!" says the Teacher.
"Utterly meaningless! Everything is meaningless."
ECCLESIASTES 1:2 NIV

Solomon was the wisest man who ever lived (1 Kings 3:12). But after a lifetime of trying everything under the sun to fill the deepest longings of his heart, the conclusion he drew is shocking: "When I surveyed all that my hands had done and what I had toiled to achieve, everything was meaningless, a chasing after the wind; nothing was gained under the sun" (Ecclesiastes 2:11 NIV).

Solomon had everything this world has to offer. *Everything*. But even a casual reading of Ecclesiastes makes it painfully clear that he was not happy. Something was missing, and Solomon knew it. No matter what he tried, all his attempts at finding happiness were nothing more than chasing after the wind.

This, of course, should come as no surprise. Nothing this world offers is big enough to fill the all-consuming hole in our hearts. Sin created the void. Only Jesus can fill it.

Even when we know Jesus, we will sometimes find ourselves struggling with the emptiness Solomon felt. Unlike him, though, we have the Holy Spirit living permanently within us. As Jesus said, "I will pray the Father, and he shall give you another Comforter, that he may abide with you for ever" (John 14:16 KJV).

In seasons of emptiness, you have the entire Trinity working on your behalf. Pray! God will bring you through.

SELFISHNESS IS THE DEATH OF FAITH

*So the Philistines were subdued, and they came no more
into the coast of Israel: and the hand of the LORD was
against the Philistines all the days of Samuel.*
1 SAMUEL 7:13 KJV

Another thought of no less importance, that comes as we think of the achievements of faith in the history of Israel, is how closely they were all identified with the public welfare, with lives devoted to the cause of God and the people. Selfishness is the death of faith. *How can ye believe who take honor one of another?*

As long as we seek to be strong in faith for the sake of our own comfort and goodness and the possession of power, even if we dream of using it all for others, when once we obtain it, we shall fail. It is the soul that at once, in its weakness, gives itself up for the sake of God and others that will find in that self-sacrifice the need and the right to claim God's mighty help. Gideon and Barak, David and Samuel, they were all men whose names and whose faith would never have been known, but that they lived for their nation and God's cause in it, that they were God's chosen instruments for doing His redeeming work in His people.

CONCERTED ACTION

Even though the people were afraid of the local residents, they rebuilt the altar at its old site. Then they began to sacrifice burnt offerings on the altar to the Lord each morning and evening.
EZRA 3:3 NLT

Jewish exiles returning from Babylon to Judah could not immediately resume their worship rituals—God's temple and altar in Jerusalem had been destroyed decades earlier. Though the temple itself would take some time to rebuild, the people decided to erect a new altar as soon as they could, "even though they were afraid of the local residents."

"Apprehension of danger should stir us up to our duty," the old-time Bible commentator Matthew Henry wrote. "Have we many enemies? Then it is good to have God our friend and to keep up our correspondence with him. This good use we should make of our fears, we should be driven by them to our knees."

Ezra 3 doesn't specifically mention prayer, but it's safe to assume the people prayed. Those Israelites who rebuilt the altar quickly reinstituted their worship of God, as "they began to sacrifice burnt offerings on the altar to the Lord each morning and evening."

Though the Jews originally felt fear, they overcame it by concerted action. That's why it's so important to maintain fellowship with other believers, as the writer of Hebrews said: "Let us not neglect our meeting together, as some people do, but encourage one another, especially now that the day of [Jesus'] return is drawing near" (10:25 NLT).

TIMES OF REFRESHING

Repent ye therefore, and be converted, that your sins may be blotted out, when the times of refreshing shall come from the presence of the Lord. And he shall send Jesus Christ, which before was preached unto you.
ACTS 3:19–20 KJV

Repentance is a discovery of the evil of sin, a mourning that we have committed it, a resolution to forsake it. It is, in fact, a change of mind of a very deep and practical character, which makes the man love what once he hated, and hate what once he loved.

Conversion, if translated, means a turning round, a turning from, and a turning to—a turning from sin, a turning to holiness—a turning from carelessness to thought, from the world to heaven, from self to Jesus—a complete turning.

When the prodigal was feeding his swine and on a sudden began to consider and to come to himself, that was repentance. When he set out and left the far country and went to his father's house, that was conversion. Repentance is a part of conversion. It is, perhaps, I may say, the gate or door of it.

— ON THE WAY TO GODLINESS —

"This is what the LORD Almighty said: 'Administer true justice; show mercy and compassion to one another. Do not oppress the widow or the fatherless, the foreigner or the poor. Do not plot evil against each other.'"
ZECHARIAH 7:9–10 NIV

In this life, godliness means everything. And this is not some mystical, ethereal thing. Godliness has to do with physical, social, and economic challenges all around us.

Throughout scripture, the Lord often demanded justice, mercy, and compassion—the protection of the most vulnerable from oppression. He denounced the plotting of evil against anyone. God didn't focus on one particular theme—He cares about every aspect of human existence and He wants His people to do the same.

While the needs of our world may seem overwhelming, God has kindly provided us with strength for the challenge: some clear, manageable steps toward doing good. Zechariah quoted the Lord's command to show mercy and compassion to each other, to avoid taking advantage of the weak, and to say "no" to any evil thinking against others. In the New Testament, James added some practical ideas: "Religion that God our Father accepts as pure and faultless is this: to look after orphans and widows in their distress and to keep oneself from being polluted by the world" (1:27 NIV).

Individually, none of these tasks are overwhelming. They just require a commitment to do what God says. And, as always, He will provide the strength to succeed. Then you will find yourself on the way to godliness.

LINKED TO THE GOD OF HEAVEN

And when the LORD saw that he turned aside to see,
God called unto him out of the midst of the bush, and said,
Moses, Moses. And he said, Here am I. And he said,
Draw not nigh hither: put off thy shoes from off thy feet,
for the place whereon thou standest is holy ground.
EXODUS 3:4–5 KJV

Look at Moses. He, too, was in communion with God. When Moses and Aaron stood before Pharaoh, the stubborn king did not see the third Person with them. If he had, he might have acted altogether differently. The idea of those two unarmed men going before the mighty monarch of Egypt and demanding that he should give three million slaves their liberty! The idea of these two men making such an extraordinary demand as that! But they were in communion with the God of heaven, and such men always succeed.

Moses was the mightiest man who lived in his day. Why? Because God walked with him, and he was linked to the God of heaven. Moses alone was nothing. He was a man like you and me; but he was the meekest of men, and "the meek shall inherit the earth" (Psalm 37:11 KJV; see also Matthew 5:5). He was famous because he walked with his God.

HUMILITY

Now Moses was a very humble man,
more humble than anyone else on the face of the earth.
NUMBERS 12:3 NIV

Humility is referenced often on the pages of scripture. For example,

- "He has brought down rulers from their thrones but has lifted up the humble" (Luke 1:52 NIV).
- "For all those who exalt themselves will be humbled, and those who humble themselves will be exalted" (Luke 14:11 NIV).
- "Be completely humble and gentle; be patient, bearing with one another in love" (Ephesians 4:2 NIV).
- "Humble yourselves, therefore, under God's mighty hand, that he may lift you up in due time" (1 Peter 5:6 NIV).

Moses may well have inspired some of these verses. Though he was God's chosen leader for the nation of Israel, he rarely acted from his own desires. Moses routinely spent time alone, talking to God about his duties and the nation he'd been tasked to serve. To be considered the humblest man "on the face of the earth" is an amazing testimony to Moses' character—and his reliance on God for strength and wisdom.

A humble attitude is the key ingredient to our success, the strength we need for the challenges of this life. When we are weak, the apostle Paul said, we are strong (2 Corinthians 12:10)—because God applies His strength to us.

And the beauty of humility is that anyone can pursue it. If you humble yourself under God's mighty hand, He will lift you up, in His perfect way and time.

—— STUDY, PRACTICE, TEACH ——

*Ezra had devoted himself to the study and
observance of the Law of the LORD, and to
teaching its decrees and laws in Israel.*
EZRA 7:10 NIV

Some time after the first wave of Jewish exiles rebuilt and dedicated the temple, Ezra made his way from Babylon to Jerusalem. Descended from the line of Aaron, Ezra was a scribe well-versed in the Law of Moses. According to Ezra 7:6, God's hand was on him—and today's scripture explains why.

While exiled in Babylon, Ezra could have given up hope. He could have let his faith dwindle or disappear. Instead, he chose to devote himself to God's Word. Not just to studying it, but also to observing (that is, practicing) and teaching it. Ezra seemed to know what the New Testament writer James would teach many years later: "Do not merely listen to the word, and so deceive yourselves. Do what it says" (1:22 NIV).

It doesn't matter where we live or what situation we find ourselves in: like Ezra, we can devote ourselves to the study, observance, and teaching of God's Word. When we do, we'll find God's hand upon our lives too. He can and will use you right where you are—and He uses those who know Him best through His Word.

THE ONLY SHEPHERD

*"My sheep listen to my voice; I know them, and they
follow me. I give them eternal life, and they shall never
perish; no one will snatch them out of my hand."*
JOHN 10:27–28 NIV

The Feast of Dedication (also known as the Festival of Lights, or Hanukkah) was instituted between the Old and New Testaments. After the invading Seleucid monarch Antiochus IV Epiphanes installed corrupt priests who desecrated the Jewish temple, the Maccabees recaptured and rededicated it to God in 164 BC. This festival specifically celebrates the miracle of the temple's candelabrum burning for eight full days on only one day's worth of oil.

In Jesus' time, the feast was commemorated with readings from Ezekiel 34, which compares good and bad shepherds. Jewish listeners would have recognized the passage as a warning against corrupt priests who could desecrate the temple again. But Jesus gave the passage new meaning.

He was surrounded by people asking Him plainly whether or not He was the Christ. Jesus replied that if they didn't believe He was the Christ, they weren't His sheep. Jesus was more than a good shepherd—He was the only Shepherd who could lead people to eternal life.

Today, many "shepherds" promise us comfort and peace. But only by listening to the one true Shepherd will we find our way home. We hear Jesus' voice when we read and study His Word.

DO NOT JUDGE BY PRESENT CIRCUMSTANCES

*Behold, I know your thoughts, and the devices
which ye wrongfully imagine against me.*
JOB 21:27 KJV

The main drift of the book of Job is to prove that temporal afflictions are not evidences of the Lord's displeasure. In my very soul I feel that if evil days shall come upon me, if poverty, desertion and disease should place me upon Job's dunghill, I shall point to that sermon with pleasure, and say to those who will tell me that God is angry with me and has judged me to be unworthy, "Nay, ye know not what ye say, for the judgment is not passed already, nor is this the field of execution; neither disease, nor bereavements, nor poverty, can prove a man to be wicked, nor do they even hint that the chosen are divided from the hearts of Christ."

O my beloved friends, settle it in your hearts that men are not to be judged according to their present circumstances, and learn like David to understand their end. It will save you from writing bitter things against yourselves in the time of trouble and prevent your scanning the works of Providence and measuring the infinite by line and plummet.

—— TRUST GOD'S PROMISES ——

Smite the shepherd, and the sheep shall be scattered.
ZECHARIAH 13:7 KJV

Some Bible students and teachers have confused this clear-cut prophecy with a similar but very different one: "I saw all Israel scattered upon the hills, as sheep that have not a shepherd: and the LORD said, These have no master: let them return every man to his house in peace" (1 Kings 22:17; 2 Chronicles 18:16 KJV).

That particular prophecy, spoken by the prophet Micaiah about wicked king Ahab, was fulfilled almost immediately (1 Kings 22:34–36; 2 Chronicles 18:33–34). In direct contrast to Micaiah's prophecy of Ahab's death, God told Zechariah that the future Messiah would be struck and His disciples would scatter.

Another prophet, Isaiah, wrote at length about the Messiah, describing how God's Anointed would be stricken, smitten, and pierced (Isaiah 53:4–5), and would suffer death for us because of our sins (53:5–6). To save His lost sheep, who had strayed away (53:6), the Good Shepherd would become the sinless Lamb of God who died, was buried, and rose again (Isaiah 53:7–10).

Jesus Himself quoted today's scripture (not Micaiah's prophecy) shortly before His arrest (Matthew 26:31; Mark 14:27). After more than five hundred years, Zechariah's prophecy came true exactly as stated.

Knowing that God can perfectly fulfill the long-term predictions He makes should give us hope in every circumstance of life. His promises of the Messiah proved true, and His promises of help and blessing to us certainly will too.

ALL-SURPASSING POWER

*But we have this treasure in jars of clay to show
that this all-surpassing power is from God and not
from us. We are hard pressed on every side, but not
crushed; perplexed, but not in despair; persecuted,
but not abandoned; struck down, but not destroyed.*

2 Corinthians 4:7–9 niv

When we read the book of Acts or the various letters of Paul, we recognize how many hardships Jesus' apostles and the early church faced. They were willing even to die for their faith. Paul himself wrote of being hungry, beaten, smuggled out of a city at night, and even shipwrecked in his service to God. Many of us would be tempted to quit if faced with such adversity.

But Paul explained how he continued to do God's work in spite of the troubles he faced. He tapped into a power source that was not his own. It was the power of God.

As men, we're tempted to use our own resources, to rely on our own hard work when we are faced with the obstacles of life. But we will encounter situations that are simply too big to overcome on our own. Then our choice is to either give up or turn to God's "all-surpassing power."

This is the power Paul described to the Corinthian Christians. In our own strength, we would be crushed, despairing, and destroyed. Through prayer and petition to God, though, we can continue. Only by faith and trust in our heavenly Father can we withstand the pressures of life's challenges.

FAITHFUL IN VERY LITTLE

*Then came the first, saying, Lord, thy pound hath
gained ten pounds. And he said unto him, Well,
thou good servant: because thou hast been faithful in
a very little, have thou authority over ten cities.*
LUKE 19:16–17 KJV

In His wisdom and for His own purposes, God gives people varying abilities. But whether a Christian sweeps the streets or serves as ruler of his country, he is expected to do his best.

Jesus told similar parables in Luke 19 and Matthew 25, describing a wealthy man planning a trip to a "far country." Knowing that he would be away for some time, he called his servants together and distributed money for them to use in conducting business. In Matthew, one servant received five talents (an amount of gold or silver) and gained an additional five; one servant received two talents, and gained two more. In Luke, several servants each received a pound (about a hundred days' wages), with one man gaining an impressive ten in return, and the next, five. In both stories, when the wealthy man returned home to collect his money, he commended the industrious servants for being "faithful in a very little." They were rewarded with much larger opportunities.

The beauty of these stories is that God doesn't expect us to match outcomes with more gifted people. He simply wants us to do our best. And that's possible for any of us. When we do, we put ourselves in line for His greater blessing.

── LIVE AS FOREIGNERS ──

*Thou art the LORD the God, who didst choose Abram, and
brought him forth out of Ur of the Chaldees, and gavest
him the name of Abraham; and foundest his heart faithful
before thee, and madest a covenant with him to give the land
of the Canaanites, the Hittites, the Amorites, and the Perizzites,
and the Jebusites, and the Girgashites, to give it, I say, to his
seed, and hast performed thy words; for thou art righteous.*
NEHEMIAH 9:7–8 KJV

By faith [Abraham] saw the unseen; in hope he lived in the future.
He had his heart as little in Canaan as in Haran; it was in heaven;
it was with God. And we, who have been called to enter into the
true tabernacle which God hath pitched—oh, shall we not obey
and go out, even though it be not knowing whither we go. Let us
separate ourselves entirely from the world and its spirit; let us, like
the Son, die to the creature, that we may live to God.

A worldly spirit in the church or the Christian is a deadly disease: it makes the life of faith impossible. Let us count it our worst
enemy and live as foreigners, who seek the city which is to come.
Let us hear the voice calling us out to Himself, to close fellowship,
to obedience as of the angels in heaven, to be a testimony and a
blessing for the world.

GOD FIGHTS FOR YOU

*For I was ashamed to ask the king for soldiers and horsemen
to keep us safe from those who hate us on the way, because
we had said to the king, "The hand of our God brings good to
all who look for Him. But His power and His anger are against
all who turn away from Him." So we did not eat, and prayed
to God about this. And He listened to our prayer.*

EZRA 8:22–23 NLV

Ezra traveled from Babylon to Jerusalem with a large group of exiles, which included women and children as well as the elderly. He'd considered asking the king for soldiers and horsemen to keep the group safe from its enemies, but he was ashamed to do so after telling the king that God would watch out for them. Rather than begging from the king of Persia, he turned to the King of the universe in fasting and prayer. And God was faithful.

Don't you appreciate Ezra's honesty? Though he didn't need to, he basically told on himself. We can take encouragement from his story.

The good news, for anyone who follows God, is that He will not only fight for His name—He'll fight for anyone who claims His name in faith (see Exodus 14:14; Deuteronomy 1:30, 20:4). God especially honors those who fast and pray to seek His will.

Perhaps it's time to spend a season in fasting and prayer over an issue you face. Take your Bible and a notebook, and spend some time alone with God. He'll be faithful to provide the spiritual strength you need to return to the daily battle of life.

CHRIST IS THERE

But [Stephen], being full of the Holy Ghost, looked up stedfastly into heaven, and saw the glory of God, and Jesus standing on the right hand of God, and said, Behold, I see the heavens opened, and the Son of man standing on the right hand of God.
ACTS 7:55–56 KJV

When Stephen was being stoned he lifted up his eyes, and it seemed as if God rolled back the curtain of time and allowed him to look into the eternal city and see Christ standing at the right hand of God. When Jesus Christ went on high He led captivity captive and took His seat, for His work was done; but when Stephen saw Him He was standing up, and I can imagine He saw that martyr fighting, as it were, singlehanded and alone, the first martyr, though many were to come after him. You can hear the tramp of the millions coming after him, to lay down their lives for the Son of God.

But Stephen led the van; he was the first martyr, and as he was dying for the Lord Jesus Christ he looked up; Christ was standing to give him a welcome, and the Holy Ghost came down to bear witness that Christ was there. How then can we doubt it?

── NO GAMES WITH GOD ──

This is the message that the LORD gave to Israel through
the prophet Malachi. "I have always loved you," says the
LORD. But you retort, "Really? How have you loved us?" . . .
"A son honors his father, and a servant respects his master.
If I am your father and master, where are the honor and respect
I deserve? You have shown contempt for my name! But you ask,
'How have we ever shown contempt for your name?' "
MALACHI 1:1–2, 6–7 NLT

The last Old Testament prophet, Malachi, urged his readers to quit playing games with God.

After the Exile, during the days of Ezra and Nehemiah, the Israelites finished rebuilding Jerusalem yet quickly turned away from the Lord. They maintained a form of religion, but their worship was a sham.

Malachi challenged the insincerity and corruption of his people with hard-hitting exhortations. Many of them took the form of a dialogue between God and the people. In these dialogues, the Lord makes a statement, only to be countered by his people: "Really? How. . . ?"

Like the New Testament book of James, Malachi is a rapid-fire series of mini sermons on practicing true religion, honoring the Lord's name, obeying God's Word, teaching what is right, doing what is just, living in light of the Lord's coming judgment, not oppressing the downtrodden, forsaking pride, fearing God, and loving Him with all one's heart, soul, strength, and mind.

Playing games with God never ends well. Let's take Him and His Word seriously.

WE SERVE AN INDESTRUCTIBLE GOD

*Lord, thou hast been our dwelling place in all
generations. Before the mountains were brought forth,
or ever thou hadst formed the earth and the world,
even from everlasting to everlasting, thou art God.*
PSALM 90:1–2 KJV

Eternity has generally been considered as divisible into two parts, which have been termed, in plain English, that eternity which is past and that eternity which is to come. And does there not seem to be an intimation of this distinction in the text?

"Thou art God from everlasting"—Here is an expression of that eternity which is past. "To everlasting"—Here is an expression of that eternity which is to come. Perhaps, indeed, some may think it is not strictly proper to say there is an eternity that is past. But the meaning is easily understood: We mean thereby duration which had no beginning; as by eternity to come, we mean that duration which will have no end.

It is God alone who (to use the exalted language of scripture) "inhabiteth eternity" in both these senses. The great Creator alone (not any of His creatures) is "from everlasting to everlasting": His duration alone, as it had no beginning, so it cannot have any end.

POSITIVE. . .IN GOD

Then Caleb silenced the people before Moses and said, "We should go up and take possession of the land, for we can certainly do it." But the men who had gone up with him said, "We can't attack those people; they are stronger than we are."
NUMBERS 13:30–31 NIV

Twelve men, the leaders of large family groups within the nation of Israel, were given the task of investigating the land that God had promised to Abraham. Compared to the sands of Egypt and the barren wilderness of the Arabian Peninsula, Canaan was a place of true beauty and productivity. They called it a land "flowing with milk and honey."

Sadly, ten of the twelve spies argued against entering the land. The people there were too strong, they said. "We seemed like grasshopper in our own eyes," they reported, "and we looked the same to them" (Numbers 13:33 NIV).

Caleb disagreed with his fellow spies. A man of great faith, he took God at His word. Caleb remembered God's protection in Egypt. He remembered God's deliverance from slavery. He remembered crossing the Red Sea on dry ground. And he knew that God had promised this land to His people.

"Positive thinking" doesn't automatically change things. But thinking positively of God's promises enhances our faith and hope in His ultimate blessing. Be positive in God, and you'll enjoy the emotional and spiritual strength of Caleb.

GOD IS KIND

*"What has happened to us is a result of our
evil deeds and our great guilt, and yet, our God,
you have punished us less than our sins deserved."*
EZRA 9:13 NIV

Everyone makes mistakes. That's a part of being human. But there are times when, even as Christians, we go beyond simple errors and into the territory of outright sin. Certainly, that's not a place we want to live. But even if we've made a foolish sojourn, we can take encouragement from the book of Ezra.

He was a priest who returned to the Jewish homeland from exile in Persia. The Israelites had been scattered decades earlier by the Babylonians, in punishment for their ongoing disobedience to God. Now, having returned to Jerusalem in waves, they were *still* sinning: "The people of Israel, including the priests and Levites, have not kept themselves separate from the neighboring peoples with their detestable practices," Ezra was told. "They have taken some of their daughters as wives for themselves and their sons, and have mingled the holy race with the peoples around them. And the leaders and officials have led the way in this unfaithfulness" (verses 1–2 NIV).

Ezra responded with an agonized prayer of confession, one that recognized God's kindness even in the punishment. It was not as much as the people deserved.

And that is how God deals with us today—kindly, mercifully, with restraint. And like the father in Jesus' parable of the lost son (Luke 15:11–32), He is always watching for us to come home.

DEALING WITH DEATH

Jesus wept.
JOHN 11:35 KJV

Lazarus, the brother of Martha and Mary—all beloved friends of Jesus—got sick and died. Jesus learned of the illness but lingered where He was a couple more days. By the time He reached the town of Bethany, Lazarus had been dead for four days.

Martha and Mary were crushed. Seeing their sadness, Jesus was "deeply moved in spirit and troubled" (John 11:33 NIV). Then He wept.

Though He knew He was about to raise Lazarus from the dead, Jesus wept. Though He had just told Martha that He was the resurrection and the life (John 11:25), He wept.

Jesus' sadness was not an example of weakness in the face of difficulty. Nor was it a lack of faith in His own ability to set things right. His weeping was a recognition of the suffering that death causes.

Death is never easy to deal with. God didn't design humanity to die, but sin brought death with it. Death, however, brings the possibility of reunification with our perfect Creator. Thanks to Jesus' death and resurrection, we are now eligible for eternal life with God.

Death is a time to weep. Resurrection is cause for celebration.

"Brothers and sisters," the apostle Paul wrote, "we do not want you to be uninformed about those who sleep in death, so that you do not grieve like the rest of mankind, who have no hope. For we believe that Jesus died and rose again, and so we believe that God will bring with Jesus those who have fallen asleep in him" (1 Thessalonians 4:13–14 NIV).

—— A BADGE IN THE HEART ——

That the righteousness of the law might be fulfilled in us,
who walk not after the flesh, but after the Spirit. For they that
are after the flesh do mind the things of the flesh; but they that
are after the Spirit the things of the Spirit. For to be carnally
minded is death; but to be spiritually minded is life and peace.
ROMANS 8:4–6 KJV

Oh, God hates a sham! It means a good deal to be a Christian, and if a person is going to be a Christian, let him put off the old man with all his deeds and put on the new man. That is the kind of Christians we need at the present time, "for to be carnally minded is death; but to be spiritually minded is life and peace."

How are you going to tell whether you are a Christian or not? Not by the fact that you are a Catholic or a Protestant, not that you subscribe to some creed that man has drawn up. We must have something better than that.

What did Christ say? "By this shall all men know that ye are my disciples, if ye have love one to another" (John 13:35 KJV). I used to wish, when I was first converted, that every Christian had to wear a badge, because I would like to know them; my heart went out toward the household of faith. But I have got over that. Every hypocrite would have a badge on inside of thirty days, if Christianity had become popular. No badge outside; but God gives us a badge in the heart.

BLESSED IN GIVING

"Should people cheat God? Yet you have cheated me! But you ask, 'What do you mean? When did we ever cheat you?' You have cheated me of the tithes and offerings due to me. You are under a curse, for your whole nation has been cheating me. Bring all the tithes into the storehouse so there will be enough food in my Temple. If you do," says the LORD of Heaven's Armies, "I will open the windows of heaven for you. I will pour out a blessing so great you won't have enough room to take it in!"
MALACHI 3:8–10 NLT

In the book of Exodus, God gave Moses instructions for giving, rules that applied to all the Lord's people as well as the foreigners among them. Some scholars suggest the people paid a total of one-third of their income in tithes and even more in offerings.

Human nature being what it is, people often balked. By the end of the Old Testament, when Malachi prophesied, God's people were "cheating" the Lord of His offerings. As a result, their herds dwindled and their crops failed or were wiped out by marauders from wicked nations.

But see how God views giving: when His people honor Him with a portion of what He's given, He throws open "the windows of heaven." In fact, God says His blessing is "so great you won't have enough room to take it in!"

Even if the promise of Malachi 3:10 was specific to the post-exilic Jews, Jesus shared a similar principle: "Everyone who has given up houses or brothers or sisters or father or mother or children or property, for my sake, will receive a hundred times as much in return and will inherit eternal life" (Matthew 19:29 NLT).

We are blessed in giving.

—— FOCUS ON THE ETERNAL ——

Therefore we do not lose heart. Though outwardly we are wasting away, yet inwardly we are being renewed day by day. For our light and momentary troubles are achieving for us an eternal glory that far outweighs them all. So we fix our eyes not on what is seen, but on what is unseen, since what is seen is temporary, but what is unseen is eternal.
2 CORINTHIANS 4:16–18 NIV

Why were the early Christians so persistent? How could they go to such great lengths for their faith, when their actions often brought persecution and even death?

The reason is simple, actually: their focus was not on the pain and trouble of the present, or even of the remaining years of this life. Instead, their eyes were on their eternal future with Jesus Christ. This is the view that we today can and should take.

No matter what trials and hardships we face, Jesus is worth it. Our brief, passing life—what the book of James calls "a mist" (James 4:14 NIV)—is only a microscopic bit of our entire experience. This life is not the end for followers of Jesus! And that is why Paul did not lose heart. That is why we do not need to lose heart.

Whatever troubles we face today will mean nothing compared to the eternal life of joy we'll one day share with our Lord.

THERE IS A SEASON

*There is a time for everything, and a season
for every activity under the heavens.*
ECCLESIASTES 3:1 NIV

Two children went for a walk with their father. One took delight in the amazing, God-created beauty all around. The other tugged and pulled and whined and complained along the way. Both were surrounded by the same incredible beauty. But only one child was able to enjoy the path his father selected.

One part of faith is the willingness to let God direct our steps no matter what path He takes us on. We must be willing to surrender control completely and live within the season He's chosen for us.

Think about it. What would happen if a farmer decided to plant his corn in the dead of a Pennsylvania winter? Or if that man chose to laugh while everyone around him was weeping? Or if he reopened a wound just as it was beginning to heal? The answers are so obvious they hardly seem worth considering. But is it possible that we do the same thing, in a million little ways, each and every day?

There will always be challenges on the road the Lord lays out for us. But when we trust Him completely and allow Him to direct our paths, we'll find that the clouds will part. The light of God will once again shine on whatever season we're in.

This truly is the path to peace and lifelong fulfillment.

—BRING SIN INTO THE LIGHT—

And said unto them, Hear me, ye Levites, sanctify now
yourselves, and sanctify the house of the Lord God of
your fathers, and carry forth the filthiness out of the holy
place. For our fathers have trespassed, and done that
which was evil in the eyes of the Lord our God, and have
forsaken him, and have turned away their faces from
the habitation of the Lord, and turned their backs.
2 Chronicles 29:5–6 kjv

When Hezekiah called the priests to sanctify the temple that had been defiled, we read, "The priests went in unto the inner part of the house of the Lord to cleanse it, and brought out all the uncleanness that they found." Only then could the sin offering of atonement and the burnt offering of consecration, with the thank offerings, be brought and God's service be restored.

Even thus must all that is unclean be looked out and brought out and utterly cast out. However deeply rooted the sin may appear, rooted in constitution and habit, we must cleanse ourselves of it if we would be holy. "If we walk in the light, as He is in the light, the blood of Jesus Christ cleanseth from all sin" (see 1 John 1:7). Let us come into the light with the sin: the blood will prove its mighty power. Let us cleanse ourselves in yielding ourselves to the light to reveal and condemn, to the blood to cleanse and sanctify.

— FOLLOWING GOD'S LEADING —

So I arrived in Jerusalem. Three days later, I slipped out during the night, taking only a few others with me. I had not told anyone about the plans God had put in my heart for Jerusalem.
NEHEMIAH 2:11–12 NLT

Nehemiah, an Israelite who served as cupbearer for the Persian king, wanted to rebuild Jerusalem, which still lay in ruins decades after the Babylonian invasion. Because "the gracious hand of God was on me" (verse 8 NLT), Artaxerxes allowed Nehemiah to pursue his desire and even promised him materials for the job.

Once in Jerusalem, Nehemiah slipped out during the night to inspect the broken walls and burned gates of the city. In one spot, the rubble was so bad that his donkey couldn't advance.

Now, with a full, personal knowledge of the need, Nehemiah went to the city officials and religious leaders in Jerusalem. "You know very well what trouble we are in," he told them. "Let us rebuild the wall of Jerusalem and end this disgrace!" (verse 17 NLT). Telling the others about his interaction with King Artaxerxes as well as the many blessings of God along the way, Nehemiah got the others to commit to the work. "Yes, let's rebuilt the wall!" they said (verse 18 NLT). And they did—under Nehemiah's leadership, the job was completed in a miraculous fifty-two days.

There's no way Nehemiah could have rebuilt the walls of Jerusalem by himself. But when he followed "the plans God had put in my heart," studying the need and assembling a good team, success was sure to follow. It's a pattern that works for all kinds of situations.

CLOTHED BY GOD

This is a faithful saying, and worthy of all
acceptation, that Christ Jesus came into the
world to save sinners; of whom I am chief.
1 TIMOTHY 1:15 KJV

Paul said he was the "chief" of sinners, and if the chief has gone up on high there is hope for everybody else.

The devil makes us believe that we are good enough without salvation, if he can; and if he cannot make us believe that, he says, "You are so bad the Lord won't have you." And so he tries to make people believe because they are so bad Christ won't have anything to do with them.

God invites you to come just as you are. I know a great many people want to come, but they are trying to get better and to get ready to come. Now, mark you, the Lord invites you to come just as you are, and if you could make yourself better you would not be any more acceptable to God. Do not put these filthy rags of self-righteousness about you. God will strip every rag from you when you come to Him, and He will clothe you with His glorious garments.

—— WHY SERVE THE LORD? ——

*"You have said, 'It is futile to serve God. What do we
gain by carrying out his requirements and going
about like mourners before the Lᴏʀᴅ Almighty?'"*
Mᴀʟᴀᴄʜɪ 3:14 ɴɪᴠ

Futile to serve God? Going about like mourners?

The ancient Jews' murmurings is completely the opposite of
Jesus' followers after Pentecost. As people who served God wholeheartedly, in a single generation they established the church across
the entire Roman Empire and beyond. Here's why:

First, they did everything thankfully. "Whatever you do, whether
in word or deed, do it all in the name of the Lord Jesus, giving
thanks to God the Father through him" (Colossians 3:17 ɴɪᴠ).

Second, they did everything as for Jesus. "Whatever you do, work
at it with all your heart, as working for the Lord, not for human
masters, since you know that you will receive an inheritance from
the Lord as a reward" (Colossians 3:23–24 ɴɪᴠ).

Third, they worked wholeheartedly knowing that God would
reward them. "Always give yourselves fully to the work of the
Lord, because you know that your labor in the Lord is not in vain"
(1 Corinthians 15:58 ɴɪᴠ).

Fourth, they deleted words like *tired* and *quit* from their vocab-
ulary. "Let us not become weary in doing good, for at the proper
time we will reap a harvest if we do not give up" (Galatians 6:9 ɴɪᴠ).

Challenges? Yes. Renewed strength? Absolutely.

— THE SLIGHTEST VARIATIONS —

For because ye did it not at the first, the Lord our God made a breach upon us, for that we sought him not after the due order.
1 Chronicles 15:13 kjv

We learn from this narrative—that all changes from the written revelation of God are wrong. There has sprung up in the church of Christ an idea that there are many things taught in the Bible which are not essential; that we may alter them just a little to suit our convenience: that provided we are right in the fundamentals, the other things are of no concern and of no value whatever. And ye think, do ye, that ye may alter some few things, that ye may change them to suit the climate, or to indulge your own ideas of taste or convenience?

But this know, that the slightest violation of the divine law will bring judgments upon the church, and has brought judgments, and is even at this day withholding God's hand from blessing us. For within a few years we might see all the kingdoms of this world become the kingdoms of our Lord and of His Christ, if we would but carry God's ark as God would have it carried, instead of marring the gospel by human inventions and leaving the simplicity of the gospel of Jesus Christ.

GOD IS GENEROUS

*And they came unto the brook of Eshcol, and cut
down from thence a branch with one cluster of grapes,
and they bare it between two upon a staff.*
NUMBERS 13:23 KJV

With the Israelites on the verge of entering their Promised Land,
God told Moses to assemble a team of spies to "search the land of
Canaan" (Numbers 13:2). These spies, one from each of Israel's
twelve tribes, were to discover what Canaan's people and cities
and landscape and agriculture were like.

You may already know the outcome of this mission: ten spies
"brought up an evil report of the land," highlighted by warnings
of "men of a great stature. . .giants. . .we were in our own sight
as grasshoppers, and so we were in their sight" (verses 32–33).
This negativity rippled throughout the Israelite community, causing fear and murmuring. Ultimately, God decreed that the com-
plainers would wander in the wilderness for forty years and die
before entering Canaan. Only the two positive spies—Joshua and
Caleb—would be spared.

What's especially sad is that Canaan was truly a land "flowing
with milk and honey" (Exodus 3:8). At Moses' command to "bring
of the fruit of the land" (Numbers 13:20), the spies—as we see in
today's verse—brought back a bunch of grapes so large it had to
be carried on a pole between two men.

That's an example of God's generosity. He was well aware of the
people already in the land, and He was perfectly capable of dealing with them. Simple obedience would have brought the Israelites
a pleasant, healthy, well provisioned land. Simple obedience brings
similar blessings to us.

PERFECT IN JESUS

*For the law having a shadow of good things to come, and not
the very image of the things, can never with those sacrifices
which they offered year by year continually make the comers
thereunto perfect. For then would they not have ceased to be
offered? because that the worshippers once purged should have
had no more conscience of sins. But in those sacrifices there is a
remembrance again made of sins every year. For it is not possible
that the blood of bulls and of goats should take away sins.*

HEBREWS 10:1–4 KJV

Perfection is not through the law; let us listen to the blessed lesson.

Let us take the warning. The law is so closely connected with
perfection, was so long its only representative and forerunner, that
we can hardly realize: the law makes nothing perfect.

Let us take the encouragement: What the law could not do, God,
sending His Son, hath done. The Son, perfected forevermore, hath
perfected us forever.

It is in Jesus we have our perfection. It is in living union with
Him; it is when He is within us, not only as a seed or a little child,
but formed within us, dwelling within us, that we shall know how
far He can make us perfect.

THAT ONE TASK

"Now my soul is troubled, and what shall I say? 'Father, save
me from this hour'? No, it was for this very reason I came to
this hour. Father, glorify your name!" Then a voice came from
heaven, "I have glorified it, and will glorify it again."
JOHN 12:27–28 NIV

There's always that one task. We cross off the other items on our
to-do list, but when we get to that one thing, we hesitate. Or maybe
it isn't an item on a to-do list, but a tough conversation with a loved
one. Perhaps it's admitting we need help to quit an addiction. It
could be switching jobs or breaking off an unhealthy relationship
or any of countless other challenges. Something about the situation
ahead is troubling your soul.

Jesus has been there. And He has given us the example to follow.

With His public ministry ending and the crucifixion ahead, Jesus
was troubled. He recognized the troublesome task. He reaffirmed
His mission. Then He requested that God be glorified.

We can do the same thing. Recognize, reaffirm, and request.
When we seek to glorify God's name with our weakness, He will
give us the strength for the task ahead. God's name has already
been glorified because we recognize our need for Him, but He
will glorify it again when we complete the task with His strength.

Whatever that one task is, God wants us to succeed. He will provide the encouragement and strength we need to glorify His name.

ALL YOUR NEED

But my God shall supply all your need
according to his riches in glory by Christ Jesus.
PHILIPPIANS 4:19 KJV

Hear what the apostle says: "My God shall supply all your need."
Look at these words carefully.

It does not say He will supply all your wants. There are many
things we want that God has not promised to give. It is "your need"
and "all your need." My children often want many things they
do not get; but I supply all they need, if it is in my power to give
it to them. I do not supply all their wants by any means. My boy
would probably want to have me give him a horse, when I know
that what he really needs, perhaps, is grace to control his temper.

Our children might want many things that it would be injurious
for them to have. And so, though God may withhold from us many
things that we desire, He will supply all our need.

BE A SERVANT

*"Remember the law of my servant Moses,
the decrees and laws I gave him at Horeb for all Israel."*
MALACHI 4:4 NIV

Thousands of Israelite individuals are named in the Hebrew scriptures, but only around forty are named again in the New Testament. The most commonly referenced is Moses, whose name appears around eighty times in the Christian scriptures, some eight hundred times altogether. Do you think he may be important for us to consider?

In today's scripture, Moses is described as "my [the Lord's] servant." The designation isn't something that Malachi coined—it appears nearly forty times in the Hebrew scriptures. At first, Moses called himself God's servant (Exodus 4:10, 13) despite telling the Lord several reasons why he couldn't obey. Later, when Miriam and Aaron bucked their younger brother's authority, the Lord twice strongly affirmed "my servant Moses" (Numbers 12:7–8). God and other main characters frequently spoke of the Lord's servant Moses in the book of Joshua, and there are other scattered usages of this description elsewhere.

Notably, "Moses" and "servant" are not typically used in reference to the Exodus but to the Law. In the former, Aaron shares center stage; in the latter, Moses is the focus. The Exodus was something to be circled on the calendar and celebrated. The Law, however, was something to know and obey daily, wholeheartedly, for all of one's life. Sadly, we rarely see that in the Old Testament except for Joshua, Daniel, and a few others also called "servants" of the Lord.

The point for us is that we can choose to be God's servants. And when we do, He gladly oversees our care and provision.

BE GENEROUS

And now, brothers and sisters, we want you to know about the grace that God has given the Macedonian churches. In the midst of a very severe trial, their overflowing joy and their extreme poverty welled up in rich generosity. For I testify that they gave as much as they were able, and even beyond their ability.
2 CORINTHIANS 8:1–3 NIV

There's an interesting story within the story of three of the apostle Paul's letters. In 1 and 2 Corinthians as well as Romans, he mentions a special offering he was overseeing. "I am on my way to Jerusalem in the service of the Lord's people there," Paul told believers in Rome. "For Macedonia and Achaia were pleased to make a contribution for the poor among the Lord's people in Jerusalem. They were pleased to do it, and indeed they owe it to them. For if the Gentiles have shared in the Jews' spiritual blessings, they owe it to the Jews to share with them their material blessings" (Romans 15:25–27 NIV).

In today's scripture, Paul singled out the churches of Macedonia for their generosity. Like the poor widow commended by Jesus for giving "all she had to live on" (Mark 12:44 NIV), these Macedonian believers, despite their "extreme poverty," gave "as much as they were able, and even beyond their ability."

Paul described the Macedonians' willingness to give as an outgrowth of God's grace. And it was certainly an attitude that God would honor—as Paul once quoted Jesus, "It is more blessed to give than to receive" (Acts 20:35 KJV).

Be generous, even when times are tight. God will certainly make up what you give up.

—— BEAUTIFUL IN ITS TIME ——

He has made everything beautiful in its time.
ECCLESIASTES 3:11 NIV

Waiting isn't easy. Nobody likes to do it. In fact, it's beginning to feel like we've lost the ability to wait altogether. Everyone is in a hurry. Nothing moves fast enough. And no matter how long we're forced to wait, even if only a few seconds, that wait is too long.

An exaggeration? Perhaps. But consider this: forty-seven percent of consumers expect a web page to load in two seconds or less. Forty percent will wait no more than three seconds for a web page to load before abandoning the site entirely. (And it took about twelve seconds to read this paragraph.)

Why are we so obsessed with doing things quickly? In such a maniacal hurry for everything? If haste makes waste, then waste is rapidly becoming the primary byproduct of modern society. But how many things are truly made better by rushing?

God has made everything beautiful *in its time*.

When our insides are a tangled ball of anxiety and confusion, when our volcanic anger is boiling just below the surface and ready to erupt at any moment, it's a clear sign that we need to slow down. We need to give God the time He needs to untangle the mess we've made of our lives.

Do you want the beautiful God-centered life Jesus made available? Then let go of the desire to have everything now. Allow God to make everything beautiful in His time.

LET ME WORSHIP

And Ezra blessed the LORD, the great God. And all the
people answered, Amen, Amen, with lifting up their
hands: and they bowed their heads, and worshipped
the LORD with their faces to the ground.
NEHEMIAH 8:6 KJV

It is in worship that the Holy Spirit most completely attains the object for which He was given; it is in worship He can most fully prove what He is. If I would that the consciousness and the power of the Spirit's presence became strong within me, let me worship. The Spirit fits for worship: worship fits for the Spirit.

It is not only prayer that is worship. Worship is the prostrate adoration of the Holy Presence. Often without words: "They bowed their heads, and worshipped." How much worship there is, even among believers, that is not in the Spirit! In private, family and public worship, how much hasty entering into God's presence in the power of the flesh, with little or no waiting for the Spirit to lift us heavenward! It is only the presence and power of the Holy Spirit that fits for acceptable worship.

—— DEALING WITH MOCKERY ——

"Hear us, our God, for we are being mocked. May their scoffing fall back on their own heads, and may they themselves become captives in a foreign land! Do not ignore their guilt. Do not blot out their sins, for they have provoked you to anger here in front of the builders."
NEHEMIAH 4:4–5 NLT

Sanballat, an enemy of the Jews, was upset when he learned that they were rebuilding Jerusalem's walls. He mocked them openly, saying: "What does this bunch of poor, feeble Jews think they're doing? Do they think they can build the wall in a single day by just offering a few sacrifices? Do they actually think they can make something of stones from a rubbish heap—and charred ones at that?" (Nehemiah 4:2 NLT).

Nehemiah didn't hurl insults back at Sanballat. He prayed, and then went back to work. Shortly afterward, the wall was finished to half its height, all the way around the city.

As Christians, we'll all face some form of opposition. But we don't have to respond in kind. Like Nehemiah, we can express our frustrations to God Himself, and leave the "vengeance" to Him (see Romans 12:19). Then get back to work.

We should expect the world to mock us. When they do, it really means they see us living differently than everybody else. "Live such good lives among the pagans," the apostle Peter wrote, "that, though they accuse you of doing wrong, they may see your good deeds and glorify God on the day he visits us" (1 Peter 2:12 NIV).

CLASSICS: D. L. MOODY

A TEACHABLE SPIRIT

*If any of you lack wisdom, let him ask
of God, that giveth to all men liberally,
and upbraideth not; and it shall be given him.*
JAMES 1:5 KJV

I remember one night when the Bible was the driest and darkest book in the universe to me. The next day it became entirely different. I thought I had the key to it. I had been born of the Spirit. But before I knew anything of the mind of God I had to give up my sin.

I believe God meets every soul on the spot of self surrender and when they are willing to let Him guide and lead. The trouble with many skeptics is their self-conceit. They know more than the Almighty! And they do not come in a teachable spirit.

But the moment a man comes in a receptive spirit he is blessed; for "if any of you lack wisdom, let him ask of God, that giveth to all men liberally, and upbraideth not; and it shall be given him."

—— REVERSAL OF FORTUNES ——

*"But for you who fear my name, the Sun of Righteousness
will rise with healing in his wings. And you will go free,
leaping with joy like calves let out to pasture."*
MALACHI 4:2 NLT

Notice that little word *but* that begins today's scripture—it indicates
a contrast with what goes before.

Malachi 4:2 follows a reference to "the wicked," those people
who cause pain and grief in our world. The prophet described a
coming day of judgment when "the arrogant and the wicked will be
burned up like straw" (verse 1). Then God's people—the ones who
fear His name and enjoy His healing, as verse 2 notes—would "tread
upon the wicked as if they were dust under your feet" (verse 3).

This promised reversal of fortunes should encourage us today.
No matter how hard, depressing, frustrating, and dangerous this
world becomes, God has something better planned. And not just
"better," but "amazing." As the apostle Paul wrote, referencing a
prophecy of Isaiah, "No eye has seen, no ear has heard, and no
mind has imagined what God has prepared for those who love
him" (1 Corinthians 2:9 NLT; see also Isaiah 64:4).

Jesus warned us of hard times (see John 16:33). *But*. . .a better
day is coming. We who fear God's name can expect the Sun of
Righteousness to rise with healing in His wings.

CHRISTIAN COMMUNITY

For the LORD will not cast off his people, neither will he forsake his inheritance. But judgment shall return unto righteousness: and all the upright in heart shall follow it. Who will rise up for me against the evildoers? or who will stand up for me against the workers of iniquity?
PSALM 94:14–16 KJV

In all ages, men who neither feared God nor regarded man have combined together and formed confederacies to carry on the works of darkness. And herein they have shown themselves wise in their generation; for by this means they more effectually promoted the kingdom of their father the devil, than otherwise they could have done.

On the other hand, men who did fear God and desire the happiness of their fellow creatures have, in every age, found it needful to join together, in order to oppose the works of darkness, to spread the knowledge of God their Savior and to promote His kingdom upon earth. Indeed, He himself has instructed them so to do. From the time that men were upon the earth, He hath taught them to join together in His service and has united them in one body by one Spirit. And for this very end He has joined them together, "that he might destroy the works of the devil."

LIVE IN FREEDOM

At the end of every seven years you must cancel debts. This is
how it is to be done: Every creditor shall cancel any loan
they have made to a fellow Israelite. They shall not require
payment from anyone among their own people, because the
LORD's time for canceling debts has been proclaimed.
DEUTERONOMY 15:1–2 NIV

This verse applies to a specific scenario in ancient Hebrew society. Individuals with great debt would indenture themselves as a means of settling that debt. But God's laws for this practice imposed an expiration date—this slavery should not become a permanent thing.

Every seventh year, the indenturing would end. Moses told the Israelites, "If any of your people—Hebrew men or women—sell themselves to you and serve you six years, in the seventh year you must let them go free. And when you release them, do not send them away empty-handed. Supply them liberally from your flock, your threshing floor and your winepress" (Deuteronomy 15:12–14 NIV). Why? Because the Hebrew people knew what slavery was—they had been under the control of the Egyptians for more than four hundred years before God Himself set them free and blessed them.

God's plan is for His people to live in freedom. Sometimes, though, we find ourselves enslaved to the past—to our own disappointments, failures, or even successes. When that happens, we'll find freedom in remembering that God has redeemed us. The saving work of His Son, Jesus Christ, is the ultimate strength for every challenge we face. "If God is for us, who [or what] can be against us?" (Romans 8:31 NIV).

GOD IS THERE

*Esther was taken to King Xerxes at the royal palace in
early winter of the seventh year of his reign. And the king
loved Esther more than any of the other young women.
He was so delighted with her that he set the royal crown
on her head and declared her queen instead of Vashti.*

ESTHER 2:16–17 NLT

A beautiful young woman once found herself in a very difficult situation. Esther, a Jew in exile in Persia, had been raised by an older cousin, Mordecai, after her parents died. When the Persian king felt disrespected by his queen, he banished her and demanded a harem to be assembled from his vast domain, stretching from India to Ethiopia. Esther was one of the women brought into the palace.

Mordecai told Esther to keep her nationality and family background to herself, which she did. After many beauty treatments and moments with the king, he chose her to his new queen. Ultimately, Esther would find herself in a position to save the Jewish people from the evil machinations of a high Persian official named Haman.

It's interesting to note that God is never mentioned in the book of Esther. But her elevation from orphan to queen is miraculous, as are many other details of the story. Though never acknowledged by name, God can be read between the lines of the entire account.

And if you follow His Son, Jesus, God is always there in your life too. No matter how dark situations may seem, you can trust that God knows, He cares, and He is working for your ultimate benefit.

—— KNOW YOUR IDENTITY ——

"I have done this to show you what should be done.
You should do as I have done to you."
JOHN 13:15 NLV

Roads in Jesus' day were dry, dusty, and probably littered with animal droppings. Since most people wore sandals, a good host would provide a servant to wash the feet of guests entering the home. It was always the lowliest servant who got this distasteful job. The master of the house would never do such a thing.

But Jesus is a master like no other. Though He had every reason to delegate to someone else, He got up from dinner, wrapped a cloth around Himself, and washed the feet of His disciples. He even washed Judas's feet, knowing full well the betrayal that was coming.

How could the Son of God lower Himself like that?

John 13:3 (NLV) says, "Jesus knew the Father had put everything into His hands. He knew He had come from God and was going back to God."

Jesus knew His identity. He wasn't concerned with impressing His disciples or proving His authority. Jesus' self-esteem was not threatened by the lowly job of foot washing. He knew, no matter how many feet He washed, that He was secure in His Father's love.

When we know our identity in Christ, we will experience the highest form of love and be willing to do the lowliest jobs. We will be ever more like our Lord.

── NO REST IN THIS WORLD ──

*For if Jesus had given them rest, then would he not
afterward have spoken of another day. There remaineth
therefore a rest to the people of God. For he that is entered
into his rest, he also hath ceased from his own works, as
God did from his. Let us labour therefore to enter into that
rest, lest any man fall after the same example of unbelief.*
HEBREWS 4:8–11 KJV

Now, while we all want rest, I think a great many people make a
mistake when they think the church is a place of rest; and when
they unite with the church they have a false idea about their position in it. There are a great many who come in to rest. The text tells
us: "There remaineth a rest for the people of God," but it does not
tell us that the church is a place of rest; we have all eternity to rest
in. We are to rest by and by; but we are to work here, and when
our work is finished, the Lord will call us home to enjoy that rest.

There is no use in talking about rest down here in the enemy's
country. We cannot rest in this world where God's Son has been
crucified and cast out.

"HOW WEAK WE ARE"

*The Lord is like a father to his children, tender and
compassionate to those who fear him. For he knows
how weak we are; he remembers we are only dust.*
PSALM 103:13–14 NLT

Paradoxes abound in the Christian life. That's why, in a book called
Strength for the Challenge, you're reading a devotional titled "How
Weak We Are."

That phrase, of course, comes directly from today's scripture,
a well-known psalm of David. God knows how weak we are, because we are—truth be told—"only dust." Since we're all prone to
pride, it's wise to remember that Adam was formed from the dust
of the ground, and only became a living soul when God breathed
into him (see Genesis 2:7). We all follow in Adam's dusty footsteps.

But our weakness becomes a strength when we look to our
Creator, Keeper, and God. As David noted, He "is like a father to
his children, tender and compassionate to those who fear him."
He is quick to fill up our weakness with His strength.

The apostle Paul picked up that theme by saying, "I take pleasure
in my weaknesses, and in the insults, hardships, persecutions, and
troubles that I suffer for Christ. For when I am weak, then I am
strong" (2 Corinthians 12:10 NLT).

How was Paul strong in weakness? By allowing God to work in
him. Or, as Jesus put it, "Come to me, all of you who are weary and
carry heavy burdens, and I will give you rest." (Matthew 11:28 NLT).

How weak we are. How strong our God is!

GOD IS PATIENT

Seeing then that all these things shall be dissolved, what manner of persons ought ye to be in all holy conversation and godliness, looking for and hasting unto the coming of the day of God, wherein the heavens being on fire shall be dissolved, and the elements shall melt with fervent heat? Nevertheless we, according to his promise, look for new heavens and a new earth, wherein dwelleth righteousness. Wherefore, beloved, seeing that ye look for such things, be diligent that ye may be found of him in peace, without spot, and blameless. And account that the longsuffering of our Lord is salvation.
2 Peter 3:11–15 kjv

Why are His chariots so long in coming? Why does He delay? The world grows grey, not alone with age, but with iniquity; and yet the Deliverer comes not.

We have waited for His footfall at the dead of night and looked out for Him through the gates of the morning and expected Him in the heat of the day and reckoned that He might come ere yet another sun went down; but He is not here! He waits. He waits very, very long. Will He not come?

Longsuffering is that which keeps Him from coming. He is bearing with men. Not yet the thunderbolt! Not yet the riven heavens and the reeling earth! Not yet the great white throne and the day of judgment; for He is very pitiful and beareth long with men!

BE WILLING

*Now finish the work, so that your eager willingness to do it may
be matched by your completion of it, according to your means.
For if the willingness is there, the gift is acceptable according
to what one has, not according to what one does not have.*
2 CORINTHIANS 8:11–12 NIV

Sometimes, the only ability we bring to a task is our willingness.

In today's scripture, the apostle Paul urged the Christians of
Corinth to complete a job: namely, the collection of a financial gift
for poor believers in Jerusalem. The Corinthians had been willing,
even eager, to be part of the relief effort, but apparently needed
some apostolic cheerleading to finish the job. Paul implored them
not to give up but to keep doing the good works they were called
to do.

At the time Paul wrote, the Corinthians had plenty. They could
give generously to the Jerusalem Christians and expect similar
treatment if they ever found themselves in straits in the future
(verse 14). But more important than their resources was the Corinthians' willingness to help. The apostle noted that the attitude
made the gift acceptable to God.

Not everyone is wealthy. But everyone can be willing. And
when we are, God accepts our efforts based on what we have, not
what we lack.

DIVINE ASSURANCE

*Be ye strong therefore, and let not your hands
be weak: for your work shall be rewarded.*
2 Chronicles 15:7 KJV

Oh, that we might learn to believe in the certainty of an abundant answer. A prophet said of old: "Let not your hands be weak; *your work shall be rewarded.*" Would that all who feel it difficult to pray much, would fix their eye on the recompense of the reward, and in faith learn to count upon the divine assurance that their prayer cannot be vain.

If we will but believe in God and His faithfulness, intercession will become to us the very first thing we take refuge in when we seek blessing for others, and the very last thing for which we cannot find time. And it will become a thing of joy and hope because all the time we pray we know that we are sowing seed that will bring forth fruit an hundredfold. Disappointment is impossible.

DO THE RIGHT THING

One day as Mordecai was on duty at the king's gate, two of the king's eunuchs, Bigthana and Teresh—who were guards at the door of the king's private quarters—became angry at King Xerxes and plotted to assassinate him. But Mordecai heard about the plot and gave the information to Queen Esther. She then told the king about it and gave Mordecai credit for the report.
ESTHER 2:21–22 NLT

We aren't sure what role Mordecai had in King Xerxes' court at this point in Esther's story. Some believe he was an officer of some sort, since he was present at the king's gate. Whatever his duty, God placed Mordecai in the right place at the right time. He overheard talk of an assassination attempt, and his response saved the king's life.

"Mordecai was not rewarded at the time, but a remembrance was written," says the old-time Bible commentator Matthew Henry. "Thus, with respect to those who serve Christ, though their recompence is not till the resurrection of the just, yet an account is kept of their work of faith and labor of love, which God is not unrighteous to forget. The servant of God must be faithful to every trust."

In this life, we see many people cheating, stealing, lying, and hurting others. Though it may seem like they "get away with murder," and that a committed Christian just can't get ahead, take encouragement from the story of Mordecai. Do the right thing and trust God to handle the rest. He can, and He will.

Classics: D. L. Moody

— FIGHT NOW, REWARD LATER —

For if ye live after the flesh, ye shall die: but if ye through the Spirit do mortify the deeds of the body, ye shall live.
Romans 8:13 KJV

If you seek the applause of men, you can't have the Lord say, "Well done," at the end of the journey. You can't have both.

Why? Because this world is at war with God. This idea that the world is getting better all the while is false. The old natural heart is just as much at enmity with God as it was when Cain slew Abel. Sin leaped into the world full grown in Cain. And from the time that Cain was born into the world to the present, man by nature has been at war with God.

This world was not established in grace, and we have to fight "the world, the flesh and the devil"; and if we fight the world, the world won't like us; and if we fight the flesh, the flesh won't like us. We have to mortify the flesh. We have to crucify the old man and put him under. Then, by and by, we will get our reward, and a glorious reward it will be.

GOD IS. . .

But without faith it is impossible to please him: for he that
cometh to God must believe that he is, and that he is
a rewarder of them that diligently seek him.
HEBREWS 11:6 KJV

The Bible's "faith chapter," Hebrews 11, provides both a definition of faith ("the substance of things hoped for, the evidence of things not seen," verse 1), and several examples of it in action—from the lives of Abel, Enoch, Noah, Abraham, and others. And verse 6, today's scripture, tells us that our faith is what pleases God.

Why? Because even though we've never seen God, we "must believe that he *is*." The implication is that God exists, and that He is actually God, not just some lesser being.

But we can gain strength from other biblical descriptions of what God is. He is knowledgeable of our lives: "For the ways of man are before the eyes of the LORD, and he pondereth all his goings" (Proverbs 5:21 KJV). He is compassionate toward us: "Thou, O Lord, art a God full of compassion, and gracious, long suffering, and plenteous in mercy and truth" (Psalm 86:15 KJV). He is powerful enough to help us in any and every circumstance: "Now unto him that is able to do exceeding abundantly above all that we ask or think, according to the power that worketh in us, unto him be glory in the church by Christ Jesus throughout all ages, world without end" (Ephesians 3:20–21 KJV).

And just think: all of this is available to you through faith.

CLASSICS: CHARLES SPURGEON

GUARD YOUR LOCKS

*Howbeit the hair of [Samson's] head began
to grow again after he was shaven.*
JUDGES 16:22 KJV

Though Samson's hair grew again, and his strength came back, and he died gloriously fighting against the Philistines, yet he never recovered his eyes, or his liberty, or his living power in Israel! Short and effective was his last stroke against the adversary, but it cost him his life. He could not again rise to be the man he had been before; and though God did give him a great victory over the Philistine people, yet it was but as the flicker of an expiring candle; he was never again a lamp of hope to Israel. His usefulness was abated, and even brought to an end, through his folly.

Whatever the grace of God may do for us, it cannot make sin a right thing, or a safe thing, or a permissible thing. It is evil, only evil, and that continually. O children of God, be not enslaved by fleshly lusts! O Nazarites unto God, guard your locks, lest they be cut away by sin while you are sleeping in the lap of pleasure! O servants of Jehovah, serve the Lord with heart and soul by His grace even to the end, and keep yourselves unshorn by the world!

—— TRUSTWORTHY FOREVER ——

*The secret things belong to the LORD our God, but the
things revealed belong to us and to our children forever,
that we may follow all the words of this law.*
DEUTERONOMY 29:29 NIV

Deuteronomy pictures the end of an era—the death of Moses and
the transition to new leadership under Joshua. As Moses' forty-year
tenure came to a close, he gave careful instruction to the next
generation, describing how to live and work and serve together
for God's glory.

Moses noted that there are some things that humans will never
know or understand. These are the "secret things" that belong to
the Lord. We can simply trust Him with those.

But the "things revealed" belong to us, and our children, and all
of our offspring. What are these things revealed? The knowledge
of God and His nature and laws that we find in His Word. These
things are ours "forever," because we worship the God of forever.

Since God has forever under control, we can follow His Word
today and every day. We don't have to wonder if the Lawgiver will
be different next week or month or year. He is unchanging—so
we can trust Him forever.

Can you find strength in the God of forever? Can you trust that
He will be available to you today just as he was for Moses and
Joshua? God has always been, and will always be, trustworthy.

— COME BOLDLY TO THE KING —

On the third day of the fast, Esther put on her royal robes and entered the inner court of the palace, just across from the king's hall. The king was sitting on his royal throne, facing the entrance.
ESTHER 5:1 NLT

At her cousin and mentor Mordecai's urging, Esther agreed to approach her husband, King Xerxes, to beg mercy for the lives of the Jewish people. Haman, the second most powerful man in the Persian empire, had hatched a plot to destroy the Jews. The king had foolishly agreed to it, not realizing that his own chosen queen was Jewish.

But Esther couldn't approach the king without an invitation—and it had been weeks since he had last requested her company. Appearing unbidden meant certain death unless the king extended his scepter, a fact that Esther made very clear to Mordecai. In the end, she did what she had to do. . .and the king was pleased to see her. He raised his scepter, and she ultimately enlisted his help for her people.

God had raised up Esther to save the Jews, but she still had to act. Few of us will ever experience the heavy burden she did. But as Christians, we do face opposition ranging from ridicule to outright persecution. Happily, we have a King who offers us an open invitation into His presence, whose scepter is always extended.

This world may be frightening, but our King is not. "So let us come boldly to the throne of our gracious God," Hebrews 4:16 tell us. "There we will receive his mercy, and we will find grace to help us when we need it most" (NLT).

PEACE IN TURMOIL

"I have told you these things, so that in me you may
have peace. In this world you will have trouble.
But take heart! I have overcome the world."
JOHN 16:33 NIV

The word *peace* may bring to mind smooth-flowing rivers, fields of grass waving in a light wind, sunshine on our faces. Maybe we equate peace with comfort, such as a perfectly broken-in chair with our favorite beverage within reach and a well-loved book in our lap.

Jesus came to give peace, but not like we ever imagined. Just before He was arrested, tortured, and killed, Jesus made a promise to His disciples: "In this world," He said, "you will have trouble."

What kind of peace can you have in the middle of trouble?

The meaning of Jesus' peace is richer than an absence of turmoil. It is the presence of blessing we get through a right relationship with God. This world may crush our hopes and dreams, but it cannot break the love God has given us.

Jesus was crucified and buried, but He didn't stay in the ground. He rose again and sent the power of the Holy Spirit to live inside us. He has overcome the world!

This life isn't everything. When we are at our weakest, we can still have peace because our strength is in our relationship with God. That's why we do as Jesus said: "Love the Lord your God with all your heart and with all your soul and with all your mind and with all your strength" (Mark 12:30 NIV).

OUR DELIVERER AND REDEEMER

*Forasmuch as ye know that ye were not redeemed
with corruptible things, as silver and gold, from your
vain conversation received by tradition from your
fathers; but with the precious blood of Christ, as of
a lamb without blemish and without spot.*
1 PETER 1:18–19 KJV

How often, like the children of Israel when they came to the Red Sea, have we become discouraged because everything looked dark before us, behind us and around us, and we knew not which way to turn. Like Peter we have said, "To whom shall we go?" (John 6:68). But God has appeared for our deliverance. He has brought us through the Red Sea right out into the wilderness and opened up the way into the Promised Land.

But Christ is not only our Deliverer; He is our Redeemer. That is something more than being our Saviour. He has brought us back. "Ye have sold yourselves for nought; and ye shall be redeemed without money" (Isaiah 52:3). We "were not redeemed with corruptible things, as silver and gold." If gold could have redeemed us, could He not have created ten thousand worlds full of gold?

STRENGTH IN SERVICE

And [Jesus] sat down, and called the twelve,
and saith unto them, If any man desire to be first,
the same shall be last of all, and servant of all.
MARK 9:35 KJV

When God said, through the prophet Isaiah, "my thoughts are not your thoughts, neither are your ways my ways" (Isaiah 55:8 KJV), He meant it. What God expects of people runs directly counter to the attitudes and passions of this world.

Our culture tells you to "go for the good life," "aim for the top," "be your own man." That's how to be strong and successful, at least in the minds of many people today.

But Jesus laid out a very different path. To be first, we should consciously make ourselves last. What does that mean? Jesus answers the question in His next phrase: we should become the servant of everyone.

This idea isn't politically correct. Being a servant doesn't sound like much fun. How am I supposed to succeed if I'm always working for someone else?

Never forget that any success we enjoy comes from God Himself (see Deuteronomy 8:18). And when He tells us to do something— even something that goes against the grain culturally—He has a good end in view. As Jesus said shortly after He spoke the words above, "Whosoever shall give you a cup of water to drink in my name, because ye belong to Christ, verily I say unto you, he shall not lose his reward" (Mark 9:41 KJV).

When we step back and serve others, God sees and blesses. Our strength is in our service.

PLANT GENEROUSLY

*Remember this—a farmer who plants only a few
seeds will get a small crop. But the one who
plants generously will get a generous crop.*
2 CORINTHIANS 9:6 NLT

Though farmers can benefit from the apostle Paul's advice in this verse, he wasn't really making an agricultural pronouncement. He was describing the joy and blessing of giving.

The very next verse contains a familiar quotation: "God loves a cheerful giver" (NIV). When we give happily—to the work of our church, to missionaries and ministries, to programs for the less fortunate, to friends and acquaintances who need a helping hand—God is pleased. And He will make sure that we never come up short. "God will generously provide all you need," Paul continued. "Then you will always have everything you need and plenty left over to share with others. As the Scriptures say, 'They share freely and give generously to the poor. Their good deeds will be remembered forever'" (2 Corinthians 9:8–9, quoting Psalm 112:9 NLT).

If you want to enjoy God's blessing, give back some (a lot!) of what He's already given you. Plant generously to receive a generous crop. Don't give simply to get, but give to bless others. When you do, you will be blessed even more.

Day 356

CHRISTIAN UNITY

Two are better than one, because they have a good return for their labor: if either of them falls down, one can help the other up. But pity anyone who falls and has no one to help them up. Also, if two lie down together, they will keep warm. But how can one keep warm alone? Though one may be overpowered, two can defend themselves. A cord of three strands is not quickly broken.
ECCLESIASTES 4:9–12 NIV

Unity is a powerful thing. The psalmist says, "Behold, how good and how pleasant it is for brethren to dwell together in unity! It is like the precious ointment upon the head, that ran down upon the beard, even Aaron's beard: that went down to the skirts of his garments. . .for there the LORD commanded the blessing, even life for evermore" (Psalm 133:1–3 KJV).

When true unity is present, the oil of God's blessing flows into, through, and out of all our efforts and interactions. Just as natural oil eases friction, the oil of God's blessing smooths over the rough spots of life, making it easy to work and play without grinding others up or burning them out.

And when three-corded unity is present—when a married couple, or two friends, or business partners are united to Christ first and then to each other—God commands a blessing that increases the love, joy, peace, patience, gentleness, kindness, wisdom, and strength of both people exponentially.

That is life as God intended. Indeed, it was His plan all along. If there is a path back to the garden, this is it. May we be so wise as to seek unity, and blessed to find it.

—— IS YOUR HEART PERFECT? ——

For it came to pass, when Solomon was old, that his wives turned away his heart after other gods: and his heart was not perfect with the LORD his God, as was the heart of David his father.
1 KINGS 11:4 KJV

We know how sadly David sinned. And yet the heart of [David] was perfect with the Lord God.

In God's record of the lives of His servants there are some of whom it is written: his heart was perfect with the Lord his God. Is this, let each reader ask, what God sees and says of me? Does my life, in the sight of God, bear the mark of intense, wholehearted consecration to God's will and service? Of a burning desire to be as perfect as it is possible for grace to make me?

Let us yield ourselves to the searching light of this question. Let us believe that with this word *perfect* God means something very real and true. Let us not evade its force or hide ourselves from its condemning power by the vain subterfuge that we do not fully know what it means. *We must first accept it and give up our lives to it* before we can understand it.

— GOD WORKS FOR GOOD —

*Many people of other nationalities became Jews
because fear of the Jews had seized them.*
ESTHER 8:17 NIV

Many people are familiar with the basic details of the book of Esther. A beautiful young Jewish woman becomes queen of Persia, then courageously stands up to an evil official who wants to wipe out God's people. But when you dig deeper into the text, there are fascinating details to be found. Such as the climactic action in chapters 8 and 9.

Haman's plot was to allow people throughout the Persian empire to rise up on a certain day, slaughtering the Jews and taking their possessions. Because the king had carelessly made the plan a Persian law, it could not be changed. It could, however, be counteracted—and Esther's bravery caused the king to issue a second order, allowing the Jews to defend themselves. That they did, killing upwards of seventy-five thousand attackers (see Esther 9:16). The Jews' strength and success stunned many people, and they "became Jews because fear of the Jews had seized them."

God can turn our seemingly impossible circumstances into smashing victories. If He did that for His Old Testament people, who'd sinned their way into Persian exile, how much more will He stand up for "those who love him" (Romans 8:28 NIV)? Don't ever forget the first part of that verse: "We know that in all things God works for the good" of His beloved children.

—— DIVINITY AND HUMANITY ——

*And she brought forth her firstborn son, and wrapped
him in swaddling clothes, and laid him in a manger;
because there was no room for them in the inn.*
LUKE 2:7 KJV

After she gave birth to Jesus, Mary wrapped her newborn in swaddling clothes. Swaddling—securing a baby's arms to their sides with a cloth—mimics the confines of the womb, providing familiarity in a harsh new environment. Parents swaddled babies for generations prior to Jesus' birth. We swaddle babies still today.

The commonness of this detail makes it stand out. The Son of God had come, but He arrived as we all do. He was not born in a palace. He was not even born in an inn. He was born in obscurity and then wrapped up like any other baby.

And yet, the detail of Jesus' swaddling served as an identifying sign to the nearby shepherds: "And the angel said unto them, Fear not: for, behold, I bring you good tidings of great joy, which shall be to all people. For unto you is born this day in the city of David a Savior, which is Christ the Lord. And this shall be a sign unto you; Ye shall find the babe wrapped in swaddling clothes, lying in a manger" (Luke 2:10–12 KJV).

We are invited to find Jesus in the same way. Mighty savior of the world, but human like us. One who is fully God and somehow fully man. The only one who could bridge the gap between God's holiness and our need.

Let us praise God for Jesus' divinity, but also for His humanity.

THE POWER OF GOD

For the preaching of the cross is to them that perish foolishness;
but unto us which are saved it is the power of God.
1 CORINTHIANS 1:18 KJV

What could be greater than God's power?

This is the power that created the entire universe out of nothing (Genesis 1:1). It's the power that's kept that universe in operation, every moment of every day, for millennia on end (Colossians 1:17). It's the power that created life and can overcome death. It's the power that underlies everything we see, touch, feel, and know.

Sadly, many people in our world think the power of God is a fairy tale, a silly superstition for weak-minded people. But, as the apostle Paul noted, those are people who are perishing, because they have never understood the "preaching of the cross."

We as Christians, though, having received spiritual sight through the grace of God, know that Jesus is "the way, the truth, and the life" (John 14:6 KJV). . .that by believing on His name, we are saved (Acts 16:31). . .that in Him, we can accomplish anything He wants us to do (Philippians 4:13).

Strength for the challenges of life begins with a recognition of the greatest power of all that comes through the message of the cross. If you have believed and received Jesus, you have full access to the power of God.

GIVE UP THAT SIN!

And Samuel said, Hath the LORD as great delight in burnt offerings and sacrifices, as in obeying the voice of the LORD? Behold, to obey is better than sacrifice, and to hearken than the fat of rams.
1 SAMUEL 15:22 KJV

Possibly, dear brother, there may be some evil habit in which you are indulging and which you excuse by the reflection, "Well, I am always at the prayer meeting; I am constantly at communion, and I give so much of my substance to the support of the Lord's work." I am glad that you do these things; but, oh! I pray you give up that sin! I pray you cut it to pieces and cast it away, for if you do not, all your show of sacrifice will be but an abomination.

The first thing which God requires of you as His beloved is obedience; and though you should preach with the tongue of men and of angels, though you should give your body to be burned and your goods to feed the poor, yet, if you do not hearken to your Lord and are not obedient to His will, all besides shall profit you nothing.

NO COMPARISON

For their rock is not like our Rock,
as even our enemies concede.
DEUTERONOMY 32:31 NIV

Shortly before he died, Moses spoke to the people of Israel, men and women he had served for forty years. The nation was soon to cross the Jordan River and enter the land promised to Abraham centuries earlier. They would do so with a new leader named Joshua.

This "Promised Land" contained several people groups, each with a false god they chose to worship. When the Israelites entered the land, Moses hoped, they would reject these fake deities and serve the one true God—the Lord who delivered them from slavery in Egypt and cared for them in the wilderness. None of the other "gods" of the Promised Land could compare to the God of Israel. Moses reminded the people that they had a Rock supporting them that was unlike any other.

Jesus used similar imagery in His parable of the wise and foolish builders (Matthew 7:24–27). The rock is a place of stability and strength, appropriate for sinking a good foundation. We do well to build our lives on the most solid rock we can find. Moses said that rock is the God of heaven. Jesus said the rock is Himself, the One sent from God.

As a Christian, your Rock is unlike any other rock out there. Those others aren't even pebbles.

— FAITHFUL IN ALL THINGS —

Mordecai the Jew was second in rank to King Xerxes,
preeminent among the Jews, and held in high esteem by
his many fellow Jews, because he worked for the good of
his people and spoke up for the welfare of all the Jews.
ESTHER 10:3 NIV

There are a couple of reasons that the Old Testament hero Mordecai rose in rank. First, he providentially foiled an assassination attempt on King Xerxes' life, which (equally providentially) was brought to Xerxes's mind just before the Jews themselves were set to be killed. Second, Mordecai inspired Queen Esther to do the right thing—to stand up for her people even though she herself faced death. That couldn't have been easy for Mordecai, given that he had raised his younger cousin as if she had been his daughter.

Mordecai always did the right thing, even though it was difficult. He chose integrity and courage over comfort and security. As he did so, God not only strengthened Mordecai's resolve but elevated him to a place of greater influence.

The small stands you make right now could lead to better opportunities, both for yourself and God's kingdom, down the road. Know that as you do the right thing, no matter who is watching or what others think, God notices. . .and He gives you the strength you need to press on.

Jesus once said, "He that is faithful in that which is least is faithful also in much: and he that is unjust in the least is unjust also in much" (Luke 16:10 KJV). Commit today to be faithful in all things.

REMEMBER THAT GOD HAS SAVED YOU

Put them in mind to be subject to principalities and powers, to obey magistrates, to be ready to every good work, to speak evil of no man, to be no brawlers, but gentle, shewing all meekness unto all men. For we ourselves also were sometimes foolish, disobedient, deceived, serving divers lusts and pleasures, living in malice and envy, hateful, and hating one another. But after that the kindness and love of God our Saviour toward man appeared.

TITUS 3:1–4 KJV

Our apostle tells us that we are to speak evil of no man, but to show meekness unto all men; and he adds this as an all-sufficient reason—we ourselves also were sometimes like the very worst of them.

When we look upon the world at this day, it pains us by its folly, disobedience, and delusion. He that knows most of this modern Babylon, whether he observes the richer or the poorer classes of society, will find the deepest cause for grief. But we cannot condemn with bitterness, for such were some of us.

Not only can we not condemn with bitterness, but we look upon our sinful fellow-creatures with great compassion, for such were some of us. Yea more, we feel encouraged to hope for ungodly men, even for the foolish and disobedient, for we ourselves also were, not long ago, like them. We feel that we must give the thought of our heart and the energy of our lives to the great work of saving men, out of gratitude to the Lord our God, who, in His kindness and love, has saved us.

— LIVE MORE IN THE FUTURE —

And I heard a voice from heaven saying unto me,
Write, Blessed are the dead which die in the Lord from
henceforth: Yea, saith the Spirit, that they may rest
from their labours; and their works do follow them.
REVELATION 14:13 KJV

Now death may rob us of money. Death may rob us of position. Death may rob us of our friends; but there is one thing death can never do, and that is rob us of the work that we do for God. That will live on forever. "Their works do follow them."

How much are we doing? We have the privilege of setting in motion streams of activity that will flow on when we are dead and gone. It is the privilege of everyone to live more in the future than they do in the present, so that their lives will tell in fifty or a hundred years more than they do now.

If they up yonder can see what is going on upon the earth, how much joy they must have to think that they have set these streams in motion and that this work is going on—being carried on after them.

SCRIPTURE INDEX

GENESIS

1:26, 31 . . . . Day 191
3:6 . . . . Day 65
4:6–7 . . . . Day 14
5:21–24 . . . . Day 237
6:13–14 . . . . Day 26
12:2–3 . . . . Day 38
12:3 . . . . Day 62
12:4 . . . . Day 38
13:6 . . . . Day 50
14:18 . . . . Day 50
14:20 . . . . Day 50
15:6 . . . . Day 50
16:13 . . . . Day 169
17:1 . . . . Day 269
18:23 . . . . Day 177
21:14, 17–18 . . . . Day 62
22:7–8 . . . . Day 74
32:20 . . . . Day 86
32:24–26 . . . . Day 86
33:1, 3–4 . . . . Day 98
37:3–4 . . . . Day 110
39:20–21 . . . . Day 122
41:15–16 . . . . Day 134
41:39–41 . . . . Day 146
45:4–7 . . . . Day 158
45:7 . . . . Day 122

EXODUS

3:4–5 . . . . Day 301
3:8 . . . . Day 326
12:13 . . . . Day 12
12:21–23 . . . . Day 170
14:7 . . . . Day 83
14:13–14 . . . . Day 182
14:15 . . . . Day 205
17:10–13 . . . . Day 194
18:8–9 . . . . Day 206
20:8–10 . . . . Day 218
25:31–32 . . . . Day 5
34:7 . . . . Day 144
39:42–43 . . . . Day 230

LEVITICUS

2:4–7 . . . . Day 242
19:2 . . . . Day 9

NUMBERS

1:3 . . . . Day 254
1:4–5 . . . . Day 254
5:5–7 . . . . Day 266
7:89 . . . . Day 81
9:1–2 . . . . Day 278
11:4, 6 . . . . Day 290
11:5 . . . . Day 290
12:3 . . . . Day 302
12:7–8 . . . . Day 330
13:2 . . . . Day 326
13:20 . . . . Day 326
13:23 . . . . Day 326
13:30 . . . . Day 211
13:30–31 . . . . Day 314
13:32–33 . . . . Day 326
13:33 . . . . Day 314
14:14 . . . . Day 23

DEUTERONOMY

5:28–29 . . . . Day 193
8:18 . . . . Day 24
11:12 . . . . Day 58
15:1–2 . . . . Day 338
15:12–14 . . . . Day 338
29:29 . . . . Day 350
31:8 . . . . Day 8
32:31 . . . . Day 362
33:1 . . . . Day 213

JOSHUA

1:8 . . . . Day 2

11:4 . . . . Day 83
11:18–20 . . . . Day 8
18:3 . . . . Day 15
20:1–3 . . . . Day 20
21:44 . . . . Day 27
23:12–13 . . . . Day 32
24:14–15 . . . . Day 173

JUDGES

2:1–2 . . . . Day 17
2:10 . . . . Day 39
2:18 . . . . Day 39
6:6 . . . . Day 44
6:15 . . . . Day 44
6:16 . . . . Day 44
6:34 . . . . Day 137
7:2 . . . . Day 51
7:12 . . . . Day 51
10:16 . . . . Day 56
11:32–33 . . . . Day 63
15:16 . . . . Day 68
15:18–19 . . . . Day 68
16:22 . . . . Day 349

RUTH

3:10 . . . . Day 75
4:10 . . . . Day 80

1 SAMUEL

1:8 . . . . Day 87
1:17 . . . . Day 87
1:26–27 . . . . Day 87
2:1 . . . . Day 133
6:20 . . . . Day 92
7:12 . . . . Day 95
7:13 . . . . Day 297
9:21 . . . . Day 99
11:6 . . . . Day 112
13:5 . . . . Day 83
13:14 . . . . Day 285
14:15 . . . . Day 83
15:22 . . . . Day 14, 361
16:2 . . . . Day 111

16:13 . . . . Day 116
17:36–37 . . . . Day 123
17:45–46 . . . . Day 123
18:7 . . . . Day 195
20:3 . . . . Day 229
22:15 . . . . Day 128
23:2 . . . . Day 135
23:4 . . . . Day 135
23:14 . . . . Day 140
24:6–7 . . . . Day 147
25:26 . . . . Day 152
25:28 . . . . Day 152
25:33–34 . . . . Day 152
26:21 . . . . Day 159
27:1 . . . . Day 164
29:6 . . . . Day 171
30:6 . . . . Day 176

2 SAMUEL

3:1 . . . . Day 183
5:24 . . . . Day 241
7:8 . . . . Day 188
7:9 . . . . Day 188
8:6 . . . . Day 195
21:17 . . . . Day 202
22:30 . . . . Day 207

1 KINGS

2:28, 30 . . . . Day 265
3:7 . . . . Day 214
3:9 . . . . Day 214
4:29, 33–34 . . . . Day 219
5:12 . . . . Day 226
11:4 . . . . Day 357
13:1–2 . . . . Day 49
17:2–4 . . . . Day 231
17:13 . . . . Day 238
17:14 . . . . Day 238
18:17–19 . . . . Day 85
19:8 . . . . Day 243
19:12 . . . . Day 260
20:4 . . . . Day 71
22:17 . . . . Day 306

2 KINGS

5:13 . . . . Day 273
6:17 . . . . Day 83, 250
11:10 . . . . Day 73
13:4 . . . . Day 255
13:15–17 . . . . Day 262
17:32–33 . . . . Day 149
18:33–35 . . . . Day 267
19:19 . . . . Day 267
20:3 . . . . Day 274
20:5 . . . . Day 274
22:13 . . . . Day 279

1 CHRONICLES

15:13 . . . . Day 325
16:15 . . . . Day 286
21:4 . . . . Day 292
21:24 . . . . Day 292
23:27, 30 . . . . Day 37

2 CHRONICLES

7:14 . . . . Day 97
15:7 . . . . Day 345
29:5–6 . . . . Day 321

EZRA

3:3 . . . . Day 298
4:14 . . . . Day 61
7:10 . . . . Day 303
8:22–23 . . . . Day 310
9:1–2 . . . . Day 315
9:13 . . . . Day 315

NEHEMIAH

2:8 . . . . Day 322
2:11–12 . . . . Day 322
2:17 . . . . Day 322
2:18 . . . . Day 322
4:2 . . . . Day 334
4:4–5 . . . . Day 334
8:6 . . . . Day 333
8:10 . . . . Day 34
9:7–8 . . . . Day 309

ESTHER

2:16–17 . . . . Day 339
2:21–22 . . . . Day 346
5:1 . . . . Day 351
8:17 . . . . Day 358
10:3 . . . . Day 363

JOB

1:1 . . . . Day 212, 248
1:6, 8 . . . . Day 212
1:8 . . . . Day 284
2:3 . . . . Day 224
2:9 . . . . Day 224
5:7 . . . . Day 283
5:8, 27 . . . . Day 248
13:15 . . . . Day 29
17:9 . . . . Day 257
21:27 . . . . Day 305
38:1–3 . . . . Day 260
38:11 . . . . Day 17
42:12–13 . . . . Day 201
42:12, 16–17 . . . . Day 284

PSALMS

5:11 . . . . Day 41
18:20–24 . . . . Day 109
19:1–4 . . . . Day 106
23:4–6 . . . . Day 11
23:5 . . . . Day 121
27:4–6 . . . . Day 107
31:19–21 . . . . Day 167
32:1–2 . . . . Day 70
33:11 . . . . Day 158
34:17–19 . . . . Day 119
37:7–9 . . . . Day 53
37:11 . . . . Day 301
49:3 . . . . Day 253
51:1–4 . . . . Day 47
51:10–12 . . . . Day 47
51:11 . . . . Day 167
55:22 . . . . Day 86
57:5, 7 . . . . Day 140

68:17 . . . . Day 83
73:18–20 . . . . Day 281
84:11–12 . . . . Day 293
86:15 . . . . Day 348
90:1–2 . . . . Day 313
94:14–16 . . . . Day 337
103:13–14 . . . . Day 342
118:1–4, 24 . . . . Day 34
119:107 . . . . Day 209
133:1–3 . . . . Day 356
147:5 . . . . Day 294

PROVERBS

1:5 . . . . Day 178
2:3–5 . . . . Day 191
3:5–6 . . . . Day 142
4:13 . . . . Day 33
5:21 . . . . Day 348
11:25 . . . . Day 145
18:10 . . . . Day 155
18:15 . . . . Day 79
21:1 . . . . Day 96
27:17 . . . . Day 151

ECCLESIASTES

1:2 . . . . Day 296
2:11 . . . . Day 296
3:1 . . . . Day 320
3:7 . . . . Day 246
3:11 . . . . Day 332
4:9–12 . . . . Day 356
4:12 . . . . Day 55
5:2 . . . . Day 246

ISAIAH

1:2 . . . . Day 45
1:3 . . . . Day 45
2:4 . . . . Day 162
5:18 . . . . Day 245
12:2 . . . . Day 4
26:3 . . . . Day 224
30:15 . . . . Day 10
30:19 . . . . Day 179

38:17 . . . . Day 141
40:10 . . . . Day 294
40:12 . . . . Day 18, 22
40:28–31 . . . . Day 22
41:10, 13 . . . . Day 30
42:1 . . . . Day 16
42:3 . . . . Day 248
49:4 . . . . Day 36
52:3 . . . . Day 353
52:7 . . . . Day 136
55:8 . . . . Day 354
65:24 . . . . Day 130

JEREMIAH

2:32 . . . . Day 77
9:23–24 . . . . Day 42
10:6, 12 . . . . Day 48, 294
17:5 . . . . Day 153
17:9 . . . . Day 20
27:5 . . . . Day 48
29:11 . . . . Day 98
31:26 . . . . Day 54
32:17 . . . . Day 54
45:1–5 . . . . Day 60
50:4–5 . . . . Day 154
51:15 . . . . Day 48

LAMENTATIONS

3:21–23 . . . . Day 66
3:24–26 . . . . Day 72
3:57 . . . . Day 89

EZEKIEL

11:19–20 . . . . Day 78
16:62–63 . . . . Day 185
18:20 . . . . Day 84
36:23 . . . . Day 233
36:26–27 . . . . Day 78

DANIEL

1:20 . . . . Day 223
2:49 . . . . Day 90
3:17–18 . . . . Day 90
4:34, 37 . . . . Day 96

5:29 . . . . Day 102
6:1–2 . . . . Day 102
6:4–5 . . . . Day 197
7:13–14 . . . . Day 108, 268
9:19 . . . . Day 114
10:6 . . . . Day 120
10:16–19 . . . . Day 120
12:2–4, 13 . . . . Day 126

HOSEA
4:6 . . . . Day 132
10:12 . . . . Day 138

JOEL
2:11–13 . . . . Day 144
2:28–29 . . . . Day 150
2:32 . . . . Day 156, 264
3:10 . . . . Day 162

AMOS
3:3 . . . . Day 105
5:24 . . . . Day 168

OBADIAH
4 . . . . Day 174

JONAH
1:9–10 . . . . Day 180
2:7 . . . . Day 186
2:9 . . . . Day 186
4:2 . . . . Day 192

MICAH
3:8 . . . . Day 198, 294
4:3 . . . . Day 162
5:2, 4 . . . . Day 204
6:8 . . . . Day 210
6:9 . . . . Day 216
7:18–19 . . . . Day 222

NAHUM
1:7–8 . . . . Day 228

HABAKKUK
1:12 . . . . Day 234
2:4 . . . . Day 240
2:20 . . . . Day 246

3:17–19 . . . . Day 252

ZEPHANIAH
1:12–13 . . . . Day 258
1:14 . . . . Day 258
2:3 . . . . Day 258
3:12, 17 . . . . Day 264

HAGGAI
1:6 . . . . Day 270
1:12–13 . . . . Day 270
2:4, 9 . . . . Day 276

ZECHARIAH
1:3 . . . . Day 282
2:8 . . . . Day 288
2:10–11 . . . . Day 288
2:12 . . . . Day 288
4:6 . . . . Day 294
7:9–10 . . . . Day 300
13:7 . . . . Day 306

MALACHI
1:1–2, 6–7. . . . . Day 312
3:8–10 . . . . Day 318
3:14 . . . . Day 324
4:1 . . . . Day 336
4:2 . . . . Day 336
4:3 . . . . Day 336
4:4 . . . . Day 330

MATTHEW
1:19–20 . . . . Day 3
2:2 . . . . Day 204
3:8 . . . . Day 138
3:16–17 . . . . Day 16
4:1–2 . . . . Day 28
5:11–12 . . . . Day 40
5:27–28 . . . . Day 52
5:44 . . . . Day 27, 210
6:7 . . . . Day 246
6:9–13 . . . . Day 129
6:15 . . . . Day 70
6:27 . . . . Day 64

7:12 . . . . Day 220
7:16–21 . . . . Day 138
7:19 . . . . Day 232
7:24 . . . . Day 240
9:29 . . . . Day 225
10:22 . . . . Day 257
10:28 . . . . Day 135
11:28 . . . . Day 57, 342
11:28, 30 . . . . Day 218
15:28 . . . . Day 203
16:16 . . . . Day 30
19:29 . . . . Day 318
22:44 . . . . Day 27
26:39 . . . . Day 105
28:19 . . . . Day 31
28:20 . . . . Day 31, 137

MARK

2:17 . . . . Day 76
3:4 . . . . Day 210
3:21 . . . . Day 88
3:33–35 . . . . Day 88
4:10–11 . . . . Day 200
4:25 . . . . Day 100
4:38–40 . . . . Day 112
6:8 . . . . Day 124
6:11 . . . . Day 136
7:15 . . . . Day 148
7:21–22 . . . . Day 148
7:26–29 . . . . Day 160
9:35 . . . . Day 46, 354
9:41 . . . . Day 354
10:44 . . . . Day 46
10:45 . . . . Day 199
12:30 . . . . Day 352
12:44 . . . . Day 331
14:51–52 . . . . Day 172
15:43–46 . . . . Day 117

LUKE

1:52 . . . . Day 302
2:7 . . . . Day 359

2:10–12 . . . . Day 359
3:8 . . . . Day 138
4:38–39 . . . . Day 196
5:4–5 . . . . Day 208
5:8 . . . . Day 208
5:17 . . . . Day 21
6:27–28 . . . . Day 220
6:32–35 . . . . Day 220
6:43–44 . . . . Day 232
7:39 . . . . Day 244
7:41–42 . . . . Day 187, 244
9:16–17 . . . . Day 256
9:24 . . . . Day 268
14:11 . . . . Day 302
14:24 . . . . Day 275
16:10 . . . . Day 363
17:6 . . . . Day 249
19:16–17 . . . . Day 308

JOHN

1:11–12 . . . . Day 57
3:19 . . . . Day 243
6:68 . . . . Day 66, 353
7:38 . . . . Day 168
7:39 . . . . Day 168
8:31–32 . . . . Day 280
8:33 . . . . Day 280
8:56 . . . . Day 72
9:1–3 . . . . Day 291
10:27–28 . . . . Day 304
11:33 . . . . Day 316
11:35 . . . . Day 316
12:27–28 . . . . Day 328
13:3 . . . . Day 340
13:15 . . . . Day 340
13:35 . . . . Day 317
14:1–3 . . . . Day 126
14:6 . . . . Day 157, 360
14:16 . . . . Day 296
14:23 . . . . Day 295
15:10 . . . . Day 109

15:16 . . . . Day 138
16:33 . . . . Day 31, 352
17:3 . . . . Day 189

Acts

1:9–11 . . . . Day 6
2:21 . . . . Day 264
2:38, 41 . . . . Day 46
3:11–12 . . . . Day 19
3:19–20 . . . . Day 299
4:1–4 . . . . Day 31
4:32–35 . . . . Day 55
5:34 . . . . Day 43
5:38–39 . . . . Day 43
6:3–4 . . . . Day 67
7:55–56 . . . . Day 108, 311
8:1–4 . . . . Day 91
8:29–31 . . . . Day 79
9:11–12 . . . . Day 111
9:13–14 . . . . Day 111
9:15 . . . . Day 111
9:17–19 . . . . Day 115
9:26–27 . . . . Day 127
16:31 . . . . Day 57
18:9–10 . . . . Day 276
20:35 . . . . Day 331
21:14 . . . . Day 105
26:20 . . . . Day 138
28:1–2 . . . . Day 139

Romans

1:11–12 . . . . Day 151
1:20–21 . . . . Day 189
4:18 . . . . Day 72
4:24–25 . . . . Day 190
5:3–5 . . . . Day 100, 163
5:6–8 . . . . Day 261
6:16 . . . . Day 24
6:23 . . . . Day 57
7:15 . . . . Day 118
7:15–19 . . . . Day 282
7:20 . . . . Day 232

8:4–6 . . . . Day 317
8:9 . . . . Day 277
8:11 . . . . Day 15
8:13 . . . . Day 347
8:17–18 . . . . Day 183
8:28 . . . . Day 1, 110, 358
8:31 . . . . Day 338
8:35–37 . . . . Day 175
8:38–39 . . . . Day 187
9:1–3 . . . . Day 93
10:13 . . . . Day 264
12:1 . . . . Day 84
12:1–2 . . . . Day 199
12:3 . . . . Day 225
12:21 . . . . Day 147
13:14 . . . . Day 137
15:25–27 . . . . Day 331

1 Corinthians

1:18 . . . . Day 360
1:25 . . . . Day 211
1:27–29 . . . . Day 125
2:1–2 . . . . Day 13
2:9 . . . . Day 336
2:16 . . . . Day 219
3:18–19 . . . . Day 223
4:12–13 . . . . Day 235
9:24–25 . . . . Day 247
9:26–27 . . . . Day 235
10:12–13 . . . . Day 259
10:13 . . . . Day 152
12:15–17 . . . . Day 271
13:1–3 . . . . Day 165
15:9–10 . . . . Day 25
15:10 . . . . Day 295
15:42–44 . . . . Day 283
15:58 . . . . Day 324
16:13–14 . . . . Day 295

2 Corinthians

1:20 . . . . Day 286
4:7–9 . . . . Day 307

4:16–18 . . . . Day 319
5:7 . . . . Day 6
5:17 . . . . Day 277
8:1–3 . . . . Day 331
8:11–12 . . . . Day 344
9:6 . . . . Day 355
9:7 . . . . Day 355
9:8–9 . . . . Day 355
12:7–9 . . . . Day 1
12:10 . . . . Day 43, 342
13:5 . . . . Day 161

GALATIANS
5:16 . . . . Day 56
5:22–23 . . . . Day 159
6:2 . . . . Day 59
6:7 . . . . Day 7
6:9 . . . . Day 7, 138, 324
6:10 . . . . Day 210

EPHESIANS
1:17 . . . . Day 146
3:20 . . . . Day 142
3:20–21 . . . . Day 348
4:2 . . . . Day 302
6:7–8 . . . . Day 26
6:10 . . . . Day 24
6:12 . . . . Day 250
6:18–20 . . . . Day 221

PHILIPPIANS
1:6 . . . . Day 286
1:21 . . . . Day 35
1:30 . . . . Day 59
2:3–11 . . . . Day 155
2:12–13 . . . . Day 69
2:13 . . . . Day 176
2:14–15 . . . . Day 289
3:1 . . . . Day 82
4:6 . . . . Day 64
4:6–7 . . . . Day 82, 181
4:13 . . . . Day 4
4:19 . . . . Day 329

COLOSSIANS
1:3 . . . . Day 181
1:29 . . . . Day 118
2:7 . . . . Day 94
3:17 . . . . Day 324
3:23–24 . . . . Day 324
4:5–6 . . . . Day 118
4:6 . . . . Day 159

1 THESSALONIANS
4:13–14 . . . . Day 316
5:17 . . . . Day 170, 217
5:18 . . . . Day 131, 170

2 THESSALONIANS
2:13 . . . . Day 101
3:3 . . . . Day 143
3:5 . . . . Day 143
6:12 . . . . Day 143

1 TIMOTHY
1:12–14 . . . . Day 166
1:15 . . . . Day 323
6:8 . . . . Day 290

2 TIMOTHY
1:2 . . . . Day 184
1:7 . . . . Day 184
1:12 . . . . Day 188
2:1 . . . . Day 215
2:3 . . . . Day 215

TITUS
1:1–3 . . . . Day 227
1:15–16 . . . . Day 236
2:2 . . . . Day 251
2:6 . . . . Day 251
3:1–4 . . . . Day 364

PHILEMON
10–11 . . . . Day 263
18–19 . . . . Day 263

HEBREWS
2:3 . . . . Day 57
4:8–11 . . . . Day 341

4:16 . . . . Day 246, 351
10:1–4 . . . . Day 327
10:25 . . . . Day 151, 298
10:36 . . . . Day 53
10:38 . . . . Day 257
11:1 . . . . Day 348
11:5 . . . . Day 237
11:6 . . . . Day 348
12:1 . . . . Day 15
12:2 . . . . Day 113
13:5 . . . . Day 38, 188

James

1:4 . . . . Day 53
1:5 . . . . Day 335
1:22 . . . . Day 303
1:27 . . . . Day 300
2:23 . . . . Day 74
3:13 . . . . Day 42
3:17–18 . . . . Day 42
4:6 . . . . Day 174
4:14 . . . . Day 319
5:16 . . . . Day 59

1 Peter

1:18–19 . . . . Day 353
2:12 . . . . Day 334
3:10–11 . . . . Day 210
5:5 . . . . Day 174
5:6 . . . . Day 302

2 Peter

2:17 . . . . Day 287
3:11–15 . . . . Day 343

1 John

1:7 . . . . Day 141
1:9 . . . . Day 148, 282
4:15 . . . . Day 288
5:4 . . . . Day 182

2 John

6 . . . . Day 239

Jude

12 . . . . Day 287
17–18 . . . . Day 287
20–21 . . . . Day 287

Revelation

1:5–6 . . . . Day 261
3:19 . . . . Day 77
14:13 . . . . Day 365
21:5–7 . . . . Day 272

━━━━━━━ CONTRIBUTORS ━━━━━━━

Besides the classic entries of D. L. Moody, Andrew Murray, Charles Spurgeon, and John Wesley, as indicated throughout this book, the following writers provided contemporary devotions:

Bob Evenhouse: Day 6, 19, 31, 43, 55, 79, 91, 103, 115, 139, 151, 163, 175, 187, 199, 211, 223, 235, 247, 271, 307, 319

Zech Haynes: Day 24, 35, 59, 82, 94, 118, 131, 166, 184, 215, 236, 251, 263

Josh Mosey: Day 3, 16, 28, 52, 76, 88, 100, 112, 124, 136, 148, 160, 172, 196, 208, 220, 232, 244, 256, 268, 280, 291, 304, 316, 328, 340, 352, 359

Paul Kent: Day 7, 38, 46, 50, 67, 83, 84, 127, 132, 143, 242, 254, 259, 278, 282, 283, 287, 292, 295, 308, 315, 326, 331, 336, 342, 344, 348, 354, 355

David Sanford: Day 4, 10, 18, 22, 30, 36, 42, 48, 54, 60, 66, 72, 78, 90, 96, 102, 108, 120, 126, 138, 144, 150, 156, 168, 174, 180, 186, 192, 198, 204, 210, 216, 222, 228, 234, 240, 246, 252, 258, 264, 270, 276, 288, 294, 300, 306, 312, 318, 324, 330, 360

Phil Smouse: Day 11, 34, 47, 70, 106, 119, 142, 155, 178, 191, 212, 224, 248, 260, 284, 296, 320, 332, 356

Lee Warren: Day 2, 8, 15, 20, 27, 32, 39, 44, 51, 56, 63, 68, 75, 80, 87, 92, 99, 104, 111, 116, 123, 128, 135, 140, 147, 152, 159, 164, 171, 176, 183, 188, 195, 202, 207, 214, 219, 226, 231, 238, 243, 250, 255, 262, 267, 274, 279, 286, 298, 303, 310, 322, 334, 339, 346, 351, 358, 363

Russ Wight: Day 14, 26, 62, 74, 86, 98, 110, 122, 134, 146, 158, 170, 182, 194, 206, 218, 230, 266, 290, 302, 314, 338, 350, 362

MORE GREAT
DEVOTIONS FOR GUYS

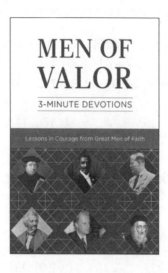

You'll find powerful lessons in courage in *Men of Valor: 3-Minute Devotions*. These 180 meditations pack challenge and encouragement into just-right-sized entries for guys of all ages, highlighting worthy Christian leaders who served God with courage—men like St. Augustine, Dietrich Bonhoeffer, Frederick Douglass, Jim Elliot, and many more.

Paperback / 978-1-64352-645-4 / $4.99